JAZZ *Myth and Religion*

New York   Oxford

Oxford University Press

1987

Jazz

Myth and Religion   Neil Leonard

Oxford University Press

Oxford   New York   Toronto
Delhi   Bombay   Calcutta   Madras   Karachi
Petaling Jaya   Singapore   Hong Kong   Tokyo
Nairobi   Dar es Salaam   Cape Town
Melbourne   Auckland

and associated companies in
Beirut   Berlin   Ibadan   Nicosia

Library of Congress Cataloging-in-Publication Data
Leonard, Neil.
Jazz : myth and religion.
Bibliography: p.   Includes index.
1. Jazz music.   2. Music—Religious aspects.
3. Music and society.   I. Title.
ML3506.L44   1987   785.42   86-18156
ISBN 0-19-504249-2

9 8 7 6 5 4 3 2 1

Printed in the United States of America

For Devin and Neil,
who in their own ways know more about jazz than I do.
And for Amy, Chris, and especially, Dottie,
who move to its related beats.

Charles Seeger tells the story of a conference of musicologists after which one of the most famous confided: "You know, I don't hate jazz; I think it's probably very important and it certainly deserves serious study. The trouble is that all jazz people treat it as holy, holy, holy!" To this, Seeger replied: "Well, now, don't you consider the area of classical music in which you specialize as 'holy' too?" "Ah," said the musicologist, "BUT IT *IS*!"

Marshall Stearns, *The Story of Jazz*[1]

Preface

This book deals with the ancient notion that music is in some sense sacred or magical. Specifically, it looks at how jazz has been regarded as supernatural and at some of the consequences of this belief. My interest is more functional than metaphysical: I am less concerned with whether jazz is at bottom otherworldly than with the fact that many listeners have regarded it as such and acted accordingly. This phenomenon has led me to studies of religious behavior, particularly those of Max Weber and his followers, and like them I have defined it broadly to include any faith in the supernatural upheld by rituals and myths. This embraces a wide range of beliefs, from those rationalized and institutionalized in established churches to informal, embryonic ones celebrated spontaneously. And it touches upon some activities ordinarily considered secular.

My first chapter discusses people who attacked early jazz for fear it had unearthly powers to pollute not only the "classical" music they held sacred but also "respectable" morality and society. The rest of the book investigates how exponents of successive jazz movements thought their musics to be supernatural in ways that dramatically altered their personal and social lives. Inspired by prophetic musicians whose powerful charisma radiated beyond the bandstand, true believers psychologically withdrew from an indifferent or hostile world and came together in sect-like groups. At their cores were small elites who had inherited the prophetic charisma and who provided the inspiration, and sometimes models, for the faithful—musicians, priest-like critics and historians, record-collecting and discographical curators, revivalists, and other celebrants and communicants. Each movement generated its own rituals of musical performance, speech, dress, humor, and initiation, as well as myths (tales of origins and heroes) which lent guidance, identity, and solidarity to the fellowship. My conclusion considers these tendencies within the context of changing spiritual values in the United States over the last century.

This examination starts, and occasionally reworks material, from my *Jazz and the White Americans* (1962).[1] That book is an historical treatment of the secular reactions to jazz between the two world wars. This one deals, in more anthropological and sociological terms, with the religious response of blacks and whites to jazz since the beginnings of the music.[2]

If there were such a thing as human objectivity, I could not claim it here, for jazz has long fascinated me. But I have tried to remain detached. I do not argue that jazz is inherently sacred or that religion lies at its heart, only that it often stimulates religious or quasi-religious feelings and behavior and answers needs commonly associated with them. I hope the results help illuminate the role of music in our lives and the nature of religiously linked behavior in this supposedly secular time.

Many of the debts incurred in the writing of this book are apparent in the text and notes, but I want to mention others here. Virtually every page benefited from the incisive comments of Charles Nanry and Drew Gilpin Faust. Stephen Dunning, Willy De Craemer, Nat Hentoff, and Roger D. Abrahams also read the manuscript and gave valuable support and advice. Dan Morgenstern listened to early versions of two chapters and pointed me toward a publisher. Genevieve Innes patiently combed the manuscript for errors. Finally, I want to thank Sheldon Meyer of Oxford University Press, who had faith in the book and did much to improve it, and Sam Tanenhaus, also of Oxford, for his careful and perceptive reading.

Philadelphia   N.L.
July 1986

Contents

JAZZ *Myth and Religion*

Church

This is the kind of lawlessness that easily insinuates itself
unobserved [through music]. . . . because it is supposed to be
only a form of play and to work no harm. Nor does it work
any, except that by gradual infiltration it softly overflows upon
the characters and pursuits of men and from these issues forth
grown greater to attack their business dealings, and from these
relations it proceeds against the laws and the constitution with
license till it finally overthrows all things public and private. . . .
for the modes of music are never disturbed without unsettling
of the most fundamental political and social conventions. . . . It
is here, then, that our guardians must build their
guardhouse and post of watch.

Plato, *The Republic*[1]

By 1922, helped by the increasingly available phonograph and
radio, jazz, or what passed for it, seemed to blare from every
street corner and living room in the land. While some classical
music lovers listened with interest, many more were appalled
and feared that the chaotic new sound represented the swan
song of America, even of western civilization. This potential
downfall was graphically dramatized in J. Hartley Manners'
1922 play *The National Anthem*, in which a group of white,
middle-class youngsters "jazzed" their way to degeneracy,
ignoring the dire warnings of the older generation. That same
year an editor of the classically oriented *Musical Courier* polled
his subscribers, mainly musicians, about jazz and reported the
results under the heading " 'Jazz'—The National Anthem(?)"

Those polled "all agreed the 'ad libbing' or 'jazzing' of a piece is thoroughly objectionable, and several of them advanced the opinion that this Bolshevistic smashing of the rules and tenets of decorous music, this excessive freedom of interpretation, tended to a similar letdown on the part of the dancers, a similar disregard for the self-contained attitude that has been prescribed by the makers of the rules of dignified intercourse."[2] This was not the first time that conservatives had been alarmed by jazzy sounding music—they had been troubled by ragtime before World War I—but now the protests were louder and voiced by many more Americans, including large numbers who viewed themselves as moderates.

The opposition to early jazz in the United States and abroad centered on a classical music orthodoxy which had many of the attributes of Ernst Troeltsch's concept of the ideal church. Troeltsch, a student of Max Weber, and his followers defined the "church type" as an objective institution fundamentally unchanged by time and human affairs. Coextensive with society, it accepts the secular order and is an integral part of the established social order. Although conservative by nature and allied with privilege, it seeks to embrace all people and to this end willingly accepts reasonable compromises. Power and status in the church extend downward through a settled hierarchy which presides over received beliefs and practices.[3] In actuality, no church or church-like organization conforms fully to this ideal, if only because real institutions are touched by time and human affairs.

We can understand much of the American classical music orthodoxy in terms of a loose Troeltschean metaphor. Largely imported from Europe, the music orthodoxy was a conservative system whose spiritual functions had been rationalized to please upper- and middle-class audiences, and too often it neglected or ignored indigenous American music. Outlining its canon, Daniel Gregory Mason, an influential composer, critic, and teacher, recalled, "The truth is, our whole view of music was based on the style of classic and romantic symphonists beginning with Haydn and Mozart and ending with Mendelssohn and Schumann."[4] But large numbers of Americans did not take easily to these composers. Walter Damrosch, who as conductor of the renowned New York Symphony Society presided like an archbishop over the Manhattan music world, wrote, "Instead of growing upward from the masses, [classical music] was carefully introduced and nurtured from above by an artistic and cultural community. . . . Its original impulses sprang perhaps more strongly from the head than from the heart."[5] This elite defined acceptable beliefs and rituals and, aided by others within the orthodox hierarchy, encouraged their proper implementation. In the professional sphere, the hierarchy descended through overlapping categories of composer, conductor, virtuoso, ordinary musician, critic, music teacher, and student. Communicants in the lay sphere included the most influential members of the Protestant, Anglo-Saxon majority: businessmen, society matrons, clergymen, educators, artists, and numerous emulators lower down on the ladder.

While the leading musicians were males, usually foreign-born, women predominated elsewhere in the hierarchy. Red-blooded males viewed music as women's work, suitable for men as recreation but not as a profession. "A strong feeling persisted," wrote Damrosch, "that music was essentially an effeminate art, that its cultivation by a man took away from his manliness."[6] Accordingly, except in the best orchestras, which consisted mainly of foreigners, the professional playing and teaching of music fell mostly to women. By 1910 there were 84,000 women and 54,000 men occupied as musicians in the United States, roughly an eight-to-five ratio. The largest single group organized in support of the orthodoxy was the National Federation of Music Clubs, which in 1910 had 400,000 members—all women.[7]

Like the Troeltschean church, the musical orthodoxy considered itself broadly inclusive, coextensive with the established social order. It was something one was born into, its tenets taken for granted in cultivated households and polite society. Young people who did not learn its doctrines at home discovered them in the classroom. As early as 1838, the Boston Board of Education inaugurated music instruction in the city's public schools with a successful program that stimulated others, and by 1900 music standards were taught in public schools across the country, often beginning in the primary grades.

Music education in colleges and universities developed more slowly, but following the example set by Oberlin College in 1837 leading institutions gradually set up courses and departments which imparted the orthodox norms. Equally influential were music programs in growing numbers of normal schools, and also conservatories, which sprang up after the New England Conservatory was founded in 1862 to train and certify practitioners.

During these years, a school of conservative music journalism emerged to spread the word. 1852 marked the appearance of *Dwight's Journal*; *The Musical Courier* followed in 1880, *The Etude* in 1883, *The Musician* in 1895, *The Musical Leader* in 1900, and the *Musical Quarterly* in 1915. The less scholarly of these read like house organs, celebrating orthodox tenets expressed in the works and words of those in the upper levels of the hierarchy. The music criticism of the general press, though less didactic, also reflected established norms, giving precedence to foreign-born composers and performers, who were regarded as the highest authorities on musical matters.

Orthodox principles descended from German Romanticism, whose mystical ideology placed enormous ethical importance on music. This had not always been the case.[8] In the eighteenth century even the greatest composers sought chiefly to please the ear. Mozart, Haydn, and Handel wrote music that was popular with a wide audience—not just with the nobles who provided their main livelihood—and thus they composed primarily to entertain rather than uplift. By the middle of the nineteenth century, however, all this had changed. The musician was no longer in the employ of princes but on his own, a free-lance composer and performer in the service of the rising middle class, which knew little of artistic niceties and willingly subscribed to the taste of the leading musicians of the day.

These artists had been educated in Neoplatonic thought, which divided experience into two realms: the secular, understandable through reason and perception; and the spiritual, approachable through religion and the arts. All art provided access to transcendence, and, according to philosophers like Hegel and Schopenhauer, this was especially true of music, which in its symphonic form was the purest, most sacred form of expression. As Theodore Thomas, the German-born conductor of the Chicago Symphony, declared: "A symphony orchestra shows the culture of a community. . . . the man who does not understand Beethoven and has not been under his spell has not lived half his life. The master works of . . . instrumental music are the language of the soul and express more than those of any other art." Thomas regarded symphonic music as "a sermon in tones . . . a powerful force" that "by its uplifting influence" led the listener to "a higher plane."[9] In a similar vein, influential critic Henry T. Finck wrote in 1910 that "no other art . . . so vividly arouses the unselfish feeling, the desire for sympathetic communion." He concluded that "one of the most important functions of music [is] that of weaning people from low and demoralizing pleasures [and] savage impulses."[10] In the eyes of the orthodoxy, then, symphonic music provided access to the ideal, rescuing listeners from their primitive selves and leading them toward righteousness. The wide acceptance of these notions testified to the great social, intellectual, and musical authority wielded by musical tastemakers.

Secure in their moral and metaphysical idealism, they were proselytizers and didacts, missionaries inspired to bring their uplifting message to America's cultural wilderness. Yet, in their desire to touch all listeners and bring them into the fold, orthodox leaders were willing to make certain compromises. One was with the banalities of American taste. Audience polls conducted at the turn of the century for all-request programs of symphony orchestras in New York and St. Louis indicated that marginally respectable pieces, like von Suppe's "Poet and Peasant Overture" and Rubinstein's "Melody in F," held far more appeal for most concertgoers than anything by Haydn, Mozart, Beethoven, or other works firmly established in the canon.[11] Such preferences could not be ignored entirely in program planning. And other concessions were necessary as well. Even the most gifted performers found it necessary to resort to show-business gimmickry to attract audiences in a climate in which listeners often talked incessantly during the demanding parts of the program and in which no symphony

orchestra could pay its way without broad subsidies from
wealthy patrons.[12]

Accommodations also had to be made with dissidents within
the orthodox ranks. After the turn of the century a schismatic
group of nationalistic composers, led by Arthur Farwell and
inspired by Dvorak's use of "plantation melodies" in the *New
World Symphony*, introduced folk material into their work.
Conservatives were appalled by the use of unlaundered Negro
and American Indian themes, but more liberal members of
the establishment, realizing the need to adapt to native circumstances, gradually formed a consensus combining European
values with those of the New World.

But while the reigning authorities were willing to tolerate
certain unfamiliar elements—when properly refined according
to accepted practices—there were limits to their accommodation, limits emphatically marked, jealously guarded, and vig-
orously defended. Clearly beyond the pale was popular music,
which flourished weed-like in minstrel and vaudeville theaters,
lower-class cabarets, saloons, dance halls, and other "unsavory"
places. For orthodox purists the sounds in such venues did
not even qualify as "music." They were a form of diabolical
noise, as impure in their way as symphonic music was sacred
in its. In a relatively moderate statement, Theodore Thomas,
who called symphonic music "the language of the soul,"
asserted that "light music, popular music so-called, is the
sensual side of the art and has more or less the devil in it."[13]
Had he been thinking of black, popular music his words would
probably have been stronger, for the unrefined music of the
Negro was a particular abomination to keepers of the classical
flame, as their response to early jazz makes clear.

This response, revealing a good deal about the church-like
nature of the orthodoxy, peaked in two waves, the first before
World War I and the second in the Twenties. The first was a
reaction to ragtime, which was born in the Nineties primarily
as a composed, written-down, syncopated piano music and
later took on orchestrated forms that provided the music for
the "dance craze" that swept the country before World War I.

The second and more tumultuous wave centered upon what was then simply called "jazz" but in varying degrees mixed conventional popular music with ragtime and the blues in syntheses that had evolved in New Orleans, Chicago, New York, and elsewhere. While the two waves were distinctive in some ways, they were broadly similar, two installments of the same church-sect argument.

In retrospect, it is hard to see why early jazz created the furor it did. Ragtime now seems exceedingly tame, and, although still not taken seriously in some quarters, it has found its way into the concert hall, its creators having been elevated to the status of "classical" composers and its compositions recorded on prestigious labels ordinarily reserved for classical music.[14] And even though the jazz styles of the Twenties have yet to attain such recognition, their sounds by now seem comfortably familiar; even conservative ears are at home with good-time dixieland music, if not its less refined ancestors.

Yet when the strange polyrhythms and exotic, blue intonations—or, more often, their dilutions—first became popular, "respectable" responses ranged from distaste to outrage. The new sounds had been objectionable when confined to the underside of society, but now they always seemed within earshot, violating the sanctity of even the purest middle-class home. Predictably, the orthodoxy turned its full wrath against jazz and its dilutions, finding allies among those ordinarily little moved by any kind of music. Thus fortified, establishmentarians condemned anything that sounded like jazz as ugly, cheap, degenerating, and threatening.

Anthropologist Mary Douglas calls this kind of treatment "pollution behavior." She points out that anything which confuses or casts doubt on the received order seems dirty and arouses demands for expurgation and that ideas of defilement are not isolated complaints but an integral part of overall cultural values, keeping deviants in line and otherwise reinforcing notions of right and wrong as well as claims of class and status.[15] Emile Durkheim, who influenced Douglas' formulation, outlined related aspects of religious behavior, showing, among other things, that belief systems tend to distinguish sharply not only between the sacred and the profane, but between two kinds of sacredness or supernaturalism: on the one hand, the pure and divine force that produces social and moral order, health, and happiness; on the other, the impure and diabolical force that brings disorder, immorality, illness, and death. Though radically antagonistic, these two kinds of sacredness can be highly ambiguous because both stem from similar supernatural sources. Indeed, each can be made from the other, and they are mutually contagious. Therefore, the well-intentioned seek to keep them strictly separate lest they mingle with disastrous results.[16]

Accordingly, the music orthodoxy attributed demonic or magic powers to jazz and most other black music and tried to isolate it from what they held sacred. As early in 1852, John Dwight, the powerful, Germanophile critic, wrote that any sort of popular music—especially that associated with the Negro—was pernicious. In his influential *Journal of Music* Dwight asserted that a tune like "Old Folks at Home" *"breaks out* every now and then, like a morbid irritation of the skin."[17] Little happened in the rest of the century to allay such apprehension, which was only confirmed by the runaway infectiousness of ragtime syncopations. In 1900 the orthodox *Etude* published an article, "Musical Impurity," which exclaimed, "The counters of music stores are loaded with this virulent poison which in the form of a malarious epidemic is finding its way into the homes and brains of our youth."[18] Still another writer urged that "In Christian homes, where purity and morals are stressed, ragtime should find no resting place. Avaunt the ragtime rot! Let us purge America and the Divine art of music from this polluting nuisance."[19] Fears escalated in the Twenties, when the malevolence of jazz seemed to strike at defenseless innocents. In 1926 the Salvation Army went to court in Cincinnati to enjoin the construction of a movie theater beside a home for unwed mothers, arguing, "We are loath to believe that babies born in a maternity hospital are to be legally subjected to the implanting of jazz emotions by such enforced proximity to a theater and jazz palace."[20]

The demonic new music seemed to destroy general feeling for classical music. In 1913 an article in the conservative *Musical Observer* explaining how ragtime ruined the technique and taste of young performers urged readers to shun it "as you would the 'Black Death.' ";[21] and fifteen years later Walter Damrosch stated categorically in *The New York Times* that the jazz contagion "stifles the true musical instinct, turning away many of our young people from the persistent, continued study of good music."[22] Worse, the demonic noise seemed to infect holy, classical music itself. Orthodox purists sought to keep the two strictly apart and were greatly troubled by the diabolical delight popular musicians took in "jazzing the classics." Frank Damrosch, the brother of Walter and a well-known musician in his own right, cited this sacrilege as proof of creative barrenness and above all as "an outrage on beautiful music."[23] Apologists for the new music belittled the conservatives' hard and fast distinctions between pure and impure. One of them wondered "why the c-sharp minor chord . . . should be so pure and holy and beautiful when used in 'The Moonlight Sonata' and poisonous and immoral when used in a ragtime piece."[24]

The most frightening aspect of jazz was its mysterious power to strike at the heart of rational conduct and moral judgment. "A person inoculated with the ragtime-fever is like one addicted to strong drink!" wrote one alarmist before the War.[25] And after the Armistice, a respected New York physician declared that "jazz music causes drunkenness . . . producing thought and imaginations which overpower the will. Reason and reflection are lost and actions of persons are directed by the stronger animal passions."[26] Still other conservatives cited "scientific data" showing that ragtime would "stagnate the brain cells and wreck the nervous system."[27]

Not surprisingly, racism, albeit muted or veiled, often lay at the bottom of such beliefs. But sometimes the horror evoked by the demoniacally infecting "coon songs" and "nigger music" brought uninhibited responses. In an article, "Ragtime, the New Tarantism," Francis Toye, a British critic, asserted that the new sounds "show precisely the kind of 'vitality' associated with Revivalism peculiar to the negro! What need have we of further witnesses? For of all hysteria that particular semi-religious hysteria is nearer to madness than any other."[28] Such feelings flourished on both sides of the Atlantic and complemented fears that jazz was part of an overall black contagion working its way into the heart of our national life. One commentator asked: "Can it be said that America is falling prey to the collective soul of the negro through the influence of what is popularly known as 'rag time' music? . . . If there is any tendency toward such a national disaster, it should be definitely pointed out and extreme measures taken to inhibit the influence and avert the increasing danger—if it has not already gone too far. . . . American 'rag time' or 'ragtime' evolved music is symbolic of the primitive morality and perceptible moral limitations of the negro type. With the latter sexual restraint is almost unknown, and the wildest latitude of moral uncertainty is conceded." This statement, appearing in a letter to the editor of the Paris edition of *The New York Herald* in 1913 and later reprinted in the *Musical Courier,* aroused a good deal of comment and indignation. Its author further claimed that "some sociological writers of prominence" and "all psychologists" agreed that America was succumbing to the evils of the Negro soul.[29] Clear and overwhelming evidence of the contagion mounted after the Armistice. The medical director of the Philadelphia High School for Girls claimed in the Twenties that "the consensus of opinion of leading medical and scientific authorities is that [jazz's] influence is as harmful and degrading as it has been all along among the savages from whom we borrowed it," and warned that if the disease continued to spread it "may tear to pieces the whole social fabric."[30]

The authors of such statements fit the familiar profile of the ethnocentric personality[31] typical of the anxious conformist who responds to a menacing world by dividing people into clearly marked categories—strong and weak, pure and impure, white (good) and black (evil)[32]—blaming vulnerable minorities for his own shortcomings and misfortunes. Ethnocentrism waxed in the Twenties in the wake of massive internal and external migrations. Changing economic circumstances brought large numbers of blacks to the North, leading to race riots and a revived Ku Klux Klan, which found numerous Northern supporters.

Unsurprisingly, this racism was closely related to sex. Established precepts held that sex, like other potentially trouble-

some, irrational activity, required careful supervision. Therefore, the well-intentioned sought to limit sexual intimacy within
the confines of marriage. Indulgence outside of this sanctified
state was thought to undermine physical and moral health and
to endanger the purity of the supposedly superior white stock.
The sexual behavior of blacks, regarded as childlike or ani-
malistic at best, challenged these restraints, threatened white
women and provided temptations for white men. Worse, the
high birthrate among blacks, which was well publicized, raised
the specter of masses of "inferiors" eventually overwhelming
whites.[33]

Jazz exacerbated these dangers. One troubled observer,
reflecting the general fear, recalled that "It was not uncommon
to see white women with colored men, especially jazz band
musicians, who seemed to exert a magnetic appeal for Caucasian women all over the country."[34] And clarinetist Buster
Bailey related that when he started playing for white audiences,
"They were afraid we'd go after their women."[35] Some whites
felt equally uncomfortable about seductive, black women singing before susceptible Caucasian men. Jazz seemed to dissolve
inhibitions, and guardians of public morality blamed it for a
variety of evils, from the rise of illegitimate births to the
bourgeoning traffic in white-slaves. A number of educational
and welfare institutions commissioned Alice Barrow, a respected social worker, to investigate behavior outside dance
halls in Midwestern towns during the Twenties. She reported
that the "nature of the music and crowd psychology bring to
many individuals an unwholesome excitement. Boy-and-
girl couples leave the dance hall in a state of dangerous disturbance. . . . The modern dance is producing little short of holocaust. The statistics of illegitimacy in this country show a great
increase in recent years."[36] And a report from the Reverend
Phillip Yarrow, head of the Illinois Vigilance Association,
claimed its agents had discovered that in 1921–22 jazz had
brought about the downfall of one thousand young women in
Chicago alone.[37]

Such outrages touched on matters too delicate for public
discourse. But other horrors evoked by the blatant impurities
of jazz dancing were vividly denounced. At the dawn of the

ragtime era, New York Chief of Police George W. Walling wrote of the bestialities in a New York "black and tan": "Whatever sign of womanhood that might have been on the women's faces once is gone now. . . . There are no bounds to license. It takes a good deal to satisfy the best of the dull-sensed Negroes in the room. They dance until the perspiration rolls down in streams on their faces, and they drink until they are stupid."[38] It was bad enough to find such behavior among blacks, but when it spread to whites, the reaction was extreme. Erotic new dances seemed overwhelming evidence of atavistic regression, reminiscent of the contagious madness of Tarantism or the St. Vitus epidemics. The sensuous gestures of the tango had been sufficiently disturbing, but outrage greeted the manias of the "Bunny Hug," "Grizzly Bear," "Baby Baboon Dance," "Devil's Ball," and "Turkey Trot," whose very names stressed their diabolical animalism.

Condemnation came from both sides of the Atlantic. In 1913 *The New York Times* reported that Canon Newboldt of St. Paul's in London had assailed ragtime in a sermon that asked, "Would indecent dances, suggestive of evil and destructive of modesty, disgrace our civilization for a moment if the professed Christians were to say: I will not allow my daughter to turn into Salome?" In behalf of middle-class respectability the *Times* declared in an editorial the following day that Canon Newboldt was no sensational preacher but a staid and respected theologian hardly given to inflammatory statements, and went on to note that "decent people in and out of the church are beginning to be alarmed" at the "rude" and "vulgar" music and "loose conduct" accompanying it with "dances defying all propriety." The editorial argued that the Canon's "example should be followed in all of the churches of England and the United States" and concluded that Americans were "drifting toward peril and the drift must be checked."[39] A decade later, a New Jersey Supreme Court Justice, J. F. Minturn, upholding the conviction of a band playing outlawed jazz, charged: "In response to its call there ensues a series of snake-like gyrations and weird contortions of seemingly agonized bodies and limbs. . . . called a dance."[40]

The point is that the orthodoxy was opposed not to ecstasy

as such, only to ecstasy that seemed alien or out of hand because improperly rationalized and channeled. Even the few orthodoxly oriented apologists for the milder forms of jazz recognized its potentially troublesome implications. After attending a ragtime performance, Hiram Moderwell, a sympathetic critic, wrote, "You simply can't resist it. I felt my blood thumping in tune, my muscles twitching to the rhythms."[41] It was this involuntary reaction that bothered conservative listeners, especially when they found themselves caught up in it, however slightly. A case in point is Gustav Kuhl, who wrote: "Suddenly I discovered that my legs were in a condition of great excitement. They twitched as though charged with electricity and betrayed a considerable and rather dangerous desire to jerk me from my seat. The rhythm of the music, which had seemed so unnatural at first was beginning to work its influence over me. It wasn't that feeling of ease in the joints or the feet and toes which might be caused by a Strauss waltz, no, much more energetic, material, independent as though one encountered a balking horse, which it is absolutely impossible to master."[42]

The rationalized ecstasies of classical music seemed refined and comfortably familiar—spiritual rather than physical. Instead of hysterically separating the listener from his senses, orthodox music appealed to higher reason. Complaining about the motor excesses evoked by jazz, a *New York Times* writer argued, "With music of the old style, even the most moving, the listener was seldom upset from his dignified posture. . . . He might feel a tingling starting at his heels and lifting the roof of his head clear up to the ceiling . . . yet the bodily anchor remained intact. The listener behaved as impassively as the radio's microphone. Nothing in his manner indicated either a struggle for self-control or an absence of decorum. The perturbation spent itself internally."[43] Not so with jazz, which reached below the belt. French critic André Saurès spoke for many on both sides of the Atlantic when he exclaimed, "Jazz is . . . the music of the guts and of all those who carry their sensibilities between their legs."[44]

In sum, the church-like music orthodoxy found that contagious jazz, springing in wild luxuriance from the black subsoil,

was blatently irrational, full of raw sensuality that defied
common decency and the sober purposefulness of the received
ethic.

This orthodoxy was, of course, dominated by whites but it had
a black auxiliary or counterpart equally if not more adamant
about the evil of jazz. Black opposition, like that of whites,
rested in no small measure on status considerations. Up
through the Thirties jazz appealed to a broad mass of blacks
at the lower end of the economic scale. Yet from its earliest
days the music was disdained or despised by many respectable
Negroes whose tastes mirrored those of the upper echelons of
the white world. Black hostility to the blues came early from
churchgoers, especially from dignified Methodists and Pres-
byterians, but also from the African Methodist Episcopal
shouting congregations and even the more ecstatic, sanctified
communicants. Varying degrees of spontaneous rapture within
these churches were acceptable, but beyond the confines of
sacred worship they seemed vulgar or sinful. Thus, jazz was
termed "the devil's music," a condemnation rooted in the strict
orthodox distinction between pure and impure music: on the
one hand there was respectable music, including the classics,
spirituals, and eventually gospel music; on the other was jazz,
along with its tributary and subsidiary forms. Moralists called
blues singers to redemption, and upstanding parents warned
their children against the jazz evil.
    Before 1900 young W. C. Handy, who later called himself
"The Father of the Blues," was forbidden by his father to take
guitar lessons because it was "one of the devil's play-things."[45]
In the Twenties novelist Ralph Ellison, then an aspiring
trumpeter growing up in Oklahoma City, knew all too well
that "jazz was regarded by most of the respectable Negroes of
the town as a backward, low-class form of expression and there
was a marked difference between those who accepted it and
lived close to their folk experience and those whose status
stirrings led them to reject and deny it."[46] Reedman Garvin
Bushell had a similar recollection of his boyhood in Manhattan:
"You could only hear the blues and real jazz in the gut-bucket

cabarets where the lower classes went. You usually weren't allowed to play the blues and boogie woogie in the average middle class home. That supposedly suggested the low element."[47] This was also true in many poorer households, like those of the God-fearing ghetto dwellers among whom Billie Holiday grew up in Baltimore. She remembered well how her mother considered jazz sinful and "would whip me in a minute if she caught me listening to it. Those days we were supposed to listen to hymns or something like that."[48]

Intellectual blacks were even more adamant about the perniciousness of jazz. The highbrow *Negro Musical Journal* warned in 1903 that ragtime "is an evil music . . . that must be wiped out as other bad and dangerous epidemics have been exterminated."[49] Four decades later, a professor at Howard University told student Leroi Jones (Imamu Amiri Baraka), "It's fantastic how much bad taste the blues contain!" As Jones explained, "Jazz was collected among the numerous skeletons the middle-class, black man kept in the closet of his psyche, along with watermelons and gin, and whose rattling caused him no end of misery and self hatred."[50] Many decorous blacks still deny jazz is art and a surprising number of black intellectuals remain ignorant of its history.[51]

Understandably, then, young middle-class black musicians have felt torn between two music worlds. In the words of Ralph Ellison, "It is seldom recognized there is a conflict between what the Negro musician feels in the community around him and the given or (classical) techniques of his instrument. He feels a tension between his desire to master the classical style of playing and his compulsion to express the sounds which form a musical definition of the American Negro experience."[52] Ellison cited two families in the Oklahoma City of his youth that embodied this tension. One produced jazz guitarist Charlie Christian, who finally turned away from orthodox music, dropping out of the high school music activities which his conventionally inclined brother Edward eagerly participated in. Another family produced singer Jimmy Rushing, the son of a businessman and a churchgoing mother, who rejected the respectable word of his parents for jazz. Still another prototypical family—in Boston some years later—

was headed by a college music teacher and produced bop saxophonist Sonny Stitt, whose brother took the opposite course, becoming a concert pianist. Other middle-class black youths were pulled in opposing directions but combined elements of each into successful careers as bandleaders, composers, or arrangers. Duke Ellington is a famous example, as are Benny Carter, Don Redman, Sy Oliver, Fletcher Henderson, and Jimmie Lunceford.

We ordinarily think of jazz as primarily the music of the black minority, and rightly so, but it is a mistake to ignore the influence the largely white, church-like orthodoxy had on its development. This establishment affected whites as well as blacks, directly and indirectly. God-fearing Negroes, modeling themselves on cultivated whites, found in orthodox values a definition of what "good" music was and of how jazz should be "refined" in order to become acceptable. For other blacks orthodox hostility to jazz gave impetus to the counter-hostility integral to the music sects that I will turn to now.

Sect

It became almost a cult after a while, and the ones who felt
themselves musically strong enough would enter it.
Drummer Kenny Clarke, on the early bop movement[1]

Jazz has had a turbulent history, perhaps as turbulent as that
of any art form in the chaotic climate of the twentieth century.
Detested by some Americans, ignored by more, exploited by
predatory businessmen, tied to the growing pains and uncertainties of the mass media, and subjected to the whims of fickle
audiences in search of endless novelty, the music has changed
extraordinarily quickly. Yet, for all the confusion accompanying its rapid development, some general tendencies are
evident. One is that broad jazz movements tend to take on
sectarian qualities, in terms of the Troeltschean metaphor.

In Troeltsch's typology the "sect-type" springs up in tension
with the church. Whereas the "church-type" is exclusive,
accommodating, and hierarchical, the sect is exclusive, relatively uncompromising, lay oriented, and minimally structured—a small group of true believers sharing faith and
fellowship. And, whereas in the church status and role are
ascribed, in the sect they rest more on merit, connected to an
awareness of transcendent truth inaccessible to outsiders and
fostering an elitist identity. Seeking self-sufficiency and inner
perfection, sectarians may welcome, even recruit, converts but
do not try to penetrate other groups, toward which their
attitudes range from indifference to hostility.[2]

There have been three jazz movements loosely fitting this

pattern. The first developed slowly and unself-consciously out of the music of ragtimers like Scott Joplin, New Orleans pioneers such as Buddy Bolden and then, in the Twenties, blues singers including Bessie Smith and instrumentalists dominated by Louis Armstrong. By the end of the Twenties their styles, variations, and various syntheses (all lumped together here as "early jazz"), began to be regarded as more than just catchy folk or popular music. Uninformed sympathizers had earlier sought to "refine" jazz for polite society and the concert hall; now knowledgeable adherents began to take it seriously as an art form in and of itself. In the early Thirties a growing cadre of critics, record collectors, and others excitedly spread the word, pointing out what was real jazz, defending it against attacks from the orthodoxy, and explaining it in ways palatable to an expanding following mostly drawn to the smooth dilutions of swing, which was rapidly becoming *the* popular music of the day. Before Pearl Harbor the maturing early sect, having survived, even flourished despite orthodox onslaughts, evolved its own hardening tradition with mystique, rituals, myths, and saints (original and latter-day)—all serving to guide and legitimize accepted beliefs and practices. But as World War II got under way all was not well among the faithful. Young musicians, feeling too constrained, departed from the fold to create a disturbing new music called bop; and fundamentalists, troubled by this aberration and the commercial impurities of swing, launched the evangelical "Dixieland Revival," which returned to untainted, original jazz.

This, then, was the situation as the second sect-like movement crystallized in the Forties around bop, which conflicted less with the church-like orthodoxy than with entrenched early-jazz forces. Whereas the early sect had gradually outgrown its folk roots, the bop movement developed more rapidly. Inspired by Charlie Parker, Dizzy Gillespie, and others who rebelled against the cliches, settled character, and restrictive rituals of early jazz and swing, bop was an electrifying new style with pyrotechnical virtuosity, harsh melodies, dissonant harmonies, and breathtaking tempos which held a powerful message for hip, streetwise youngsters. After a period of gestation in Harlem, it migrated downtown to West Fifty-

second Street, where its circle of devotees, now including
whites, widened into a full-fledged sect during and after World
War II. In the process it generated its own rituals, mythology,
and critical machinery which helped define its values and
defend them from a thunderous attack from early-jazz loyalists.

The intersectarian battle over bop did not spill over into the
nonmusical world as much as the church-sect controversy over
early jazz had in the Twenties, but within its limits it was
equally intense and raised similar issues. Conservatives complained that bop was shrill, anarchic, impure, and contagious—
dangerous to music and morality alike. Elder prophet Louis
Armstrong called it "jujitsu music" and ruinous to jazz.[3] And
trumpeter Max Kaminsky reported, "it had such an upsetting
effect on my nervous system that it actually made me feel
nauseous."[4] The boppers seemed like incompetent upstarts
reaching for sensational effects, not only through outlandish
music but through bizarre speech, dress, humor, and also
through drugs. Upholders of early jazz and the orthodoxy
tried to expunge the new pollution, telling the world of its
evils and doing what they could to keep it from the public ear.
In 1946 radio station KMPC in Los Angeles, following the
precedent of forerunners in the Twenties, banned bop on the
grounds that "it makes degenerates out of our young listeners."
And *Time* magazine called it "hot jazz overheated, with over-
done lyrics, full of bawdiness, references to narcotics, and
double talk."[5]

As the Fifties wore on the dispute predictably quieted down.
Having lost some of its original zeal, the bop movement settled
into a tradition of its own and split into two factions: "cool,"
which watered the music with conventional elements; and
"funky," or "regressive," hard bop, which sought a return to
the sounds or spirit of the Forties. But despite the ardor of
the regressives, the lines between early jazz and bop, once
sharp, now blurred. Increasingly musicians synthesized the
two styles, both were played on the same stage at concerts and
festivals, and formerly partisan publications treated both sym-
pathetically. Bop, in effect, had now joined early jazz in the
increasingly respectable jazz world.

But as it did so a new "scourge" appeared. By 1960 the "new

thing" or "free jazz" emerged in the work of restless youngsters moved little by formulas of bop. The new prophets, including Ornette Coleman, Cecil Taylor, and eventually (and most notably) John Coltrane, sought to liberate jazz from limitations—melodic, rhythmic, and especially harmonic—of the older styles. The departures of the "free-jazz sect" (for lack of a better name), sometimes appearing in militant program music linked to the civil rights movement and other social upheavals of the Sixties and Seventies, generated a new version of the jazz mystique and rituals which stressed African roots and pointedly abandoned the old hip attitudes in favor of a serious artistic demeanor. It also developed its own myths, critics, and fringe devotees who spread its evolving doctrines. The boppers, to say nothing of the declining number of early-jazz holdouts, were puzzled and appalled by these strange new experiments.

The intersectarian fight which the "new thing" elicited was even smaller than the bop feud a generation earlier, although it raised similar issues. Again authoritarian voices warned against wild new noises that seemed devoid of organization and meaning. Trumpeter Roy Eldridge, a style-setter in the late Thirties and Forties, declared of Ornette Coleman: "I listened to him all kinds of ways. . . . I even played with him. I think he's jiving, baby. He's putting everybody on. They start with a nice lead-off figure, but then they go off into outer space. They disregard the chords and they play odd numbers of bars. I can't follow them."[6] Some veterans were more vehement, refusing to play with or, even listen to, the newcomers. In Los Angeles, star bop tenorman Dexter Gordon, arriving late for a job with his band, found young Ornette Coleman sitting in and sent him packing in the middle of a number. And in 1962 the bartender-manager of the Coronet Bar, a hotbed of hard-bop sentiment in the Bedford-Stuyvesant area of Brooklyn, summarily fired Cecil Taylor's band after the first set on opening night. Unintimidated, the group remounted the stand after the break but was forced to leave by outraged habitués, one of them brandishing a switchblade. Yet, as before, the opposition of entrenched forces had little effect in the long run and served mainly to close the ranks of the schismatics. In the course of time, however, these rebels became increasingly established and by the Eighties were taking their place in the overall jazz denomination. And this denomination was more and more accepted by the evolving musical establishment, which, in its continuing spirit of accommodation and inclusiveness, had long since begun to make room for the sounds of the advancing twentieth century.

These, then, were the three jazz sects. They did not necessarily grow in similar ways; each had its distinctive character and pace of development. Yet they shared broad similarities with Troeltsch's "sect-type." Some of these are implicit in the above summary, and later I will discuss others in detail. But for now, I will spell them out in general terms.

Jazz movements suggest a blend of what Bryan Wilson calls gnostic and introversionist sects[7]—gnostic in that they are inspired by positive, intuitive knowledge of the supernatural, and introversionist in that they withdraw socially and psychologically from unsympathetic, outside worlds in order to nurture and practice their beliefs. Animated by the messages of prophetic musicians and aided by distinctive myths and rituals of performance, initiation, language, dress, and humor, they rebel against the prevailing musical system, aggressively distancing themselves from its banalities, corruptions, formalities, and supporters. Organization is simple, especially at first, with esteem and role resting on merit constantly reviewed by watchful peers.

Sectarian structure also depends on race. The ecstasy and fellowship of the music sometimes dissolve ethnic barriers, but both Jim Crow and "Crow Jim" (anti-white feelings among blacks) can be as strong in the jazz community as elsewhere in American society. Until recently blacks and whites did not customarily perform together, especially on records or broadcasts. And dance halls, theaters, and musicians' unions were generally segregated in a familiar pattern of pollution behavior, made all the more vehement by the unfathomable nature of the music. I do not mean to underemphasize this segregation in the following pages, but my main concern is with correspondences in the behavior of black and white followers who, despite obvious ethnic differences, demonstrated similar kinds of sect-like behavior. Thus, black and white jazz subgroups can be seen as related parts of a given jazz movement, much as black and white congregations and conferences of Methodists are related parts of an overall denomination (i.e., a mature sect).

In addition, organization depends on sex. Although not untouched by women's liberation, jazz fellowships remain heavily masculine in character and tone, particularly at their core. Women function in secondary roles as pianists, singers, dancers, den mothers, homemakers, breadwinners, and sex objects, but seldom are first-line musicians. The mystique and working conditions discourage domestic ties and reward the men's macho attitudes. Many performers feel a need for aggressive self-confidence on the bandstand, in the street, and in clubs in the midst of gangsters, vice, heavy drinking, and drugs. Even in the best of times, jobs are scarce for men, and far scarcer for women who compete in the face of ridicule or ostracism. One measure of the masculine tone of the jazz world is its fraternal argot, which is full of macho terms. And for many devotees the music itself is by definition masculine. As one pianist asserted in 1973, "Jazz is a male language. It's a matter of speaking that language and women just can't do it."[8]

The sexual division of labor and prestige in music is ancient and in most systems upheld by powerful taboos. In some African cultures women are still not allowed to play, hear, or even look at certain magically endowed instruments except in special, ritual circumstances.[9] And until recently women were seldom seen in symphony orchestras. Yet extremes of male dominance did not come immediately to jazz. Like other ecstatic movements, jazz brotherhoods initially permitted women to play prominent ritual roles, relegating them to lesser functions only as the fellowship matured.[10] In the early days, women stars such as Bessie Smith and Billie Holiday shone as brightly as male performers. But this is no longer the case. Many women now believe they must play twice as well to attract half the attention their male counterparts receive. Contemporary guitarist Sonny Sharrock, whose wife, Lynda, a singer, has failed to break through the sexual barrier, told critic Valerie Wilmer, "If a woman is going to invade the holy territory of the artist, she's in for a lot of trouble. . . . I know that people refuse to give Lynda any recognition at all." Wilmer herself, one of the few female jazz writers, observed that even when a woman performer is noticed, she is measured in masculine terms: " 'You play like a man' was always the ultimate compliment a female musician could receive, fractionally better than the other painful cliche—'you sound good for a woman.' "[11] Not a few jazzmen, as we'll see, feel that women's extreme susceptibility to the emotional power of the music makes them unpredictable front-line performers and potentially dangerous distractions both on and off the bandstand, a view shared by many in the classical-music world.

Not all jazzmen think this way, of course. Given their broad range of beliefs and practices, there is seldom unanimity on such questions and no one person or group can be called representative.[12] Nevertheless, usually there is a consensus rooted in a pattern of priority and influence flowing from the core outward. Elite musicians and critics set the style and pace, dramatize ideals, and to some extent serve as role models. Their music and words are commanding and familiar while the evidence of more peripheral communicants remains relatively scanty. I have relied mainly on the examples of the better known figures, although in the final chapter I will focus on those who in varying degrees followed their leads.

Jazz sects, along with many of their religious counterparts, are, to use Victor Turner's terms, "liminal" or "liminoid," existing on the fringes or in the cracks of the social structure. They consist of adolescents, apprentice musicians, ethnics, or artists (sometimes all at the same time) in the fissures or on the edges of the received order. Flourishing in egalitarian, simply organized groups and guided mainly by peers, they operate at a remove from many ordinary responsibilities and preconceptions and freely question conventional standards of behavior and belief. Their climate is charged with potency and potentiality that encourages experimentation, spontaneity, improvisation, and imagination in art and in conduct.[13]

In New Orleans, after 1900, teenage clarinetists Sidney Bechet and Albert Nicolas, drifting away from the influence of family and school, acquired their education informally. Barely out of knee pants, they sat on the curb in front of their houses, playing their horns and exchanging musical ideas that were then traded with other youngsters. All of them were enthusiastic members of the "second line" who performed behind their heroes in local marching bands on secondhand or homemade instruments. In those days, musicians were often "ear men," unable to read music, and improvisation and spontaneity were essential, especially in the heady world of jazz novices, with its impromptu music and adolescent pranks. Fledgling cornetist Louis Armstrong learned his profession in often violent honky-tonks and dance halls in the company of colorful prostitutes and hustlers with names like "Mary Jack the Bear," "Steel Arm Johnny," and "Black Benny," the latter a drummer and trickster who looked after younger musicians when he was not in jail himself. ("He was devilish and everybody loved him," Armstrong recalled.)[14] In this liminal environment apprentice musicians shaped their imaginations and outlooks without orthodox guidance, but not without models, for there were plenty of commanding figures, and fortunate novices were tutored by their idols.

In Chicago, during the Twenties, restless white youngsters at Austin High School, on the West Side, found insufficient emotional nourishment at home or school and discovered special meanings in jazz. Cornetist Jimmy McPartland who, along with saxophonist Bud Freeman and clarinetist Frank Teschmacher, made up the nucleus of this group, recalled how they stumbled on records by the New Orleans Rhythm Kings at the local malt shop: "I believe the first tune we played was 'Farewell Blues.' Boy, when we heard that—I'll tell you we went out of our minds. Everybody flipped. It was wonderful. So we put the others on. . . . We stayed there from about three in the afternoon until eight at night, just listening to those records one after another, over and over again. Right then

and there we decided we would get a band and try to play like
these guys."[15] Turned-off teenagers became true believers,
bound in musical fellowship. Soon they discarded much of
their formal, musical training (along with the violins most of
them had studied) and went about becoming jazzmen. Prohibition Chicago was a world of dangerous, mob-owned speak-
easies, big spenders, fast women, speedy cars (Frank Teschmacher died at twenty-six in an automobile crash), and heavy
drinking (which infected many musicians). Young jazzmen
learned about music and life as it came, regarding the best
players of the day as models, in similar fashion to apprentice
jazzmen before and after them.

These experiences were shared in varying degrees by other
young enthusiasts. Some were novices who performanced only
for a small circle of friends or at the junior prom, but who
nonetheless participated in the rituals of the jazz community.
Others were non-musicians who in their own ways shared in
the ecstasy, lingo, faddish dress, and hip humor. For casual
young followers, as well as for the most devoted, jazz gave
meaning to expanding sensibilities intensified by the aggressive
and sexual impulses of adolescence.

Devotees of whatever age, however, were liminally suspended between conventional categories, high and low culture
(the dance hall and the concert hall), and, more significantly,
between black and white worlds. This was especially true of
recognized musicians used to marginal working conditions,
nomadic night people playing at irregular hours in places that
discouraged conventional social life and responsibilities. In
good circumstances, they played for weeks in a single place,
but more often were booked for one-night stands, living and
sleeping on crowded buses and eating on the fly between
performances sometimes five hundred miles apart. Tours could
last for two months or longer. Stan Kenton's band was on the
road eleven months a year for most of its long life. And during
the hot summer of 1937 the Benny Goodman band played
thirty consecutive nights, typically finishing at one o'clock in
the morning. If the next booking was more than two hundred
miles away, they piled into the band bus and arrived at their
destination late in the morning, exhausted. As Goodman

remembered, "After eight hours bumping around in a bus, trying to catch a few winks of sleep, the only thing you wanted to do was to crawl into bed and get some sleep before it was time to go to work again. There are more towns in America that I have only seen after dark than I care to think about."[16] His band was more fortunate than most; some spent weeks on the road without a night in a real bed. Such circumstances, often marked by heavy drinking, casual sexual contacts and disrespect for "square" listeners, reinforced marginal behavior more familiar to black jazzmen from the underside of society than to white players.

These circumstances helped the jazz fraternity breed a deep sense of understanding and fellowship. Performers felt a profound mutuality that stemmed from moments of musical ecstasy, sometimes during formal presentations in dance halls, clubs, or theaters, but more commonly in informal gatherings, especially in what used to be called jam sessions, which in the right circumstances produced transcendent occasions of ser-endipitous improvisation. The fellowship developed in such moments suggests what Turner terms "communitas," a spiritual bond nourished in liminality and based on otherworldly experience or knowledge. Communitas, he explains, is usually considered sacred because it transgresses the rules that govern institutionalized relationships. It leads to unprecedented feel-ings of potency fueled by extraordinary interpersonal com-munication simultaneously operating at different levels of awareness—"wholeness wholly attending," in deep understand-ing and reciprocity.[17]

During the Twenties, a lonely Artie Shaw, then in his late teens, was the clarinetist in a Chinese restaurant in Cleveland. The work was uninspiring until one night a young pianist, Claude Thornhill, sat in, entrancing Shaw. At the end of the evening, Shaw drove him home and later remembered: "We parked on the street in front of his hotel; and there we sat until six A.M. During that time we talked and talked and *talked*. He must have been pretty bottled-up too, at the time, for he seemed to need all this talk as much as I did. We parted at daylight. Although I had only known him for one night, I felt far closer to him than to anyone I had ever known in my life before." Shaw found in his new friend the first non-Jew with whom he could dicuss "the enormous gulf between myself and all gentiles." Although they worked different hours, they found time to talk over endless cups of coffee, and on days off, Shaw recalled, "We used to take long rides out into the country or along the lake shore, gabbing our heads off about everything and anything under the sun and/or moon—not only about music but also about a little thing called Life. Once in a while I brought my horn and we'd go somewhere where there was a piano and stay up for hours on end playing any and all sorts of music, just by way of exchanging further ideas or occasionally collaborating on an original piece."[18] Eventually Thornhill joined the band at the restaurant, and later he and Shaw collaborated in other groups during a long friendship. Commenting on such relationships from another viewpoint, singer Anita O'Day averred, "I can tell you now that musical intimacy is on a completely different plane—deeper, longer-lasting, better than the steamiest sexual liaison. Passion wears out, but the closer you work with a really rhythmical, inventive swinging musician, the closer you become."[19]

Not all communitarian feelings in jazz were so narrow, intense, or enduring. Sometimes they pervaded whole bands or existed, however superficially, among large numbers of listeners. But whatever their depth or degree, they were a powerful socializing force, bringing devotees together, providing reassurance despite the players' diffidence and in the face of outside hostility, and smoothing over internal friction. Under communitarian influence, followers whose interests and outlooks otherwise had little in common found themselves in close contact and mutual sympathy, sharing gnostic truths which reached into their existential cores.

Jazz movements develop, I believe, along lines laid out by Max Weber and his followers. Weber demonstrated, among other things, that religious innovations come in "breakthroughs" inspired by prophets who generate feelings of ecstasy, of being in touch with a deity or other supernatural source. At first the message attracts only a small group of apostles, but as it spreads the original circle expands into a congregation which, though simple at first, becomes increasingly complex. Eventually it begets priests and other functionaries who rationalize the prophecy and related values, clarifying, specifying, and systematizing the myths and rituals to meet contemporary demands, and writing them down in gospels, which has the effect of closing the canon and making them more accessible and palatable to a growing following. Thus, the prophecy, however watered-down, eventually becomes comfortably incorporated into the larger culture.[20]

Similarly, jazz sects begin in cults then move in a churchly direction. By cult I mean a loose group almost without organization, not so much a brotherhood as a transient, fluctuating collection of individuals drawn together by ecstatic experience. The cult requires little, if any, common discipline and permits other religious affiliations. It demands only loyalty to the source of the attraction and appropriate rituals which may be part of a broader system of belief. In short, the cult represents the extreme of personalized, non-institutionalized religious activity, which tends to become more formal and complex as it develops.[21]

Jazz sects start out in the cultic ferment of prophetic figures, like Bix Beiderbecke, Charlie Parker, and Ornette Coleman, men with messages and auras powerful enough to break through accepted customs and beliefs. Such charismatics change not only musical tastes but the outlooks and life-styles of listeners who fall under their spell. Before long the prophet acquires a small, elite following, mostly musicians, but gradually, as his message spreads in personal appearances, by word of mouth, and through recordings, he attracts a highly personalized and unstructured following composed of aesthetically adventurous individuals whose taste is volatile but who remain zealous while in the fold. Cultists demand stylistic purity of their idols and shun listeners who accept tainted music or musicians. For the most part, however, they readily tolerate other belief systems—including those of other art forms (including modern classical music) or religions (Christianity, Judaism, Islam, as well as more exotic faiths)—so long as they do not threaten the jazz life. Moreover, jazz cults, untroubled by most kinds of deviance or odd behavior, condone or even encourage them so long as they do not interfere with the music or its devotions. The cult asks only that believers revere the proper music, idols, and objects, and in some instances follow tacitly approved practices of dress, vocabulary, and association.

If it survives long enough, the jazz cult, like its religious counterparts, tends to merge with similar groups, becoming part of a more formal, increasingly structured body, a sect. Admirers of, say, Bix Beiderbecke extend their fascinations to Louis Armstrong and Duke Ellington, or the other way around. And, as the movement grows, its membership expands and differentiates. Elitists find discerning newcomers in their midst, gifted young musicians and critics whose hearts are in the music first and last. Newcomers also include less committed enthusiasts, fellow travelers, including musicians, writers, record collectors, hipsters, and others absorbed in the music but maintaining important links to the outside world. From these ranks come believers, some accredited by the establishment, who perform priest-like functions, rationalizing and certifying sectarian rituals and myths in broadly acceptable ways: critics, who explain and evaluate the new sounds; historians, who put the plots, characters, and settings of the music's past into meaningful order and perspective; and curators, including collectors and discographers, who preserve sacred objects and verify the details of the emerging canon. As the rationalization evolves, jazzmen with classical training come forward to blend the music with comfortably familiar forms of classical and popular music. Their dilutions attract large numbers of casual communicants—occasional record buyers, concert and club patrons, and recreational dancers—whose essentially conventional tastes are still adventurous enough to be intrigued by the now temperate sounds. The fringe followers acclaim the most celebrated diluters (mostly white), ignoring superior artists (mostly black), whose undiluted music has more power. Thus Paul Whiteman, a classical violinist bitten by the jazz bug during World War I, "refined" the new sounds into confections which made him the "King of Jazz" during the Twenties; in the next decade clarinetist Benny Goodman, at home with both Mozart and jazz, streamlined jazz of the Twenties so adroitly that he became wealthy and famous as the "King of Swing"; during the Fifties, pianist Dave Brubeck, who had sat at the knee of modernist composer Darius Milhaud, mixed jazz with classical and popular music in ways that put him high on the record charts and on the cover of *Time* magazine; and in the Seventies Miles Davis, a pioneer in the departures of the Fifties, led a "fusion" of jazz and rock music that brought him celebrity and fortune. The original prophets or their finest disciples are not displaced by such events, particularly in the opinion of elitists, but they rarely receive the popular rewards accorded celebrated diluters.[22]

The population of listeners has a fluid membership. Elitist, fellow travelers, and marginal or casual fans—these are far from hard and fast categories. Many a casual listener, first attracted to the music through accessible dilutions, draws closer to the core after discovering purer sounds. And there are departures as well as arrivals. At the cult stage some devotees drop out when the novelty wears off and friends move on to other kicks. Then, too, as the fellowship moves in a churchly direction, it leaves behind early believers who object to compromises and reassert original purities, as in the Dixieland Revival of the Forties or the "hard-bop regression" in the succeeding decade.

At the other end of the fellowship Young Turks, chafing under restrictive sectarian cliches and rituals, seek out new prophets whose radical messages break through settled modes, thereby creating new cults and antagonizing unbending loyalists. Thus, in the early Forties, restless young jazzmen were mesmerized by the experiments of Charlie Parker and Dizzy Gillespie, much to the horror of aging idols, like Louis Armstrong, who had changed the face of jazz a generation earlier. And in the early Sixties adventurous young players and listeners, dissatisfied with tired bop formulas, discovered fresh enchantment in Ornette Coleman and John Coltrane, dismaying elder statesmen like Dizzy Gillespie and Dexter Gordon.

As sects mature in settled and formal ways, they join sympathetic groups evolving along churchly lines and grow increasingly open and tolerant. By now most of the original sectarian zeal has dissipated, along with much of the old exclusiveness. Time wears sharp edges smooth. Intractable positions and rigorous definitions soften, old antagonism fade into a spirit of acceptance, even cooperation, a fixed establishment broadens to accommodate and include.

Today churchly movement abounds in the jazz world as old sectarian enmities cool and fade. The initial thrust of post–free jazz is not nearly so radical as that of its predecessors. Many avant-gardists now believe that free-jazz iconoclasm of the Sixties was too sweeping, particularly in its abandonment of traditional harmonic sequences. Reedman David Murray, who has returned to a big-band format with instrumental sections, tightly written arrangements, and repeated harmonic patterns, argues that it is time for jazz to return to ignored traditions. And Julliard-trained trumpeter Wynton Marsalis, seeking to reinstate some of the old harmonic rules, maintains that "Without the obstacles improvisation is nothing."[23] The distinction between jazz and classical music has been blurring for years and is now impossible to make in much avant-garde work. And many musicians who in an earlier era would have identified themselves exclusively with jazz now draw on numerous native and national traditions and find the term "jazz" too restrictive. Ornette Coleman, unhappy with the category of "jazzman," recently said, "I've always classified myself as a composer who also performs music."[24] Members of both classical and jazz camps now comfortably perform together and increasingly share similar skills and backgrounds. In 1984 Marsalis, who has played with Art Blakey's Jazz Messengers and also at the Mostly Mozart Festival, won Grammy awards for recorded solo performances in both jazz and classical categories. Seminal jazzmen, including former radicals Richard Davis, Archie Shepp, and Max Roach, are finding places on university and conservatory faculties. And the music has established beachheads at the Smithsonian and at the National Endowment of the Arts, which awarded $1.3 million of its $13-million music budget for 1983–84 to jazz projects.[25] As all this indicates, structural development now centers less on church-sect opposition or intersectarian battles than on amalgamation and synthesis in a churchly framework.

*   *   *

In sum, until recently jazz movements resembled sects, gnostically focused on spiritual knowledge accessible only to insiders and introversionist in their desire to withdraw socially and psychologically from an unsympathetic outside world. Jazz sects were multiethnic, male-oriented, liminal groups that began as loose, zealous cults, inspired by charismatic musical prophets, and gradually evolved in a churchly direction as their music, myths, and rituals become increasingly rationalized and moderated in ways that attracted a growing conventional following.

3 *Prophets*

The innovative jazzmen who inspired jazz sects were prophetic performers whose role harked back to the shaman, a figure traceable to paleolithic times and still functioning in hunting and food-gathering cultures. A visionary and healer linked to the wizard and the medicine man, the shaman is marked by his capacity to evoke ecstasy and is the medium through which the gods speak to man.[1]

A classic account of shamanic performance appears in Waldemar Bogoras' description of a seance among the Chuckchee of Siberia. Bogoras tells of the shaman occupying a special "master's place" near the back wall of a dark, crowded room after the evening meal; smoking strong tobacco, gyrating rhythmically while beating a drum, he employs ventriloquism and sleight-of-hand, singing repetitous, sometimes wordless songs especially identified with him or as part of a repertoire recognized and reacted to by his audience in words and gestures. As the spirit enters his body, the shaman moves and chatters ever more violently until the climactic moment when he communes with the supernatural before returning to his body for final incantations. Other shamen use different musical instruments and not uncommonly drugs, spiced water, or aromatic plants which help generate the magic "heat" indicative of ecstasy. "Getting hot," evidenced by emotional excitement, perspiration, or some other sign, is seen as an indication of superhuman power to produce ecstasy or trance.[2]

Much of this behavior occurs in the performance of jazzmen. One thinks of a possessed Buddy Bolden transfixing the patrons of Longshoreman's Hall in New Orleans; a perspiring Louis Armstrong, eyes shut and horn tilted up at a forty-five degree angle, galvanizing the faithful at the Sunset Cafe on Chicago's South Side; Charlie Parker hugging his saxophone to his stomach and fixing the rapt audience with a sightless stare while "blowing snakes" in the Yacht Club on Fifty-second Street; an intense John Coltrane mesmerizing the crowd at the Five Spot in lower Manhattan with one of his riveting, marathon solos. One of the best examples is King Oliver in 1923 at Lincoln Gardens in Chicago. An imposing figure who dominated the altar-like bandstand, he started performances by directing a stream of King Bee tobacco juice into the cuspidor, which he then beat with his foot to set the rhythm, and proceeded to blow the powerful, poignant sounds he was famous for. In the course of the evening he augmented his magic with a variety of tricks, such as making his cornet sound like a human or animal voice. Visiting musicians, gathered around the bandstand, were fascinated, and behind them entranced dancers performed Dionysian gyrations under a large, revolving crystal ball that scattered specks of light around the dark, closely packed hall. After forty-odd minutes of "High Society" or "Dippermouth Blues," he might peer down at the acolytes ranged before him and say with a wink, "Hotter than a forty-five." Then he would drink deeply from the bucket of strongly sugared water he kept on the bandstand.[3]

Needless to say, the presentations of the jazzman and shaman differed greatly in format, skill, kinetics, preparation, and modes of dress. But there were also broad similarities. Both worked in the evening, occupied semi-sacred spots along the walls of crowded rooms, made magic sounds, and used sleight-of-hand, rhythmic movements, music, and stimulants to get "hot." The shaman transported listeners to upper and lower worlds where they visited gods or consorted with the dead, and jazzman, like other performing artists, transported their audience to heights and depths inaccessible through ordinary experience.[4]

As with his shamanistic forebear, the jazz prophet's chief characteristic is his power to evoke ecstasy, the source of his charisma or magic attraction, giving him the power to legitimize his message with the sanction of a higher authority. The jazz hero resembles Max Weber's "exemplary prophet," who makes

no binding demands but offers an inspirational model. He is
not the instrument of the deity so much as its vessel and
inspires an elitist following among those seeking superior
religious status.[5]

The jazz player's charisma was most evident on the bandstand. Singer Ethel Waters testified that stride pianists such as
James P. Johnson "stirred you into joy and wild ecstasy. They
could make you cry. And you'd do anything and work until
you dropped for such musicians."[6] In the Twenties fledgling
guitarist Eddie Condon and his friends were mesmerized at a
performance of King Oliver's band. "It was hypnosis at first
hearing," wrote Condon. "Everyone was playing what they
wanted to play and it was all mixed together as if someone
had planned it with a set of micrometer calipers; notes I had
never heard were peeling off the edges and dropping through
the middle; there was a tone from the trumpets like warm
rain on a cold day. Freeman, McPartland, and I were immo-
bilized; the music poured into us like daylight down a dark
hole."[7] A generation later, a Columbia student and apprentice
jazzman, Bob Dorough, was seized by the charisma of Charlie
Parker. "Oh, it was *crazy* how we dug Bird." He and his friends
followed their hero everywhere, sometimes getting a special
reward. "I mean, even tho' we thought of Bird as a sort of
god, it seems he was occasionally induced to visit and blow
with lesser mortals . . . and sometimes, *you'd get to play three or
four tunes with Bird! Wow!* DONNA LEE! CONFIRMATION!
HALF-NELSON! [pieces associated with Parker]. . . .
Not to buy his every recorded solo, we collected tapes and
exchanged them—and *listened* to them. We loved every note
he played. We loved the squeaks of his reed. It was like
idolatry—it was crazy. We were Bird-happy, Bird-struck, Bird-
bent." Dorough began to devote himself almost entirely to the
music, at the expense of his schoolwork, and shortly dropped
out of college for a musical career.[8]

But if the jazz prophet's magnetism was strongest onstage,
his charisma often spread elsewhere. With or without his
instrument he could electrify the atmosphere. Pianist Fats
Waller needed only to enter a room to cause smiles. "His face
would light up with such an expression that it was transmitted

to everybody in the room," wrote clarinetist Mezz Mezzrow. "He was so magnetic with such a robust personality that you could never be sad in his presence."[9] Duke Ellington radiated glamour. "There was some sort of magic to him you wouldn't understand," declared drummer Sonny Greer. "In my whole life, I've never seen another like him. When he walks into a room, the whole place lights up."[10] Sometimes the charisma was even more enigmatic as in the haunting attraction of the introverted, saintly John Coltrane. But whatever the prophet's personality, the magic was an extension of his ecstatic music.

The charisma grew with mythical tales about the prophet while he was still alive. Many stories concerned his otherworldly connections as revealed in superhuman appetites and capacities. Trumpeter Howard McGhee testified of Charlie Parker, "I saw him drink a quart of whiskey and take a handful of benzedrine tablets. A handful of them, and swallow them and drink whiskey and then smoke pot, and do the other things he was doing besides [that is, heroin], and *stand up like a man*. . . . what I saw him take would kill an average man. . . . I was amazed."[11] Another well-known performer with an incredible tolerance for alcohol was bassist Oscar Pettiford. "He could be falling-down drunk," reported pianist Dick Katz, "but he'd always come up with something. He had an almost superhuman quality about him. I don't want to get too mystical, but I was around him a lot."[12]

The prophet's absentmindedness further contributed to his otherworldliness. Teddy Hill, the manager of Minton's Playhouse, a bop headquarters in the Forties, recounted how house pianist Thelonious Monk would show up an hour early for the first set and then be missing when it began, only to be found an hour later off alone in a back room lost in composition. In distracted moments he seemed oblivious both to time and space. As Hill said, "He just doesn't seem to be present unless he's actually talking to you and then sometimes all of a sudden in the middle of a conversation his mind is somewhere else. He may be still talking to you, but he is thinking about something else."[13] All of this reinforced the image of a naive genius. Perhaps the best example is Bix Beiderbecke, whose young face had the look of a consumptive Romantic poet (especially in the well-known photograph of him at eighteen) and who often seemed totally preoccupied with transcendent concerns. "Everybody loved Bix," said fellow bandsman Russ Morgan. "The guy didn't have an enemy in the world but he was out of this world most of the time."[14]

Zaniness also contributed to prophetic charisma, suggesting that the nonconforming hero was possessed by an otherworldly vision. The jazz realm had its full quota of clowns and eccentrics whose crazy feats and stunts affronted convention but charmed followers. Charlie Parker disciple August Blume declared, "I worshiped the guy, because a man like him comes along once in ten lifetimes. Sure he did crazy things. . . . I guess the only thing he never did was invent the A-bomb."[15] (In bop argot "crazy" meant great and conferred the highest esteem.) But the hero's madness could go too far. Founding prophets Scott Joplin and Buddy Bolden ended their days tragically in mental institutions, and some latter-day giants, including Charlie Parker and Bud Powell, spent time in asylums. The true believer shook his head over such events, but interpreted them as further evidence of the prophet's trascendence. Commenting on Bolden's fate, Louis Armstrong wrote, "People thought he was plumb crazy the way he used to toss that horn. The sad part is Buddy actually did go crazy a few years later and was put away in an insane asylum in Jackson, Mississippi. He was just a one-man genius that was ahead of 'em all . . . too good for his time."[16]

Thus the afflicted jazz giant was cast in the role of psychotic genius, consumed prematurely by his fidelity to the ideals of the jazz world and posthumously reborn in myth to symbolize them. While he was still alive, however, his charisma helped obscure his personality. Even if he was a familiar figure, he remained curiously unknown, psychologically distant. Duke Ellington, for instance, though constantly in the spotlight, was almost inscrutable even to musicians who toured with him day after day. He cleaned them out at poker on payday, worked closely with them musically, yet remained essentially enigmatic and aloof. Lester Young was even more so. John Hammond, a critic and promoter as responsible as anyone for Young's place in the jazz pantheon, summed up twenty years of

acquaintance in this way: "For the first seven I was nothing
less than a worshipper at the shrine. . . . My enthusiasim knew
no bounds, but I was not alone in finding it next to impossible
to carry on a conversation with him. His world was a special
one, and I was never to be a part of it."[17] Bix Beiderbecke also
remained strangely distant even to his closest associates who
were awed by his musical genius and did not presume to
examine his personality. At the end of Beiderbecke's career,
long-time apostle Hoagy Carmichael found that nobody seemed
to know who or what the cornetist really was. At first Carmichael exempted himself, but then had to admit, "A terrible
thought struck me. I didn't know either."[18]

Perhaps he unconsciously did not want to peer past the
prophetic cloak and discover mere humanity. Restrictions on
personal contact helped generate reverence among admirers.
Erving Goffman has noted how "In the matter of keeping
social distance, the audience itself tends to cooperate in a
respectful fashion, in awed regard for the sacred integrity
imputed to the performer." In effect, the mystery conceals
mortal flaws and the fact that "behind the mystery there is no
mystery."[19] "Authority," explained Charles Cooley, "especially
if it covers intrinsic personal weakness, has always a tendency
to surround itself with forms of artificial mystery, whose object
is to give the imagination a chance to idealize."[20] Thus,
worshipers gave jazz heroes considerable breathing room. John
Lewis, a disciple of Charlie Parker, declared, "Bird was like
fire. You couldn't get too close."[21] Yet even when the genius'
flaws became obvious, the charisma might remain. Nat Hentoff
has told how "A brilliant drummer, drunk, hit an alto saxophonist hard in the mouth at a New York club one night. 'I
didn't hit him back because he was high,' said the altoist.
'Besides, I love him for what he plays, not for what he is.' "[22]
At bottom, then, the music and the man were separate, existing
on two different planes, the sacred and the profane. As long
as the prophet provided ecstasy, his followers tolerated or
mystified most of his mortal failings.

Some even made him a deity. One night Fats Waller, in the
midst of one of his clowning piano rituals, spotted his idol,
Art Tatum, in the house and, according to Rex Stewart, jumped

up "like he'd been stung by a bee," and announced gravely, "Ladies and gentlemen, God is in the house tonight. May I introduce the one and only Art Tatum." (Another version had Waller announcing, "I just play the piano. But God is in the house tonight.")[23] Certain musicians who were accorded divinity were not above exploiting it. Charlie Parker once refused to take the stage, telling an imploring club owner, "You can't put me on the bandstand. I'm God." But in more sober moments he made no such claim. Once when one of his long-suffering managers, despairing at his childish intransigence, yelled, "I quit. You think you're God," Parker, immediately deflated, replied in a sweet and serious tone, "Man, I was born out of a pussy just like you."[24]

Successful religious prophets view themselves not as the deity, but as its agent,[25] and jazz luminaries are no exception. As drummer Billy Higgins put it, "Music doesn't come from you, it comes through you."[26] Singer Abbey Lincoln agreed, "Sometimes I hear the sound coming from me and I know I'm not controlling it. It's like being a medium. It uses me."[27] But such declarations did not prevent followers from eagerly deifying their idols, or discourage some performers from claiming divine sanction, particularly in the heady climate of the Sixties. Tenor player Albert Ayler, regarded by believers as an evangelical preacher-prophet, a visionary singing in tongues, declared in an open letter to Imamu Amiri Baraka (Leroi Jones), "It was revealed to me that we [he and his brother Donald] had the right seal of God almighty on our forehead," marking them as spiritual purifiers.[28] Sometimes the sanction was claimed for a specific performance, as when the word went out that John Coltrane had communicated with God before recording "A Love Supreme."[29]

Many jazzmen regarded stylistic innovation in religious terms. Dizzy Gillespie thought that "There is a parallel with jazz and religion. In jazz a messenger comes to the music and spreads his influences to a certain point, and then another comes and takes you further. In religion—in the spiritual sense—God picks certain individuals from this world to lead mankind up to a certain point of spiritual development."[30] And pianist McCoy Tyner, one of many post-boppers who blended his Muslim faith with his belief in the jazz ideal, or gnosis, regarded Charlie Parker and John Coltrane as emissaries charged with bringing sacred truths to earthlings. "John and Bird were really like messengers. In other words, God still speaks to man."[31]

Like the Weberian prophet, the jazz genius was a powerful agent for change, with charismatic power to defy the status quo and sweep whole groups into new paths. Ralph Ellison recalled how in 1929 Lester Young, tall and intense, newly arrived in Oklahoma City, "left absolutely no reed player and few young players of any instrument unstirred by the wild, excitingly original flights of his imagination. Who else but Lester Young, who with his battered horn upset the entire Negro section of the town. One of our friends gave up his valved instrument for the tenor saxophone and soon ran away from home to carry the new message to Baltimore, while a good part of the efforts of the rest was spent trying to absorb and transform the Youngian style."[32] Earlier, Louis Armstrong had made a similar impression in New York. In a dramatic confrontation at Harlem's Apollo Theatre he overwhelmed reigning trumpeter Joe Smith, and after the triumph, trumpeter Louis Metcalf reported, "They were sayin' 'Now here's another *King*!' And the house was his. It was a real thrill for me because Louis comin' out of New Orleans and me from St. Louis were both of the same style, and he was backin' up everything I had been trying to tell—only *he* made them understand."[33]

The prophet articulated for the inarticulate. He said dramatically and convincingly what his admirers felt most deeply but could not say themselves, things bottled up inside struggling to get out. Gerald McKeever, a would-be musician, recalled being devastated by the sounds of John Coltrane. "I was sitting there, digging . . . screaming. . . . I *felt* so much of what he was saying, I had so much I wanted to say to the whole world . . . and *I didn't know how to get it out*! He was *my God*!"[34] In the Twenties, Bix Beiderbecke did the same for his disciples. As Mezz Mezzrow wrote, "When you're a kid and your first

millennium falls on you, when you get in a groove that you
know is *right* for you, find a way of expressing something deep
down and know it's *your* way—it makes you bubble inside. But
it's hard to tell outsiders about it. It's all locked up inside you,
in a kind of mental prison. Then, once in a million years,
somebody like Bix comes along and you know the same
millennium is upon him too. . . . That gives you the courage
of your convictions—all of a sudden you know you aren't
plodding around in circles in a wilderness."[35]

Once the prophet's revelation had reached the audience, his
image further elaborated and reinforced the message. The
image, a mixture of fact and fiction reflecting the emotional
requirements of the following, showed the hero as an embodiment of the mystique. Referring to Bix Beiderbecke, Eddie
Condon declared, "Nothing which has been invented about
him is as accurately symbolical as the everyday things he did.
Without effort he personified jazz; by natural selection he
devoted himself to the outstanding characteristics of the music
he loved. He was obsessed with it . . . he drove away all other
things—food, sleep, vanity, desire."[36] Jimmy McPartland reverently agreed, "His main interest in life was music, period. It
seemed as if he just existed outside that."[37] The same was said
of Charlie Parker. "He was all music," averred trumpeter
Kenny Dorham. "When he played he couldn't play enough,
and nothing stopped his playing."[38] Other accounts said that
he played for days on end without sleep, a habit which dated
back to the early days of the music. A New Orleans veteran
told how Jelly Roll Morton would sit at the keyboard all night
and added, "We used to ask him, when do you sleep—he fool
[*sic*] at the piano so much."[39]

Followers were in awe of such single-mindedness, and aspiring musicians sought to emulate it along with the prophet's
sounds and technique. They also copied his walk, talk, and
clothing. In the beginning of his career cornetist Rex Stewart
found himself alone and adrift in New York. "Then," he
recalled, "Louis Armstrong hit town: I went mad with the rest
of the town. I tried to walk like him, talk like him, eat like
him, sleep like him. I even bought a pair of big policeman
shoes like he used to wear and stood outside of his apartment

waiting for him to come out so I could look at him. Finally I got to shake hands and talk with him."[40] Not all worshipers were so faithful in their emulation, but in one way or another the prophet's example determined much of what they did, musically and otherwise.

For young liminars settling into the new faith, and for veterans as well, the prophet dramatized the ongoing verities of the music and mystique. Merely listening to him in person or on records was sometimes enough to reinforce one's faith, but to perform along beside him was something else again, an experience dearly sought after, and those lucky enough to achieve it often found themselves playing far over their heads. Attesting to Buddy Bolden's serendipitous influence, trombonist Albert Gleny wrote, "You couldn't help from playing good with Bolden."[41] Performing with Beiderbecke had a similar effect. "The thing about Bix's music is that he drove a band," avowed clarinetist Pee Wee Russell. "He more or less made you play better. Whether you had any talent or not he made you play better."[42] Dizzy Gillespie, a charismatic hero in his own right, freely admitted, "I guess I probably played my best with Charlie Parker. He would inspire you; he'd make you play better."[43] Lesser prophets had a similar influence. Speaking of Count Basie, sideman Johnny Mandel explained, "The band doesn't feel good until he's up there. He makes everybody play differently. There's no going against him; it's almost like having a big father on the bandstand. And not just with his own band. I was working with a poor band Buddy Rich was leading in 1945. One night Basie sat in and suddenly everyone was playing differently."[44]

Accounts of the prophet's magic were uplifting and reassuring, even when his mortal failings were painfully evident. And hardship and suffering only enhanced his charisma, for in the jazz sect, as elsewhere, sorrow had a sanctifying power.[45] But some admirers preferred to belittle or ignore their idol's defects and tribulations. True believer Angelo Ascagni, who had more than ample firsthand opportunity to observe Charlie Parker's agonies and shortcomings, asserted, "I always felt safe with Bird. You get a kind of well-being because he was so sure of himself. He always knew where he was going and why and why he was there."[46] Cocky or not, or troubled or not, the charismatic could make admirers feel larger than life. Bill Cole, one of John Coltrane's hagiographers, told of a visit he and a friend paid to the great man, and concluded, "When we both walked out of Trane's hotel room, we both felt as though we were ten feet tall."[47]

The prophetic artist was a messenger from beyond who demonstrated the mystique, inspired the following, embodied the sectarian values, and provided a rallying symbol. In liminal jazz groups, lacking conventional guidelines and governing hierarchies, he provided followers noted for their individualism and idiosyncrasies with definition, justification, and discipline.

Gnosis

"I am a devout musician."
Charlie Parker, upon being asked by an English reporter about
his religious affiliation

"Music is a religion to me, and it's also a love affair."
Singer Sheila Jordan[1]

From the earliest times, loud sound has evoked feelings of awe, fear, and divine power, and has been used to praise gods, its sacred or magical force gradually transferred from natural sounds, like thunder and wind, to man-made devices such as drums, horns, church bells, organs, and other musical instruments.[2] Thus music—organized sound—has long been associated with religious purposes and meanings. And even in our own time, when reason has cast out much traditional supernaturalism, music retains its supernatural power.

The heart of the sectarian gnosis was the positive, intuitive knowledge that jazz was holy or magic. For most black devotees this was only natural, for even if they were unaware of the sacred associations of its antecedents in African and colonial cultures, it was common knowledge that much of it came from the church. New Orleans veterans testified that cornetist Buddy Bolden, reputedly the first jazz musician, had come by his inspiration in religious services. "Each Sunday, Bolden went to church and that's where he got his idea of jazz music. They would keep perfect time by clapping their hands," said guitarist Bud Scott.[3] Trumpeter Mutt Carey agreed: "Hell, that music was swinging all the way back to Bolden's time, and before that in the Holy Roller churches where he got it from."[4] And since then, other jazzmen have found inspiration in a similar source. In the Twenties young Dizzy Gillespie, raised as a respectable Methodist in a small South Carolina town, often sneaked over to the sanctified church on Sunday evenings to witness enthusiastic worship frowned upon by his parents. "Like most black musicians," he wrote, "most of my inspiration, especially with rhythms and harmonies, came from the church. I first learned about rhythms there and all about how music could transport people spiritually . . . and I've just followed that ever since."[5] Bassist Charles Mingus, growing up in Los Angeles a few years later, had a similar education. "A lot of my music," he said, "comes from the church. All the music I heard when I was very young was church music." His father went to a Methodist church, where Mingus and his sisters sometimes played in a trio. But his stepmother took him to Holiness services which were "too raw for my father. He didn't dig my mother going there. At the Holiness church the congregation gives their testimonial before the Lord, they confess their sins and sing and shout and do a little Holy Rolling. Some preachers cast out demons; they call their dialogue 'talking in tongues' or talking in an unknown tongue (language that the Devil can't understand). People went into trances and the congregation's response was wilder and more uninhibited than in the Methodist church. The blues was in the Holiness churches—moaning, riffs and that sort of thing between the audience and the preacher."[6]

A good deal of such ecstasy—reminiscent of a shamanic seance with its rhythmic kinesis, music, words, and audience participation—carried over into jazz. And in some ways the jazzman was like a preacher.[7] Guitarist Danny Barker noted, in connection with Bessie Smith, "If you had any church background, like people who came from the South, as I did, you would recognize a similarity between what she was doing and what those preachers and evangelists from there did, and how they moved people. Bessie did the same thing on stage . . . she could bring about mass hypnotism."[8] Charles Mingus liked to think of the bandstand as something like a pulpit. "You're up there . . . trying to express yourself. It's like being a preacher in a sense."[9] Art Davis, who played bass with John Coltrane, compared him to an evangelical spellbinder. During his riveting solos, "People would just be shouting, like you go to church, a holy roller or something like that. . . . You could hear the people screaming."[10]

Given these associations, it is understandable that some jazzman went back to the church to charge their creative batteries. This was especially true of the hard-boppers of the Fifties and later who emphasized the religious roots of their music with titles such as "The Preacher," "Sermonette," "The Congregation," "Wednesday Night Prayer Meeting," "Moanin'," and "Ecclesiasticus." Others even composed liturgical jazz, the best known examples being Duke Ellington in his three sacred concerts and Mary Lou Williams in her jazz masses. Still others performed nonliturgical jazz in churches or church-like environments. Shortly before his death, John Coltrane and his wife, Alice, considered, as she said, "setting up a center that would be like a church . . . a place for musical meditation and maybe someone would feel like praying. It would bring others a kind of fellowship based on the music."[11]

Yet at bottom it was not any such association that made jazz sacred or magical. Its supernaturalism existed independently, in its mysterious power to evoke ecstasy. The responses it drew varied according to the listeners' background, sex, age, psychological makeup, and social situation, but all believers found in it some degree of transcendence or catharsis—particularly in the blues. Stride pianist Willie "The Lion" Smith wrote, "You could say the blues are really a sacred thing with [blacks]. . . . They sing and play what their heart tells them to express. If one is in trouble, and downhearted, he can really express the blues. That's where the spiritual thing comes in."[12] And singer Alberta Hunter declared, "To me, the blues are— well, almost religious. They're like a chant. The blues are like spirituals, almost sacred. When we sing the blues, we're singin' out our hearts, we're singin' out our feelings. Maybe we're hurt and just can't answer back, then we sing or maybe even hum the blues. Yes, to us, the blues are sacred. When I sing:

'I walk the floor, wring my hands and cry. Yes, I walk the floor, wring my hands and cry' . . . what I'm doing is letting my soul out."[13]

Followers of other jazz had similar reverence. Guitarist Eddie Condon told how during the Twenties his fellow white converts in Chicago treated the music of King Oliver and Louis Armstrong "as if it were a new religion just come from Jerusalem."[14] Still others regarded it as a form of sacred expression or affirmation. Saxophonist Ornette Coleman believed that a dedicated performance was "just showing that God exists."[15] And Charles Mingus explained how he and Eric Dolphy "used to really talk and say words with our instruments. . . . We had different 'conversations,' we'd discuss our fear, our life, our views of God—which is still our main subject today." Later he emphasized, "I believe in God. . . . And that's what the music is about, man."[16] Not all followers "believed in God"—certainly not Mingus' god—but many shared sacred feelings about the music. Speaking of his mainly white coterie in Chicago during the Twenties, pianist Art Hodes explained, "We lived with the beat. Our mistress was music. We worshiped her as a god. In the morning when we'd start in on the vic (phonograph) 'til late at night when we were exhausted and had to sleep, we had but one desire—to play, to play better this minute than we had the last, to hear something played that would knock us out."[17]

Such devotion was not uncommon among true believers. Pianist George Wallington, one of the few white performers to find a place in the early bop movement, remembered, "In the years between '42 and '43 [*sic*], the fellows lived only to play. We were obsessed by the new music. There was such pleasure in the faces. We would play our regular jobs until three in the morning, then go to an after-hours place till seven and then wait around a few hours till Nola Studios would open at nine, rent a studio and practice some more. Our bodies were sustained by enthusiasm, and when they alone could not carry through a weaker physique, a little barbiturate pill helped. . . . I remember Bird tapping on my window at five in the morning to get me up to play."[18] Not surprisingly, this devotion bred a certain asceticism, leading performers to do without the ordinary amenities, even necessities, rather than stint on the quality of their instruments or amount of practice time. Some players carried their horns with them constantly, practicing every free moment. Lester Young hung his horn on his bedstead so that he could get up and try ideas that came to him in his sleep. And John Coltrane, after finishing an exhausting two-hour set, repaired to the men's room or kitchen, the only refuge in some clubs, to practice his horn until it was time to go on again.

Such devotion demanded that the sacred music be kept as free as possible from impurities. Drummer Jo Jones, who liked to counsel younger musicians, advised that "Music is not only a God-given talent, but it is a God-given privilege to play music. There shouldn't be any debauchery attached to it, and it should be presented in the exact spiritual vein originally intended."[19] Not all jazzmen were so puritanical, but most believed in the importance of purity, and directed a form of pollution behavior toward outsiders who were indifferent or hostile to the gnosis. Much of this was aimed at the upholders of conventional culture ("squares"), but it was also intended for heretics who had "sold out" to commercial interests. There could be no dilution of the sacred; attempts to alloy it could only void the true magic. "If you start taking what's pure in a man and you start putting it on a bill of sale, you somehow can't help but destroy it," warned New Orleans master Sidney Bechet.[20] Few jazzmen could remain entirely uncommercial because hard times and unsympathetic audiences forced compromises, but the ideal remained even among backsliders. Benny Goodman recalled his scuffling days before making a fortune as the "King of Swing." "The musicians who played hot were pretty much a clique by themselves. They hung around the same places, made the same spots after work, drank together and worked together whenever they had the chance. . . . None of us had much use for what was then known, and probably always will be, as commercial musicians."[21]

Purists also avoided members of other jazz sects. Each group had its own hangouts where its version of the music reigned and its rituals could be exercised without undue disturbance from outsiders. Even in neighborhoods where jazz clubs were cheek-by-jowl true believers had no doubt about who belonged where. Critic Leonard Feather, an early champion of bop, wrote, "52nd [Street] was a divided world for many of us, particularly for musicians. Those of us who were interested in jazz passed by Leon & Eddie's as if it didn't exist. By the same token, I was seldom in Jimmy Ryan's. It represented a different kind of music. It was like a foreign territory. To me 52nd Street was the Onyx, Three Deuces, Famous Door, Kelly's Stable, Spotlite, etc. Everything else, including 21, was not forbidden territory, but foreign."[22] (Leon & Eddie's featured commercial entertainment, Jimmy Ryan's, dixieland jazz.) Sometimes such places were forbidden, too, as trumpeter Johnny Carisi, a recent convert to bop, discovered when he was thrown out of Eddie Condon's, a dixieland stronghold in the Village, for playing "too uptown."[23]

And just as the faithful learned to steer clear of profane or alien locations, they regarded as sacred the areas where their own rituals took place. The bandstand, especially, was inviolate, as were the things on it. Said pianist Cecil Taylor, "Obviously for me, the stool upon which I sit when I'm playing could be considered an altar."[24] Ideally, at least, there was no room for impurity here. Charlie Parker, who did not necessarily practice what he preached, told one disciple, "Baby, don't never get up on the bandstand with no differences on your mind. Keep the bandstand like it was a pulpit—clean. If you get any differences among you cats, leave them in the audience. When you come down, you can resume your differences."[25] Also unwelcome on the stand were the unindoctrinated and incompetent, including unqualified musicians and most women—a custom consistent with Durkheim's finding that religious rituals are generally performed on consecrated ground from which un-initiated persons, especially women and children, are excluded.[26]

Clearly the bandstand suffered profanations, but true believers still liked to think of it as a special space, and the demand for an inviolate performance area was strong even among followers outside the hard core. In his study of Chicago dance musicians during the Fifties, Howard S. Becker reported that the players regarded the bandstand as a refuge from the square world.[27] In situations where they *had* to play down among the audience, they did their best to remain free of outside disturbance and contagion. One of Becker's subjects, speaking of a job at a wedding where there was no bandstand, recalled: "We set up in a far corner of the hall, Jerry pulled the piano around so that it blocked off a small space, which was thus separated from the rest of the people. Tony set up his drums in this space, and Jerry and Johnny stood there while we played. I wanted to move the piano so that the boys could stand out in front of it and be next to the audience, but Jerry said, half-jokingly, 'No, man. I have to have some protection from the squares.' So we left things as they were."[28] They eventually needed more room, however, and some of them had to move out in front of the piano, but not before building a barricade of chairs to avoid contact with the dancers.

For many musicians the square world "out in front" was a profane one altogether different from their sacred one—where all sorts of bizarre things might happen. On any given night there might be a persistent drunk demanding "Melancholy Baby," a threatening gangster, a racial incident, or a stabbing. Out of conviction or callousness many musicians ignored even the most troublesome incidents that occurred in the audience. Nat Hentoff remembered a dance where the Duke Ellington band was playing: "There was a scuffle in front of the stand and a man was knifed. As he fell, the band continued playing without the slightest break. Only a few of the musicians showed moderately open interest, and I can still see alto saxophonist Johnny Hodges, who was in the middle of a solo when the knife came out, not indicating by so much as a change of expression that anything untoward was happening."[29] In other circumstances, some musicians demonstrated their protective obliviousness, or disdain, by turning their backs to the audience while performing, refusing to announce numbers, avoiding eye contact, or otherwise ignoring those who did not understand or respect the music. Thus, just as "respectable" citizens, troubled by the ways jazz confused and contradicted their values, had called it dirty and demanded expurgation, jazzmen had their own form of pollution behavior directed at what they deemed the impurities of the "square" world.

Some sectarians regarded jazz as magical rather than sacred. The distinction between these two categories is often vague, since both refer to supernatural powers that possess an inner logic. But, as Victor W. Turner suggests, the sacred implies a personal deity—a god, ghost, or ancestral shade; magic bespeaks an impersonal force rooted in a specific ritual.[30] I have tried to observe the distinction here, although, of course, musicians do not necessarily do so.

Music has long been related to magic, despite attempts since Pythagoras, or earlier, to demystify it. In the case of jazz, even schooled players—those exposed most rigorously to European rationalizations—insist on its fundamentally supernatural nature. While he admits that jazz can be discussed in logical terms, pianist Cecil Taylor, a graduate of the New England Conservatory of Music, maintains that "part of this music is not to be analyzed exactly. It's about magic and capturing spirits." And this supernatural aspect is what fascinates him. "Music has those qualities which transform the environment," he believes. "It certainly transforms the players." Taylor himself once worked on a book, *Mysteries*, which emphasized that "Art works in really mysterious ways."[31]

Especially mysterious was the nature of musical performance. When things went right, it took its own course, without apparent guidance or plan, sweeping the musicians up in its inscrutable path. A performer might come in off the street, cold or unprepared, and be caught up unconsciously in the serendipitous flow, inexplicably playing notes beyond his ken. Pianist Chick Corea once told how as a youngster he joined the band of his idol, Miles Davis, and asked, "When are we going to rehearse?" Davis replied "in a hoarse whisper, 'Just play what you hear.' Uh-oh, [Corea] thought. . . . I got up on stage with that one instruction: Play what you hear. The band started off like a rocket ship in the first piece. It was 'Agitation.' I'll never forget it. I just hung on. It was like the shock of suddenly traveling at five hundred miles per hour. I knew they were playing tunes, but they had the tunes so facile and abstracted that even a musician's ear couldn't tell what chord changes were going by." But unexpectedly he found himself in his element. Exhilarated and relieved after the first set, he went to the bar where, "Miles came up behind me and whispered in my ear, 'Chick, you're a muthafucker.' That did it! What more could I ask for? I stayed with the band for three years."[32]

Serendipitous events of this sort (Duke Ellington called them "mystic moments" when performers' "muses were all one and the same")[33] were not limited to impressionable aspirants breaking into the big time. They also happened to established musicians, and even in the inhibiting, now-or-never atmosphere of the recording studio. Such was the case with Louis Armstrong's masterpiece "West End Blues" in 1928. It emerged from a mixture of previously used and spontaneous material in a partially arranged framework, but with extraordinary results that even the participants were not fully aware of at the time. "When it first came out," remarked pianist Earl Hines, "Louis and I stayed by that recording practically an hour and a half or two hours and we just knocked each other out because we had no idea it was gonna turn out as good as it did."[34] Other musicians experienced similar inspirations, overwhelming and incomprehensible (if not as dramatic), as they were unconsciously swept into a magic flow.

Nor were serendipitous feelings limited to performers. The story of jazz abounds with accounts of listeners, from fringe followers to elitists, caught up in the musician's spell. Recalling the Twenties, bandleader Paul Whiteman described "fat-faced business men who never in their lives listen to any music except cheap, thin, popular tunes; rouged young-old women who had never once heard a real concert. Something happened to them . . . that shook off their false faces and made them real and human, spontaneous and alive for once."[35] For others, the music held far more. Critic Nat Hentoff remembered

A cold winter afternoon in Boston, and I, sixteen, am passing the Savoy Cafe in the black part of town. A slow blues curls out into the sunlight and pulls me indoors. Count Basie, hat on, with a half smile, is floating the beat with Jo Jones's brushes whispering behind him. Out on the floor, sitting on a chair which is leaning back against a table, Coleman Hawkins fills the room with big, bursting sounds, conjugating the blues with a rhapsodic sweep he so loves in the opera singers whose recordings he plays by the hour at home.

The blues goes on and on as the players turn it round and round and inside out and back again, showing more faces than I had ever thought existed. I stand just inside the door, careful not to move and break the priceless sound. In a way I'm still standing there.[36]

Something of the enchantment came from the physical presence of the performer with his spontaneous synthesis of musical, verbal, and body languages, proxemics, sensitivity to audience feelings, and dramatic intuition. But the most important ingredient was what pianist McCoy Tyner called "the magic of sound," or, as critic Bill Cole put it, "the magic of sound—that aspect that takes you to another level."[37] Part of this came through in recordings, even the old 78's, on which everything conspired to destroy fidelity. Gunther Schuller has noted, "For imaginative and sensitive ears . . . even in old acoustical records, the sound of the King Oliver band, for example, in its heyday was an extraordinarily beautiful, rich and full one, mellow in timbre like a fine wine. All the good players from Louis Armstrong, through Coleman Hawkins, Ben Webster, Charlie Parker—to Sonny Rollins and beyond— yes, even Lester Young—are characterized by a larger-than-life sound and projection."[38]

As all this indicates, the sacred or magical nature of jazz expressed itself in ecstasy, which liberated the self from the confinements of ordinary space and time and aroused feelings of supernatural vitality or power. Ecstasy is related to many emotions, most obviously those linked to sex, art, battle, and sports, and it can be induced with the help of hypnosis, drugs, hyperventilation, and other agents that detach consciousness from the senses. But essentially it is something "other," incomprehensible to ordinary understanding and experience,[39] and as such has important religious ramifications, its most powerful and enduring forms providing the prophetic sparks which ignite sectarian beginnings and stimulate concern in established circles about its blatantly irrational nature.

Marghanita Laski distinguished between two kinds of ecstasy: "intensity experiences"—generally brief, tumescent, and followed by a cathartic afterglow of purification, renewal, or refreshed awareness—and more extended, lower-keyed transports.[40] Intensity experiences were common in jazz, and perhaps trombonist Bob Brookmeyer was right when he claimed that jazz is "the most ecstatic form of creativity. No form of music is as intense emotionally for the men making it as jazz. It is an immediate, sensate emotion that does not last. With a painter or sculptor, creation is a slower building process. In these and other arts you reach a pitch but only at certain times. In jazz, when you're playing with the right people, you can hit that pitch frequently in a night, and when you do, it's a thrill exceeded only by making love."[41] Intensity experiences in jazz ranged from the relatively mild sort touched upon in the first chapter in connection with ragtime to the agitated kinds elicited by more powerful musicians. The latter, especially, could be dramatic and unsettling. Trumpeter Max Kaminsky related how upon first hearing Louis Armstrong, his "dazzling virtuosity and sensational brilliance of tone so overwhelmed me that I felt as if I had stared into the sun's eye. All I could think of doing was to run away and hide until the blindness left me."[42] A generation later Charlie Mingus recalled, "When I first heard Duke Ellington in person, I almost jumped out of the balcony. One piece excited me so much I screamed."[43]

Far less dramatic are Laski's passive, gradual ecstasies, which can be consciously cultivated in solitary meditation and may result in what she calls "the discovery of a continuous and expanding focus in the trigger to the experience.[44] In the early Forties, John Lewis, a reflective, middle-class college student in Albuquerque, underwent such a period of enchantment as he listened to weekly radio broadcasts by the Jay McShann band that were beamed nationwide from the Savoy Ballroom in Harlem. He was impressed, above all, with one of the saxophonists: "The alto solos on those broadcasts opened up a whole new world of music for me. . . . The alto saxophonist was ahead of anybody in jazz. He was into a whole new system of sound and time. . . . I didn't learn that it was Charlie Parker until after the War."[45] Lewis had peak experiences during successive broadcasts, illustrating Laski's point that gradual enchantments can be punctuated by brief intensity episodes that hasten and broaden the overall ecstatic feeling.

Laski further demonstrated that ecstasies, intense or otherwise, can be marked by contrasts, for instance, between extreme passivity and high agitation. Speaking to this point, Evelyn Underhill maintained that the "passivity of concentration is . . . the necessary preliminary to spiritual energy: an essential clearing of the ground. It withdraws the tide of consciousness from the shores of sense."[46] Without meditation, the excitement which follows is not as profound or as powerful. John Coltrane sometimes retreated into the silence of his bedroom for a period of solitary contemplation before going out for an intense evening on the bandstand and, as I will show later, other jazzmen found various ways to prepare themselves psychologically for performances.

Another kind of contrast had to do with wild mood swings, from depths to heights, perhaps related to manic-depressive shifts. Laski spoke of "desolation ecstasies" in which the final exultation is made more acute by comparison to the hopelessness which precedes it.[47] It is no secret, of course, that pain and sorrow often come before renewal; out of trials and affliction emerge spiritual knowledge and liberation. Downhearted blues provides an obvious case in point, the performer pouring out his or her feelings and emerging emotionally relieved and regenerated, having touched upon transcendent truths which the listener might share. Carl van Vechten told of Bessie Smith singing at a party in his Manhattan apartment in the Twenties: "She asked for a glass of straight gin, and with one gulp she downed a glass holding nearly a pint. Then, with a burning cigarette depending from one corner of her mouth, she got down to the blues, really down to 'em, with Porter [Grainger] at the piano. I am quite certain that anybody who was present that night will never forget it. This was no actress; no imitator of a woman's woes; there was no pretense. It was the real thing—a woman cutting her heart open with a knife; until it was exposed for all of us to see, so that we suffered as she suffered, exposed with a rhythmic ferocity, indeed, which could hardly be borne. In my experience this was Bessie Smith's greatest performance."[48] A more authoritative description of Bessie's ecstasies came from fellow blues singer Alberta Hunter, who remarked that despite Bessie's "raucous and loud" voice, "she had a sort of tear—no, not a tear but there was *misery* in what she did. It was as though there was something she had to get out, something she just had to bring to the fore."[49]

The cathartic response to jazz or the blues could be mild and sweet, in its own way reminiscent of St. Augustine's response to hearing some hymns: "The tunes penetrated into my ear and truth floated into my heart, a feeling of piety and intimacy gushed over me; tears were streaming, and I felt at ease."[50] But the overwhelming raptures triggered by Bessie Smith, Armstrong, Parker, and Coltrane made devastating demands. As critic Whitney Balliett said of Cecil Taylor's ecstatic outbursts: "Each step of the way is an equal mixture of passion and thought, which in catharsis fashion, is virtually *forced* upon the listener—an exhilarating if bone-trying experience."[51] Yet, demanding as it is, the final effect was of expurgation or revitalization. As old-timer Reese D'Pree advised one young truth seeker, "Son, the blues regenerates a man."[52] And veteran pianist Art Hodes once explained, "The blues heal you. Playing the blues is like talking trouble out. You have to work the blues out of you."[53] Still other players, whose music was less influenced by the blues, found it similarly revitalizing or medicinal. Pianist Mary Lou Williams occasionally interrupted her performances to implore inattentive audiences, "Listen, this will heal you."[54] And Billy Strayhorn wrote of Duke Ellington, "He's constantly renewing himself through the music."[55]

The magic of the music was further evident in its sexual ramifications. The belief prevailed that it had mysterious powers of sexual arousal, particularly over certain female sensibilities. One contemporary musician made to Valerie

Wilmer the familiar claim that although sex was not the main impulse behind the music, it sometimes aroused women to the point where they sought to share the jazzman's charisma in bed: "The woman feels that she must have this. The thing that he's projecting, it's coming from somewhere else, but it comes through him and projects to the woman out there. She feels that the spirit is strong but she can't collect that thing where it's coming from, and so she has to collect the person its coming through!"[56] In any case, many musicians liked to please female listeners. Percussionist Art Lewis remarked, "Sometimes you might play *to* a woman. You might see a certain woman in the audience and you do try to project to her. For a musician it's very beautiful to see a woman in the audience, it's very inspiring sometimes. It can be distracting though, because you can't concentrate like you would like to. . . . When women come up to you [afterward], It's like 'O.K., I did something for you, now you do something for me.' And usually it's sex."[57] Other jazzmen found the woman's contribution to the exchange more spiritual. Trumpeter Cootie Willilams maintained that "All great jazz musicians, every one of them, have had many loves and girls in their lives. People don't read about these things in books, but a girl *is* jazz music. They throw something into the mind that makes you produce jazz."[58] Duke Ellington had a related sentiment in mind in composing "A Drum Is a Woman."

Art Lewis was not alone in believing that the sexuality aroused by the magic could be distracting, and more ascetic players found it more deleterious still, some arguing that it undermined the performer's emotional life and artistic discipline. "Jazzmen get a screwed-up sex life, and that sucks up a lot of their energy," said Ornette Coleman, who believed that when the woman's message of arousal came back to the bandstand, the musician "is going to forget what he's up there for, and he's going to start saying, 'Wait, man, where'd that bitch go that I had my eyes on when I was cooking?' You don't know how many times I've come off the bandstand and had girls come up to me and hand me a note with their address on it. . . . I'm telling you this whole sex thing has more of a negative effect on the music than drugs, I'm sure of it."[59]

Not a few musicians were uneasy about women being around the bandstand, to say nothing of being on it, even during rehearsals; and women were made acutely aware of male uneasiness. One woman who contravened this pollution behavior by playing regularly in her husband's band to, the consternation of fellow sidepersons, bitterly told Valerie Wilmer, "All they want to do is fuck you. They can't because I'm up there with him—plus I have the *audacity* to be up there on the stage—so they can't really deal with it and they have to put out some negative comment."[60] Beyond this, some bandsmen were bothered by the presence of female musicians in or around their offstage activities, inhibiting their salty talk, macho drinking, casual sexual relationships with admirers from the audience, and gambling. Noting Billie Holiday's extraordinary craps winnings in the Count Basie Band, trombonist Benny Morton pointed out, "A lot of men didn't like to play with women, because they feel they usually take away their luck."[61] In general, then, women could be unsettling influences, on or off the bandstand, because of their alleged susceptibility to the music and because their inherent supernatural powers cast a hex on the musicians' behavior.

At home, too, women were potential threats, since the sexual and emotional fulfillments they offered could lead to distracting loyalties and responsibilities. True believers went out of their way to see that domestic conformity did not cut into the pure interests of the music. Jazz was a demanding profession and many performers felt a conflict between it and their love life. But for many of the faithful it was a one-sided conflict. Explaining his recurrent marital difficulties, Louis Armstrong said, "You got to live with that horn. That's why I married four times. The chick didn't live with that horn."[62] And a drummer recently told Valerie Wilmer, "You must realize that the music is first and a woman is next. [The jazzman] is not going to give up the music for a woman, but he could give up the woman for the music."[63] Therefore, many women lived with musicians as inferior partners even though they were the family's primary breadwinners, having taken steady jobs so that their husbands could devote themselves fully to performing.

Sometimes the conflict was reversed, female performers

ending relationships with men who threatened their devotion to the music. "I can't think about anything else, never could. The people I've been with have been very jealous of the music. And the music is part of me," declared singer Sheila Jordan. "If I find somebody who knows what you're [*sic*] into and tries to pull you away from it, you'll let that that person go." She was not alone in attempts to reconcile her domestic and professional commitments. "I'm not really sure whether it's possible to have a really normal family life and career as a singer," Maxine Sullivan lamented after a marital breakup. The mystique of the music and the working conditions it imposes denies lasting domestic ties for many performers of both sexes.[64]

As might be expected in such circumstances, the sectarian subgroup has taken over some of the feelings and functions usually assigned to the family. In making this point, Valerie Wilmer quotes bassist Sirone (Norris Jones) as saying that in some jazz bands, "[Y]ou establish the love and everything of a family and then you go inside yourself and go to the depths of your inner self."[65] Threats to such "domestication" are deeply resented, even in the more commercial groups. The Stan Kenton Band (on the road for 329 days one year and logging over 60,000 miles) developed a strong "family" feeling on the bus which was their home, a feeling that was interrupted when Kenton provisionally allowed a few wives and girl friends to travel briefly with their men. The experiment had to be abandoned after complaints from unaccompanied bandsmen strenuously objecting to intrusions into the band's "domestic" equilibrium.[66] Thus the music sanctified the group and gave spiritual identity to its members. The point is not that this prevailed generally in the fellowship, but that when circumstances were right the magic of the music defied the most entrenched conventional institutions and provided substitutions for some of the pleasures and security they offered.

When initially felt by receptive listeners, the magic might bring about conversion to the gnosis. Such turnabouts, like the ecstasies stimulating them, could be immediate and unexpected or gradual and willed, but more often than not were a mixture of the two. And like religious or quasi-religious conversions in general, they all seemed to have periods of preparation in which growing patterns of suppressed feelings worked toward consciousness, joining other stirrings already there, usually in an atmosphere of anxiety or personal crisis. Such conversions altered not just musical taste but entire outlooks. In the words of Anthony F. C. Wallace, they involved "mazeway reformulations," redefinitions of the total image of the self and of the world about it which allows the individual to cope with stress at all levels. Although the image is readjusted from time to time to square with new experience, it doggedly resists broad changes which threaten internal consistency and communication. But if the image is retained too stubbornly in the face of overwhelming contradictions, anxiety builds and eventually produces symptoms such as depression, guilt, or drug abuse, or complaints about personal failure and intolerable social pressures—all familiar in the jazz commmunity.[67]

Potential jazz converts (mostly youngsters, as are most candidates for religiously tinged conversions) may respond to anxiety with a form of regression that permits conscious access to primal, nonlogical thinking. Regression ripens for them a new outlook ushered in by an ecstatic, musical experience strong and authoritative enough to sweep aside the remaining claims of the old mazeway. Whatever the final results of the convert's attempts to bring reality into line with the new mazeway, his initial feelings bring him joy, relief, and liberation from old dilemmas and torments.[68]

We cannot trace this entire procedure, of course, but there is evidence of it in the following statement by Nat Hentoff describing experiences shared variously by many other jazz devotees:

> My own introduction to the jazz life began with a record of Artie Shaw's "Nightmare." I came from a home where any overt expression of emotion was calculated and measured lest it roar out of control. In a record store one afternoon, however, I shocked myself by yelling in pleasure at the first bars of "Nightmare." . . . From Shaw I went to Duke Ellington, Louis Armstrong, Fats Waller, blues singer Peetie Wheatstraw ("The

Devil's Son-in-law"), and I was hooked. I knew how irretrievably lost I had become when, at thirteen, I went to see a Count Basie stage show on the afternoon of one of the high holidays, and never made it to the synagogue at all. Neither God or my father struck me dead, though the latter thundered for weeks. In any case, my record collection continued to grow.[69]

Here, as in other liminal conversions, are the suggestions of ambivalence and repression, ecstatic illumination, rejection of convention, parental disapproval, and feelings of joy and certainty as the revelation takes command. Hentoff's mazeway shift, affecting not just his musical taste but his whole personality, religious upbringing, ethnic background, and family relationships, was gradual, a cumulative process marked by an initial revelation and subsequent peak episodes, reminiscent of John Lewis' revelations during the Savoy broadcasts.

Charles Mingus also had a gradual conversion, to the world of Charlie Parker. At first, he did not know what to make of the new music, but slowly, at the insistence of his wife, he came to love it. "He put something else in there," Mingus discovered, "that had another kind of expression . . . more than just, say, the blues or the pain that the black people have been through. And in fact he brought hope in. . . . I knew I had an uplift to life from hearing his playing. In fact, I immediately gave up what I believed in, which came from classical and from Duke, and I felt a whole change in my *soul* when I joined in and accepted that I liked Charlie Parker."[70]

Other conversions centered on a more specific episode of sudden illumination. In 1924 Hoagy Carmichael, a student at Indiana University rebelling against the world of his parents and a burgeoning jazz pianist, was overwhelmed by a Bix Beiderbecke solo: "Boy, he took it! Just four notes. . . . But he didn't blow them—he hit 'em like a mallet hits a chime—and his tone, the richness. . . . Whatever it was he ruined me. I got up from the piano and fell on the davenport."[71] Thereafter, life was never the same: "Those four notes that Bix played meant more to me than everything else in the books. When Bix opened his soul to me that day, I learned and experienced one of life's innermost secrets to happiness—pleasure that it had taken a whole lifetime of living and conduct to achieve in full."[72] In the bop era, pianist Hampton Hawes underwent a similar metamorphosis during a Charlie Parker solo: "It was so strong, so revealing that I was molded like a piece of clay stamped out on the spot."[73] In such episodes the effect of the music, especially its rhythms, disarmed defenses culturally implanted in troubled, highly impressionable listeners, allowing positive feelings to break through. As they did, the overwhelming truth of the gnosis burst in, for the moment, at least, melting doubts and dissolving worries as the convert was reborn into the jazz life.

Thereafter, he returned regularly to the music for reaffirmation and guidance, for order and understanding. Sidney Bechet attested that it was "always the music that explained things. . . . You come into life alone and you go out of it alone, and you are going to be alone a lot of the time when you're on this earth—and what tells it all, it's the music. You tell it to the music and the music tells it to you."[74] "Every time I got into trouble, it was because I strayed from the music," wrote Mezz Mezzrow. "Whenever I latched onto the music, I flew right. I was beginning to sense a heap of morals in all of this."[75] For true believers the music was unshakable, a rock of integrity and security in a world of corruption and uncertainty. There was no deceiving the inviolate or its tools. "You can't fool the drums," declared Jo Jones, who regarded them as holy.[76] He was not alone. "The trumpet is a sacred instrument," averred Miles Davis, who viewed music with similar gravity.[77] Whether new convert or seasoned player, the jazz performer found in the music and its accessories ongoing transcendence and deliverance from an alien world full of emptiness and insecurity.

I have already noted that jazz music and its ideal, or gnosis, generated powerful and mysterious feelings of brotherhood, particularly during rituals like jam sessions—the noncompetitive sort. Louis Armstrong spoke of evenings at the Sunset Cafe in Chicago in the Twenties when the musicians would lock the doors after hours and play for themselves: "Now you talking about jam sessions . . . with everyone feeling each other's note or chord, et cetera . . . and blend with each other instead of trying to cut each other . . . nay, nay, we did not even think of such a mess . . . we tried to see how good we could make music sound which was an inspiration within itself."[78]

These feelings were not necessarily confined to the giants of the music; lesser figures could also share the fellowship and serendipity. Tenor player Art Engler remembered an occasion at Jimmy Ryan's on West Fifty-second Street in the Forties: "All the great tenormen in town seemed to be around—Ben Webster, Chu Berry, you name them. I was there, too, and I was scared stiff. But I *had* to play. I forget the tune, but suddenly somebody doubled up the time. And with all these great cats around me, I couldn't hold back. I was so excited, I just started blowing and I blew beyond what I could normally play. I could hear Chu, Ben and others urging me on. And soon there were three tenors going like mad, me in the middle. God, you'd come out of a session ten feet off the ground. . . . It always ended as one big happy party with everybody loving everybody else. It was so beautiful and exciting."[79] Nor were such feelings limited to the gentle or sympathetic performers. Hard-bitten bassist Oscar Pettiford, no sentimentalist, exclaimed after jamming with bop guitarist Charlie Christian, "We had a wonderful time blowing with Charlie. I never heard anyone like that who could play with so much *love*—that's what it was, pure *love of jazz* and great happiness just to be called part of this thing called music."[80]

To most listeners in the Forties, bop was dissonant and abrasive, anything but tender and affectionate, but when asked once if it were fighting music, two of its founders emphasized it was not. Drummer Kenny Clarke replied, "No, no, by all means, no!" and trumpeter Dizzy Gillespie added, "It was love music."[81] Even the bitterest hard-boppers, whose dissonances lacerated unattuned ears, felt the same way. Nat Hentoff told of one who descended from the bandstand after a strong set one night and said, "There was a lot of loving going on up there." Their music seemed to have more than its share of anger but, as Hentoff commented, even the angriest performers could not "hate all night on their horns."[82] No matter how hardboiled the player or how raw his music, when things went right it evoked a profound sense of understanding and respect among insiders—or to use Victor Turner's word, "communitas," liminal fellow feeling that seems to spring from something ultimate and mutually engage individuals at many levels simultaneously. Although communitarian feelings in jazz emerged most readily in small, spontaneous gatherings, they were also evident in more formal, structured situations and larger groups. Sidney Bechet remembered them in the New Orleans street bands: "We were working together. Each person, he was the other person's music: you could feel that really running through the band making itself up and coming out so new and strong. . . . That's some kind of discovery in a way."[83] Communitas of some sort was present in all successful bands, indeed it had to be for their music to jell. "There has to be understanding and teamwork among musicians," explained Max Kaminsky. "They inspire each other and build on each other's ideas. The richness and the excitement comes from the interplay of ideas. They comment on and develop what the man has just said in his solo. And they have to be able to improvise collectively so that each part makes a beautiful sensible whole."[84]

The musicians did not have to be personally close, but they had to know and understand one another artistically or the magic would not emerge in their sounds. Not just in performances, but in rehearsals, too, where its appearances were prepared for. Rehearsals in Duke Ellington's band were collective undertakings. "When we're all working together," he explained, "a guy may have an idea and he plays it on his horn. Another guy may add to it and make something out of it. Someone may play a riff and ask, 'How do you like this?' The trumpets may try something and say, 'Listen to this.' There may be differences of opinion on what kind of mute to use. Someone may advocate extending a note or cutting it off. The sax section may want to put an additional smear on it."[85] In the end Ellington had the final say in making the suggestions come together effectively. Yet he and other composers-arrangers were successful only if they were deeply aware of the capabilities and character of the musicians. They wrote for the man, not the instrument, and knew how to make his magic blend in with the whole. Good arrangers, from the time of Jelly Roll Morton and earlier, have known how to let the musicians surpass themselves and make the band become more than the sum of its parts in a serendipitous, communitarian flow. Communitas helped cut down the disciplinary problems endemic in jazz bands. Highly individualistic artists voluntarily followed a sometimes tacit but clearly defined code, sacrificing egotistical demands for the opportunity to participate in the fellowship of rituals. In such bands, the leaders tended not to be autocrats but, rather, first among equals. "Basie is still a sideman at heart," observed cornetist Rex Stewart. "He doesn't think like a leader at least not in terms of laying down the law."[86] He did not have to, for as the band's singer, Jimmy Rushing, put it, "We were like a band of brothers."[87] There was occasionally ill feeling, of course, but the strong communitarian bonds, rooted in gnostic commitment, created an atmosphere of understanding and tolerance reducing the frequency of blowups. And even when it was necessary to crack down on a bad actor, subtle pressure frequently sufficed. Duke Ellington brought miscreants into line with calculated embarrassments. If a sideman appeared for a show drunk, he might be given the first difficult solo—a challenging demand even for a sober performer. Musicians in other groups took disciplinary problems into their own hands. In the early Forties, members of the Earl Hines band, including a number of future bop stars sharing strong fellow feelings, resorted to peer pressure in attempts to bring the highly unreliable Charlie Parker into line. Singer Billy Eckstein recalled that Hines dealt Parker a series of stiff, but ineffectual, fines for missed performances, and then the sidemen took over:

> We got on him too, because we were more or less a clique. We told him "When you don't show, man, it's a drag because the band don't sound right. You know, four reeds up there and everything written for five." We kind of shamed him. So one time we're working in the Paradise Theater in Detroit, and Bird says, "I ain't gonna miss no more. I'm going to stay in the theater all night to make sure I'm here." We answered, "Okay. That's your business. Just make the show, huh?" Sure enough,

we come to work the next morning; we get on the stand—no
Bird. As usual, we think. . . . We played the whole show, the
curtains closed, and we're coming off the band cart, when all
of a sudden we hear a noise. We look under the stand, and
here comes Bird out from underneath. He'd been under there
asleep through the entire show!"[88]

Occasionally feelings of brotherhood ran strong enough
even to break through racial barriers. Rex Stewart reported
on one such interlude in Manhattan during the late Twenties:
"This was a beautiful period for the music and the players.
There was little jealousy and no semblance of Jim Crow or
Crow Jim at the sessions. Musicians were like a fraternity of
brothers, despite their being aware of the distinction that was
strongly maintained by white agents, bookers, and the public.
The jazzmen were bound together by their love for the music—
and what the rest of the world thought about fraternizing did
not matter."[89] It is hard to believe that the color line could
vanish thus, even if only briefly, so perhaps Stewart's memory
was touched here by a rosy, gnostic glow. But there have been
other times as well when ecstatic feelings have helped banish
ethnic barriers, as during the New Orleans revival of the
Forties when worshiping whites rediscovered and canonized
sometimes bewildered black veterans. And during the Forties,
according to white trumpeter Red Rodney, "There was hardly
any ill feeling at all. I don't remember any. The attitude was
just great. The camaraderie was wonderful. . . . this was
the one area in American life where there was honestly and
sincerely no prejudice whatsoever. Nothing. We lived together.
Ate together. Thought together. Felt together. . . . And then
the black revolution came in. . . . feelings became very hostile."[90]
However euphoric, such fraternal moments testify to the
extraordinary power of the music and the communitarian
impulse that emanated from it.

Audiences too shared in the gnostic fellowship, most obviously when the ecstasy flowed back and forth across the
bandstand in a mutually inspiring fashion. "If everyone is
frisky, the spirit gets to me and I can make my trombone
sing," declared New Orleans old-timer Jim Robinson. "I want
people about me. It gives me a warm heart that gets into my

music."[91] We shall see later how jazzmen inspired good dancers, and vice versa. But after the arrival of bop, when jazz became more of a listener's music, audiences still provided an enthusiastic or influential—if more pasive—feedback. Whether they sat in silent rapture, gyrated wildly, or screamed involuntarily, listeners as well as performers contributed to the spell in the Forties. Saxophonist Sonny Criss recalled how hip West Coast listeners furthered serendipitous moments: "There were many nights when I played above my head. Way above my head. . . . The audience were special people. They were artists, writers, actors, and so forth. They were very into the music. They inspired all the musicians to play their asses off."[92] Supporting testimony came later from John Coltrane: "It seems to me that the audience in listening is in an act of participation, you know. And when somebody is moved as you are . . . it's just like having another member of the group." Whether or not the listeners truly understood did not matter, as long as there was some feeling of communication, Coltrane explained, adding, "the emotional reaction is all that matters."[93]

The sense of mutual, ecstatic understanding helped inspire the supernatural feelings which lay at the center of the gnosis and animated the rituals that are the subject of the next chapter.

Rituals

By rituals I mean prescribed, repeated practices and patterns relating to the music and to gnosis.[1] While some rituals are exercised by solitary individuals, my concern is mainly with rituals performed in groups. The key word here is *performance*, which in Dell Hymes' definition "occurs when two or more persons take responsibility for a presentation." To be successful, Hymes adds, the performer has to know what to say and how to say it. In other words, he needs not only a good grasp and interpretation of his material, but also a command of the expressive techniques needed to be authoritative and engaging.[2] Hymes is concerned mainly with linguistic performance, but his notions can be extended to various ritual presentations of jazz groups.

Musical Performance

Some of the materials of the jazzman's performance rituals are obvious. Each musical style had its own distinctive formulas—from the twelve-bar, *AAB* structure, microtonal usages, and *I-IV-I-V-I*-type chordal sequences of the classic blues, to the reliance on melody, key feeling, special sensitivity to fellow performers, and the rhythmic and harmonic liberties that marked free jazz. And aside from procedures bearing on melody, harmony and rhythm, there were those governing timbre, tempo, solos, and the use of different instruments. Selections played frequently acquired their own special introductions, obbligatos, cadenzas, conclusions, and the like. There were also rituals for training, practicing, rehearsals of sections and whole bands, and recordings.

It was no mean feat for the jazz performer to master the requisite musical patterns and synthesize them in his own distinctive terms. But the problem of presenting them author-itatively and convincingly, of taking responsibility for executing them effectively before an audience, could be even more challenging because it required an ability to mesh several expressive codes—musical, kinetic, proxemic, and sometimes linguistic. This involved putting one's skills, ego, and reputation at stake, especially in improvisation. "I feel my whole musical life is on the line with each performance," said saxophonist Art Pepper.[3] And one bass player explained, "It's like going out there naked every night. . . . I mean we're out there *improvising.* The classical guys have their scores whether they have them on stands or have memorized them. But we have to be creating, or trying to, anticipating each other, transmuting our feelings into the music, taking chances every goddamned second. That's why when jazz musicians are really putting out, it's an exhausting experience. It can be exhilarating too, but always there's that touch of fear, that feeling of being on a very high wire without a net below." A member of Thelonious Monk's group recalled, "I got lost one night and I felt that I had just fallen down an elevator shaft."[4]

Improvisation demanded that the performer be relaxed enough to let his ideas flow, yet at the same time have great intensity and concentration. It was absorbing and draining work and musicians learned to handle its demands in various ways. For some drugs seemed to help. There is no evidence that they actually stimulated creativity, but in the short run they relieved stress and allowed the player to focus fully on the ecstatic task. In the early years, musicians turned mainly to alcohol or marijuana. Clarinetist Mezz Mezzrow recalled his first marijuana glow on the bandstand: "I found I was slurring much better and putting just the right feeling into my phrases— I was really coming on. All the notes came easing out of my horn like they'd already been made up, greased and stuffed into the bell, so that all I had to do was blow a little and send

them on their way. . . . I felt I could go on playing for years
without running out of ideas or energy. . . . I began to feel
very happy and sure of myself."[5] By the Forties, stronger
drugs were used, particularly heroin. It "let's you concentrate
and takes you away from everything," asserted one performer.
"Heroin is a working drug, like the doctor who took it because
he had a full schedule so he could work better. It lets me
concentrate on my sound."[6] Pianist Hampton Hawes said
of early bop and its practitioners: "It was intense but beautiful music and I began to see why a lot of them had to stay
stoned. . . . In order to play it every night they had to adjust
to so many inner changes, blow their minds so far out to
encompass the quick-shifting harmonies and note-patterns and
at the same time block the hostility from critics and fellow
musicians (Louis Armstrong, one of the original brothers,
complaining, *Them cats play all the wrong notes*), and all the shit
going on out front of the stage (*crazy niggers playin' that wild
music*)—that there was a tremendous drive to turn inward, stay
blind, blot it all out."[7] In effect, the drug helped the musician
to get "out of this world," to escape the frustrations caused by
troublesome colleagues, uncomprehending audiences, dishon-
est middlemen, racial antagonisms, bad working conditions,
and personal anxieties, so that he could give his full attention
to the rituals of performance.

And just as the musician had to "get up" for his presentation
with the right blend of confidence, relaxation, concentration,
and intensity, he had also to "get down" afterward, to return
from his ecstatic high the ordinary world. Once again, there
were different ways of doing it, but drugs were helpful to some
performers. One was Anita O'Day. "It's a different world when
the music stops," she said. "The show's over and nothing's
happening. You try to make it continue."[8] As trombonist Bob
Brookmeyer explained, "Reaching that high a pitch intensifies
everything else. If it's been any kind of good night, you're
roaring by the time you have to stop playing. Where do you
go afterwards? . . . It's an arrested orgasm. Some guys try to
prolong the feeling of ecstasy. Others want to cut it off, and a
lot of drugs are designed to cool you down."[9] (I have used
drugs here to indicate the nature of performance anxiety—

and later I will discuss them in connection with initiation rituals—but I do not mean to overemphasize their place in jazz. The image of the jazzman as junkie has been exaggerated. There were plenty of "clean" musicians about, even during the high tide of abuse in the Forties. And among those addicted the results were not always disastrous. Some users managed to keep their habits under reasonable control over years of indulgence without apparent damage to their playing.)

Much of the anxiety of improvised performance had to do with its incomprehensible nature. Trumpeter Roy Eldridge recalled how he would sit down before taking the stand and "run over in my mind what I was going to do. But when I got out there I didn't try to make the B-flat or whatever I was thinking of, because I'd go right into a void where there was no memory—nothing but me. I knew the chords and I knew the melody, and I never thought about them. I'd just be in this blank space, and the music came out anyway. It wasn't always easy." Playing in the Gene Krupa band before a large audience petrified him: "I'd fall to pieces. The first three or four bars of my first solo I'd shake like a leaf, and you could hear it. Then this light would surround me, and it would seem as if there wasn't any band there, and I'd go right through and be all right. It was something I never understood."[10] The great players went into a trance, putting the rituals and even their fellow performers out of their minds. Louis Armstrong told his trombonist Trummy Young, "When I go on the bandstand I don't know nobody's out there. I don't even know you're playing with me. Play good and it will help me. I don't know you're there. I'm just playing."[11]

The rituals were essential, and became second nature to the good performer. Without them he would not have been able to play at all, much less with others. Without the knowledge of consensual procedures of rhythm, harmony, melody, and timbre, and the ability to exercise them—however implicitly or unconsciously—there could be no music, as musicians who assiduously practiced them and their applications were acutely aware. But it would not do to focus on them unduly in performance. Saxophonist Sonny Criss, honored in the late Forties to be playing with his idol Charlie Parker for the first time, anxiously concentrated on bop's challenging new technical procedures, until Parker put him straight: "I was trying really hard. He said to me, 'Don't think. Quit thinkin'.' "[12] It was not enough to *play* the rituals; one had to *use* them to express one's self, master them and then put them in the background upon beginning to play.

Although certain fixed practices were crucial, one could not simply fall back on routine and remain in custody of the magic, for the mysteries of creativity flourished not in the comfortable realm of the old and familiar but on treacherous, uncharted frontiers. Jazz was as fluid and unpredictable as the raw experience it drew on. "Life has many changes," declared Charles Mingus. "Tomorrow it may rain, and it's supposed to be sunshine 'cause its summertime, but God's got a funny soul—he plays like Charlie Parker—he may run some thunder on you, he may take the sun and put it up at night, the way it looks to *me*. You know, I mean, when people live so that they're only playing one mood, one emotion there's something dangerously wrong there because it's like insanity in a way."[13] Not insanity, perhaps, but staleness; in jazz as elsewhere the artist must press into new areas with new problems and risks if he is to stay on the cutting edge. Trumpeter Buck Clayton summed it up when he declared, "If you don't do something new, then you might as well forget it."[14]

Given the mysteries, uncertainties, and challenges of improvisation, performers had to sharpen their skills, bring the proper ingredients together, and hope for the best. The magic could not be commanded, only coaxed by those with talent and the proper frame of mind, receptive to unexpected paths to transcendence. Every performer had his own way of evoking it. "Not long before I play, I take a large whiskey," explained violinist Stephane Grapelli. "Improvisation—it's a mystery. . . . When I improvise and I'm in good form I'm like somebody half sleeping. I even forget there are people in front of me. Great improvisers are like priests: they thinking only of their god."[15] And pianist Dick Wellstood stated, "I'm one of those persons who rely on divine spirit—on what they call inspiration. When it comes by itself, you don't have to worry. But when it doesn't come, you have to fall back on all kinds of patterns and figures"[16]—rituals used in the artists' attempts to summon the muse.

Not all performers are so mystical about improvisation, of course, but to all it is inexplicable and absorbing, related to what psychologist Mihaly Csikszentmihalyi calls "flow," a mental state in which events follow one another in unified, organic fashion without our conscious interference. We feel in control of the situation yet fully immersed in it, oblivious to distinctions between self and surroundings, stimuli and response, past and present. Consciousness and behavior seem as one, and life becomes engrossing and meaningful.[17] Flow is quite at home in the performing arts, liminal or at least "liminoid," insofar as they create environments of enchantment in which anything can, and indeed should, happen.[18] And clearly it had an important place in jazz improvisation, emphasizing potency and potentiality as it sweeps the performer along in its stream. Pianist Mose Allison had something like this in mind when he said, "That's the challenge every night; trying to work toward that spot where it's all *flowing*. Sometimes it comes easy, sometimes it comes hard, sometimes it doesn't come at all."[19] But all performers knew when it was at hand and the power of its spell.

Aside from fostering freedom and flow, jazz performance rituals organized, guided, and reassured. The soloist might be an isolated high-wire artist without a safety net, but he did not start from scratch every time he picked up his instrument; rituals told him, unconsciously or not, what sort of steps to take, what order to take them in, and how quickly to move. Sometimes, though, as doctrine hardened into dogma, the ritualization process went too far. Once fresh patterns turned into sterile cliches that became sacred in themselves, fixed and inviolate in ways that inhibited spontaneity—as with the rigid dixieland formulas of the Forties or bop cliches of the late Fifties. But when still fresh and creatively used, they were liberating frameworks or "groundworks" helping performers and listeners tap wellsprings of imagination and ecstasy.[20]

* * *

Many of us brought up in conservative faiths, honoring sober, rational worship, think of rituals as solemn and deliberate, never lighthearted or playful. But in many cultures festivity has an important place in religion, and ludic and serious rituals go hand in hand. Jazz took the juxtaposition of the two for granted. During performances a comedy number might follow one that had reached empyrean heights, or vice versa. The darkest blues could have humorous lines, and lighthearted songs might have an underlying seriousness. The link between the playful and sober has existed from the music's inception, most obviously perhaps in New Orleans funerals which perpetuated one half of the African custom of "rejoicing at death and crying at birth."[21]

New Orleans wakes often lasted well into the night, with much singing, sobbing, writhing and fainting, activity that continued the next day at the church. The solemn march to the graveyard was more dignified, but on the way back to town, after the body was put to rest, the company exulted. Mourners, mere hours after being prostrate with grief, danced joyfully along with the rest of the party in festivities that lasted all evening. Veteran New Orleans trumpeter Bunk Johnson related how

> On the way to the cemetery with an odd Fellow or a Mason— they always buried with music you see—we would always use slow, slow numbers such as "Nearer My God to Thee," "Flee as a Bird to the Mountains," "Come Thee Disconsolate." We would use most any 4/4, played very slow; they walked very slow behind the body.
>
> After we would get to the cemetery, and after that particular person were put away, the band would come on to the front, out of the graveyard . . . and then we'd march away from the cemetery by the snare drum only until we got about a block or two blocks from the cemetery. Then we'd go right into ragtime.
>
> We would play "Didn't He Ramble," or we'd take all of those spiritual hymns and turn them into ragtime—2/4 movements, you know, step lively everybody. "Didn't He Ramble," "When the Saints Go Marching In," that good old piece "Ain't Gonna Study War No More," and several others we would have and we'd play them just for that effect.
>
> We would have a second line there that was most equivalent

to King Rex parade—Mardi Gras Carnival parade. The police were unable to keep the second line back—all in the street, all on the sidewalks, in front of the band, and behind the lodge, in front of the lodge. We'd have some immense crowds following.[22]

Such events took place in other cities, too. Pianist Eubie Blake recalled his days as a young second-liner in Baltimore before the turn of the century: "Let me tell you about the funerals! You know some big shot would die, some big-time guy—especially if the guy had been in the army before, a Negro, I mean—well, the people would sing and the band would play, you know, funeral music, dirges. Now on the way back, see, they play the very same melodies—he's buried now, see—in ragtime. Oh, how they'd swing! Now there just wasn't any way I could stay away from this music."[23] During funerals in New Orleans, Baltimore, and elsewhere, certain tunes were played at certain times in prescribed keys, with prescribed rhythms, harmonies, timbres, and tempos.

Even when the impulse behind jazz was frivolous, to fool around or blow off steam, the rituals had a religious aspect. In such frivolity, as Durkheim put it, "man is carried beyond himself in the general excitement; in the collective effervescence he feels transformed and transforms his environment."[24] But in festivity proper, as distinct from mere frivolity, the transformation is more pronounced, more comprehensive. Theologians Joseph Pieper and Harvey Cox regard festivity as the meeting place of opposites: real and ideal, temporal and timeless, physical and spiritual, sacred and profane. In this view the mortal celebrant touches something eternal or at least universal, thus enlarging his imagination, creativity, and his relationships with the past and with other men. He becomes part of an epic, raising his sense of personal worth and cosmic awareness.[25] Rituals of festivity and jazz have joined naturally in many different circumstances, from old-time New Orleans funerals, to jazz festivals (especially during commemorative concerts celebrating the myths and rituals of past prophets), and, most significantly perhaps, in ballroom dancing.

Until the rise of bop in the Forties, jazz was primarily festive dance music with important communal functions, sometimes presided over by charismatics, such as King Oliver at Lincoln Gardens in Chicago during the Twenties. Ralph Ellison has described the dancing led by singer Jimmy Rushing a few years later in Oklahoma City: "The evenings began with the more formal steps, to popular and semi-classical music, and proceeded to become more expressive as the spirit of jazz and the blues became dominant. It was when Jimmy's voice began to soar with the blues that the dancers—and the musicians— achieved that feeling of communion which was the true meaning of the public jazz dance. The blues, the singer, the band and the dancers formed the vital whole of jazz as an institutional form."[26] Ellison goes on to explain that "jazz and the blues did not fall into the scheme of things being spelled out by our two main institutions, the church and school, but they gave expression to attitudes which found no place in these and helped to give our lives some semblance of wholeness. Jazz and the public jazz dance was a third institution in our lives, and a vital one; and though Jimmy was far from being a preacher, he was, as official floor manager or master-of-the-dance at Slaughter's Hall, the leader of a public rite."[27]

Related festivity prevailed in less formal circumstances. Pianist Mary Lou Williams recalled afternoons in the Forties at Minton's in Harlem (at night one of the incubators of bop): "Minton's Playhouse was not a large place, but it was nice and intimate. . . . During the daytime, people played the jukebox and danced. I used to call in often and got many laughs. It is amazing how happy those characters were—living, dancing and drinking. It seemed that everybody was talking at the same time; the noise was terrific. Even the kids playing out on the sidewalk danced when they heard the records. That's the way we were then—one big, happy family on 118th Street."[28]

Much in jazz, festive or not, exemplifies Johan Huizinga's concept of play as a "free activity standing quite outside ordinary life as being 'not serious,' but at the same time absorbing the player intensely and utterly. . . . It proceeds within its own proper boundaries of time and according to fixed rules and in an orderly manner." Jazz performance generated what Huizinga calls the "play mood," one of "rapture and enthusiasm, and sacred and festive in accordance with the occasion," a mood in which "a feeling of expectation and tension accompanies the action, mirth and relaxation follow."[29]

Jazz also had the play attributes set forth by Roger Caillois: *agon* (competition)—as in cutting sessions; *alea* (chance)—in improvisation; mimicry—in the voice-like timbres of the horns; and *ilinx* (literally "vertigo," but extended here to other forms of sense deprivation, including ecstasy). Combinations of these characteristics find balance between what Caillois calls *paidia* (spontaneity and intuition), basic to improvisation, and *ludens* (intention, order, and discipline), demanded by harmonic, melodic, and rhythmic rituals.[30]

Agonistic "cutting sessions" were duels between individuals, distinct from the noncompetitive jam sessions already discussed—although one sometimes grew out of the other. Agonistic confrontations might start with impromptu needling among friends or friendly enemies, attempts by unknowns to gain recognition, or efforts of regional titans to become king of the hill, but once under way they were "serious" duels, fueled by fondness for competition and transcendent feelings of flow generated in intense play. No matter whom the battle involved, it could generate great psychic energy, high drama, and serendipity. Art Pepper told of a night at the Blackhawk in San Francisco when Sonny Stitt came in and threw down the gauntlet: "We both play alto, which . . . really makes it a contest. But Sonny is one of those guys, that's the thing with him. It's a communion. It's a battle. It's an ego trip. It's a testing ground. And that's the beautiful part of it . . . just the joy of playing with someone great." Stitt called for "Cherokee," a demanding number with notoriously difficult chord changes, at the time used to test a player's nerves and skill. He counted it off at breakneck speed and, as Pepper said,

> he was flying. We played the head, the melody, and then he took the first solo. He played, I don't know, about forty choruses. He played for an hour maybe, did everything that could be done on a saxophone, everything you could play, as much as Charlie Parker could have played if he'd been there. Then he stopped. And he looked at me. Gave me one of those looks, "All right, suckah, your turn." And it's my job; it's my gig. I was strung out. I was hooked. I was drunk. I was having a

hassle with my wife, Diane, who'd threatened to kill herself in our hotel room next door. I had marks on my arm. I thought there were narcs in the club, and I all of a sudden realized that it was me. He'd done all those things, and now I had to put up or shut up or get off or forget it or quit or kill myself or do something.

I forgot everything, and everything came out. I played way over my head. I played completely different than he did. I searched and found my own way, and what I said reached the people. I played myself, and I knew I was right, and the people loved it, and they felt it. I blew and I blew, and when I finally finished I was shaking all over; my heart was pounding; I was soaked in sweat, and the people were screaming; the people were clapping, and I looked at Sonny, but I just kind of nodded, and he went, "All right." And that was it. That's what it's all about.[31]

In this episode, with its free activity outside of ordinary life and logic, its utter absorption, its special boundaries of space and time, fixed rules, and orderly manner, its Cailloisian *agon*, *alea*, *ilinx*, all balanced between *paidia* and *ludens*, creative play occurred in what Huizinga terms "the sphere of festival and ritual—the sacred sphere."[32] Not all play, or even its "higher forms," is necessarily sacred or magical, but it often has such associations in the minds of the devout, conforming to Hugo Rahner's claim that "to play is to yield to a kind of magic, to enact oneself the absolutely other . . . to give lie to the inconvenient world of fact. . . . The mind is prepared to accept the unimagined and incredible, to enter a world where different laws apply, to be relieved of all the weights that bear it down, to be free, kingly unfettered and divine."[33]

This magic comes mainly from the feeling of flow, in which events seem to follow one another organically without human intervention. Drummer Jo Jones noted how "it was a very strange thing at those jam sessions in Kansas City. Nobody ever got in anybody's way. Nobody had to point a finger and say, 'You take it now. You take the next chorus' . . . the guys would just get up on the bandstand, and spiritually they knew when to come in. . . . They just felt which one was coming next."[34] Within ritual patterns of melody, harmony, and rhythm, these all-absorbing proceedings seemed autotelic and continuous, as if nothing else mattered. Pianist Mary Lou Williams remembered stopping in at the Sunset Club in Kansas City one midnight to find the musicians jamming on "Sweet Georgia Brown." Sensing a long night, she went home to clean up. When she returned an hour later, the musicians were still improvising on the same tune.[35] Sammy Price, another pianist, recalled a session in which a single song went on for three hours, wearing out more than one rhythm section as successive hornmen took extensive solos.[36] Not uncommonly these sessions lasted until noon the next day as contests. Some members of the audience dropped in and out, but true believers hung on until the end, betting on their favorites and taking a loud part in determining winners.[37]

A successful showdown with a recognized performer provided a local youngster with a quick route to fame. Such events were the talk of the hip part of town; still more dramatic was the arrival of an out-of-towner to challenge the local champion. Scott Joplin and Jelly Roll Morton traveled about the South and Midwest toppling established heroes and accumulating reputations like gunfighters. But their duels paled before later, epic confrontations between regional champions evoking fierce local pride and loyalty. Tales of battles between tenor players Coleman Hawkins (representing the East) and Lester Young (the hero of the Southwest) live vividly in jazz mythology. The first memorable confrontation took place in 1934 when Hawkins, then with Fletcher Henderson's band, stopped overnight in Kansas City. Word went out that he was in a well-known club taking on the local talent, and Young and other Kansas City tenor men, including Ben Webster and Herschel Evans, arrived quickly to take up the challenge. According to Mary Lou Williams, Hawkins (nicknamed "Bean")

> didn't know the Kaycee tenor men were so terrific, and he couldn't get himself together though he played all morning. I happened to be nodding that night, and around four A.M., I awoke to hear someone pecking on my screen.
> I opened the window on Ben Webster. He was saying, "Get up, pussycat, we're jammin' and all the pianists are tired out

now. Hawkins has got his shirt off and is still blowing. You got
to come down."

Sure enough, when we got there, Hawkins was in his singlet,
taking turns with the Kaycee men. It seems he had run into
something he didn't expect.

Lester's style was light, and, as I said, it took him maybe five
choruses to warm up. But then he would really blow; then you
couldn't handle him on a cutting session.

That was how Hawkins got hung up. The Henderson band
was playing in St. Louis that evening, and Bean knew he ought
to be on the way. But he kept trying to blow something to beat
Ben and Herschel and Lester. When at last he gave up, he got
straight in his car and drove to St. Louis. I heard he'd just
bought a new Cadillac and that he burnt it out trying to make
the job on time. Yes, Hawkins was king until he met those crazy
Kansas City tenor men.[38]

The second duel took place in a Harlem club five years later
when Hawkins, just back from a long European sojourn and
supposedly rusty and out of touch, had the crowd behind him.
The story goes that he bided his time, sitting catlike and sipping
a drink at the club where the best tenor men in town flaunted
their talents. Finally, after several nights, he made his move at
three one morning. Young was playing behind his friend,
singer Billie Holiday, and after she made an oblique but
unmistakable remark about Lester being without a peer, Hawkins slipped out, returned with his horn, and began to play
along softly on the blues she was singing. Looking around
surprised, she signaled Young to take charge, and the battle
was joined. Rex Stewart recounted that Young "really played
the blues that night, chorus after chorus, until finally Hawk
burst in on the end of one of his choruses, cascading a harmonic
interruption, not unlike Mount Vesuvius erupting, virtually
overpowering Lester's more haunting approach. When Hawk
finished off the blues, soaring, searing and lifting the entire
house with his guttural, positive sonority, every tub began
cheering, with the exception of Lady Day, Lester, and her pet
boxer, Mister. They, like Arabs, folded their tents and stole
away."[39] As before, this was a hometown decision, and the
victor remained on the scene to bask in his enhanced charisma,

while the vanquished disappeared, his stature diminished for the time being at least.

Cutting sessions, whether battles between titans or seriocomic rivalries between friends, followed familiar rituals, varying little from city to city. It was generally understood that if a musician took out his instrument at certain times, he was challenging an adversary, and once the duel was on no quarter was given or expected. Sometimes a brash neophyte mounted the bandstand with one of the giants, but wiser aspirants thought twice before jumping into the breach, knowing they might easily become laughingstocks. Still, the unknown musician who had the gall, courage, and talent to get up on the stand with an established performer and hold his own was accorded recognition in the local elite and landed better jobs.

During the Thirties in New York, where the biggest reputations were made, the testing rituals worked as follows for blacks (and in a similar way for whites). The new arrival, having found a place to live, would seek out the local musicians' hangout, instrument case in hand. Friends from home might help him get started, but essentially he was on his own. Eventually, he would be asked to "show out" before intensely curious colleagues. If his playing was mediocre, he melted anonymously into the following, but if he presented a serious challenge, the alarm would go out, and the best local talent would soon show up, for, as Rex Stewart explained,

> if this cat was really good, it was the duty of every tub to drop whatever he was doing and rush to the club. And nobody ever did fall into New York City and cut the entire field—some brother always came to the rescue of New York's prestige.

> These sessions, as every other aspect of life, had a pecking order. The giants seldom deigned to compete with the peasantry. Instead, they sat around getting their kicks, listening with amusement as the neophyte struggled to justify his claim to entry into the charmed circle of the (for want of a better word) establishment.

> The blowing would start, and the pilgrim's status was soon established—he was either in or out. If he was in, he would be toasted at Big John's bar, and friendships were formed that assured his being invited to sit in a session with the big shots,

who did their serious blowing at the Hoofer's Club, downstairs in the basement of the same building.[40]

Established New York jazzmen were not alone in their reluctance to play with unknown youngsters until the challenge was genuine. In most towns, unrecognized figures had to work their way up through smaller clubs before taking on the big-timers, and, in general, ambitious tyros who ignored the rituals of the pecking order immediately regretted their transgressions. A luminary such as Charlie Parker might find five or more supplicants at front tables waiting for a chance to sit in. To discourage such nuisances, recognized performers developed intimidating procedures. Sometimes they permitted a newcomer on the bandstand and then called for a number with bewildering chord changes, in an unusual key, and a devastating tempo. After a brave beginning, the swamped pretender would have to drop out, setting a sobering example for other aspirants. One of them was Trumpeter Joe Newman: "I was really afraid to get up there. . . . The guys would put in a key maybe like an F-sharp or something, anything where the fingering doesn't lay right on the horn. Everything you touch, it's not that, it's something else. And if you don't really know your instrument and know the theory of music, you just can't play it. Every note you touch is wrong. You can't really hear those keys like that."[41] There were other tricks as well. "To make things tough for outsiders," explained drummer Kenny Clarke, "we invented difficult riffs. Some of our tunes used the 'A' part of one tune, 'I Got Rhythm,' but the channel came from something else, say 'Honeysuckle Rose.' The swing guys would be completely hung up on the channel [the third, or *B*, section in the *AABA* structure of a song]."[42] And when this happened, all but the hardest hopefuls packed up their instruments and melted into the audience. As singer Dave Lambert remembered, "The musicians petered off, and the men were separated from the boys. One of the very fast tunes sometimes played for this weeding process was written by Bud Powell and was a variation of 'Cherokee' [the challenging piece Sonny Stitt called for in his confrontation with Art Pepper]. The number was aptly titled 'Serenade for Squares.' "[43] But this habit was not necessarily as harsh as it sounds, nor it was a device for blocking out all strangers. "There's no truth to the story that we purposely played weird things to keep musicians outside of the clique off the stand," Kenny Clarke later claimed. "All we asked was that the musician be able to handle himself. When he got up on the bandstand, he had to know."[44] He had to know what to play and how to play it; in other words, he needed a vital interpretation of the music and a command of the appropriate codes to express it.

Needless to say, not all agonistic jazz play reached epic proportions, and not all of it ended in clear-cut victory or defeat. Sometimes the result was a standoff, as in the duel between Art Pepper and Sonny Stitt. And there were often honors for combatants who did not measure up. Sometimes an underdog had only to keep his wits about him and do his best under fire in order to emerge creditably, for to play to the hilt was, in the proper circumstances, to share in a catharsis. As W. Bruce Cameron suggests, "In a very real sense the session is a ritual of purification for [the performer]—a self-cleaning and the reaffirmation of his aesthetic values."[45] Even the vanquished did not necessarily feel humiliated. It was enough to participate in the exhilarating flow, to learn a useful lesson, or be able to tell others how one had jammed with the major leaguers. After being bested by drummer Chick Webb one night, an exhilarated Gene Krupa told a friend, "Chick gassed me . . . I was never cut by a better man."[46] Nor were the rewards always limited to the duelists. The triumph and prestige of the victor in agonistic play flowed easily to his supporters.[47] His victory was theirs too, since he represented their interests and honor, and his success reaffirmed their outlook, taste, and judgment—reinforcing conviction and solidarity. Of the 1941 sessions at Minton's, Kenny Clarke wrote, "One night after weeks of trying Dizzy [Gillespie] cut Roy Eldridge. It was one night in many, but it meant a great deal. Roy had been top dog for years. We closed ranks after that."[48]

And just as there were battles between individuals representing different schools and regions, there were contests between bands that spoke for different constituencies. Informal duels could grow out of chance meetings. In turn-of-the-

century New Orleans, bands encountering one another in the
street would play simultaneously, vying for the approval of
crowds that gathered to judge the results and reward the
victors with food, drink, and patronage. In Manhattan, during
the Twenties, bands visited clubs for the express purpose of
cutting the presiding group and taking its job. But the most
famous battles were formally staged in dance halls like Harlem's
Savoy, which in 1929 put on "the greatest, most sensational
Battle of Jazz ever staged, anywhere—any place—any time,
South vs. North."[49] Each region was represented by three
bands—including Duke Ellington's orchestra upholding the
honor of the North—that attracted five thousand enthusiasts
who jammed the Savoy at eighty-five cents a head. Nine years
later, Chick Webb's band bested Count Basie's in a battle that
seesawed back and forth until Webb's final, overwhelming
drum solo carried the night. As in the battles between individuals, such confrontations took place within accepted rituals of
play and produced similar results. The victors emerged with
enhanced charisma and the losers were consoled with having
shared in the magic flow. And again the audience loudly
participated in determining the winner and sharing the spoils.
"Handkerchiefs were waving, people were shouting and stomping, the excitement was intense," reported the *Amsterdam News*
of the Webb–Basie duel.[50] It was talked about for months
afterward, especially Webb's winning heroics, which like other
celebrated agonistic feats was embellished in the telling as it
found its way into a growing mythological canon.

Appearance

Individual jazzmen, particularly the better known figures,
sometimes developed their own form of dress, implying a
unique identity beyond ordinary fashion and judgment.[51] But
in the jazz community, as in other groups with vocational
mystiques, there were distinctive, shared patterns of appearance. In addition to band uniforms, costumes of performance,

and rituals that contributed to unity, discipline, and identity, there were voluntary fashions that had significance on and off the bandstand. Jelly Roll Morton and his New Orleans cohorts favored boxback coats, Stetsons, tight pants with razor-sharp creases, and Edwin Clapp shoes; Harlem stride pianists sported derbies and homburgs, elegant canes, and double-breasted overcoats with bright silk handkerchiefs tucked into their breast pockets; boppers were famous for wide-lapeled, pinstriped suits, berets, goatees, and thick, horn-rimmed ("bop") glasses; early free-jazzmen looked like professional pallbearers with dark business suits, white shirts, narrow, conservative ties, and short hair; and some musicians of the Sixties and Seventies wore African-inspired costumes and hairdos.

How to explain such trends? Current hypotheses regard dress fashions as outlets for imagination and caprice, reactions to boredom with stale custom, symbols of repressed sexual impulses, or assertions of troubled egos within socially sanctioned departures.[52] While these explanations may make sense in connection with fads of jazz dress, the notion of imitation seems more to the point. When Dizzy Gillespie turned up on the job once with a button missing from his coat, several of his followers appeared the following evening missing the same button. And when Charlie Parker, who sometimes slept in his clothes, appeared in rumpled suits, his disciples did likewise. "The preposterous lengths some guys would go to," declared bassist Buddy Jones. "Fellows would take their good clothes and roll them up into a ball to get them creased, because they saw Bird walking around in a suit he had forgotten to have pressed."[53] It is no secret that imitation provides a sense of security, telling us we are not alone but members in good standing of an admired group, sharing its standards and rewards. Nor is it news that when persons of low status copy the styles of those above them, the elitists alter their own fashions to avoid looking like their imitators.[54] Accordingly, hard-core jazz sectarians dressed in a manner that set them apart from outsiders, emphasizing their distinction and separateness, and when the squares or fringe members started to imitate their look, insiders found other ways to underscore their elitism.

Rituals of appearance reinforced the identity and solidarity of the group most faithful to the ideal. They were forms of symbolic behavior, reassuring insignia for the devout and models for those aspiring to the elite. As a teenager growing up in East St. Louis, Miles Davis discovered how a man's style extended beyond his music: "I was fascinated by the musicians, particularly the guys who used to come up from New Orleans and jam all night. I'd sit there and look at them, watch the way they walked and talked, how they fixed their hair, and of course how they played."[55] Here were men who knew what they were about and looked like it—appearance was an integral part of the overall impressions they projected. Growing up in Los Angeles during the same years, Art Pepper was struck by drummer Lee Young, Lester's brother, a celebrity among the faithful on Central Avenue who dressed in a way that thrust him forward confidently in the street: "He was a hep black man with processed hair. He was light complected, very sharp, with diamond rings; he wore clothes well and was a cat you'd figure would conduct himself in any situation."[56] This image provided Pepper with reassurance, direction, evidence that the jazz mystique prevailed, and guidance on how it should be implemented.

These were not isolated instances. Throughout the jazz community the distinctive performer sent strong messages to diffident novices, who imitated his appearance in the confidence that it led not just to acceptance, but to truth.

Language

Like his dress, the jazzman's speech was highly eclectic, combining Black English with the jargons of gambling, prostitution, larceny, music, and the dance.[57] Successive versions of this rapidly changing parlance started as semi-secret codes, vocational idioms which were proud symbols of the jazz community's identity and separateness. As Louis Armstrong explained in the Thirties, "Jazzmen have a language of their own, and I don't think anything could better show how much they are apart from the regular musicians and have their own world that they believe in and that most people have not understood."[58]

But the incomprehensibility of this speech did not necessarily limit its appeal, even among those who understood it only fractionally. For fringe followers and outsiders intrigued by the jazz life (if not always by its music), its novel argot enhanced its demimondial glamour. And its words spread to the outside world in a pattern of imitation and replacement, with insiders finding new words for those debased by general usage. In 1946 clarinetist Mezz Mezzrow said that the term "swing . . . was cooked up after the unhip public took over the expression 'hot' and made it corny by getting up in front of a band and snapping their fingers in a childish way, yelling, 'Get hot! Yeah, man, get hot'. . . . This happened all the time. . . . It used to grate on our nerves because it was usually slung in our faces when we were playing our hottest numbers. . . . That's the reason we hot musicians are always making up new lingo for ourselves."[59] New terms for marijuana seemed to emerge hourly: "muggles," "weed," "tea," "grass," "reefer," "muta," "hemp," "gay," "pod," "pot," "golden leaf," "cool green," "stuff," "gauge," and so on. Similarly, boppers coined words for being in the know: "hip," "fly," "booted," "down," "ready," and others. Although a few in-words remained fashionable over relatively long periods, for instance, "dig," "jive," and "gig," there was usually a turnover in usage when musical styles changed, as in the Forties when the loose, overblown argot of pre–World War II jazz was contracted into the economies of bop talk. To be "on drugs" came to be simply "on"; to "split the scene" was shortened to "split"; and to "flip one's wig" became to "wig."

Beginning as more or less secret idioms, successive jazz argots were not entirely the outgrowth of separatist impulses. Their unconventionality stemmed in part from the speakers' inarticulateness or the incapacity of ordinary language to express extraordinary feelings. Unable to convey his deepest emotions in the received idiom, the performer invented terms of his own. "Jazzmen come to grips with emotions so strong," wrote Robert Reisner in 1959, "that they are unable to cope with them in ordinary adjectives. They are gassed, fractured, killed, tore up. A wonderful instrument is too much, the end, gone."[60] Such words help proper meaning only for those already aware of the intended referents, those who knew about the music's evocations.

Verbalizing his feelings led the jazzman to "the edges of language"[61] and far away from standard usages, with their emphasis on clarity and precision. Like the poet and prophet, he used metaphor, oxymoron, and synecdoche to probe the unknown or unexpressed in ways puzzling to unattuned ears. Yet every insider knew what Lester Young meant when he said he "felt a draft," or told an unfamiliar drummer, "Don't drop no bombs behind me, baby. Just give me that *titty-boom titty-boom* all night on the cymbal and I'm cool." Nor was the aficionado puzzled when Charlie Parker declared, "I lit my fire. I greased my skillet and I cooked."[62] And he knew about the rhyming slang in which "jack the bear" meant "nowhere," which in turn meant off the "scene" or out of it. He also knew that "bread" referred to dough (money), and about the reversals in which words like "mean," "bad," "dirty," "lowdown," and "crazy" conferred status, while others like "sweet," "pretty," "square," and "straight" were pejorative. The ecstatic areas on experiential frontiers were "out of this world," or "far out." To "swing" was to "jump," "rock," "ride," or "stomp"; and words like "hot," "burn," and "cook" (all suggesting shamanistic "heat") referred to ecstatic performance. The meanings or shadings of most of these expressions were heavily contextual. Nowhere is this more obvious than in the uses of "cool" and "like," the latter employed as almost every part of speech and as a punctuation mark.[63] To exclaim "Like!" was to express the otherwise unsayable, comprehensible only to those who already knew the message.

Jazz talk not only meant, it *created*. As I. A. Richards, Kenneth Burke, and others have pointed out, language is a form of "symbolic action" that both expresses and formulates, imposing order and significance on experience.[64] This was notably evident in the jazz world's use of nicknames. Ned E. Williams related that Duke Ellington had

a penchant for pinning nicknames on those most closely asso-
ciated with him, usually nicknames that stick. Thus Freddy
Jenkins, the little trumpet player . . . became Posey, Johnny
Hodges . . . is called Rabbit by those closest to him.

The late Richard Jones, Duke's valet for years, jumped only
to the call of Bowden, and Jack Boyd, erstwhile manager of the
band, whose given name is Charles, for no explainable reason
was always just Elmer to Duke. It was Elmer in turn who dubbed
Ellington as Dumpy, and I can't remember when I've called
him anything else in direct communication. It may be a signal
honor, but Duke went into a big corporation routine for me,
never refers to me except by my first initials, N. E. Another
leader while playing trumpet for Ellington, won the name which
he still uses professionally, Cootie Williams, and there are many
other instances.[65]

Such bynames stimulated and evoked as well as described. Dub
a man "King," "Duke," "Count," "Pops," "Satchelmouth,"
"Rabbit," "Dumpy," or "Elmer" and you create not just a label
and image but an attitude of affection, respect, or derision and
encourage behavior that goes with it. Nicknames also helped
establish identity and shape perceptions, expectations, and
social relationships. When used tactfully, bynames could indicate things that could not be said directly. To call someone
"Dizzy," "Muggsy," or "Mousey" in some contexts was to court
open offense, but in the rituals of nickname usage these terms
were socially sanctioned outlets for aggression absorbed in
friendly banter.[66]
There were times when jazz talk, like the music itself,
conveyed feelings in a process resting heavily on associational
linkages.[67] What you said might matter less than how you said
it, with semantics depending largely on spontaneous integra-
tion of appropriate linguistic, kinetic, proxemic, and other
ritualized codes. The jazz community's verbal games, often
resembling musical cutting sessions, are cases in point. Among
American blacks in general, speech duels take the form of
"playing the dozens," "signifying," "rapping," "chopping," and
"capping."[68] Akin to these, the jazzman's verbal jousts might
occur or begin in, brief moments of kidding, needling, or
good-natured horseplay, but usually they were episodes in

serious, ongoing rivalries over music, women, and other things. This competitive play might last for months, even years, particularly in successful big bands where players were together day in and day out for long periods. Fletcher Henderson's wife, Leora, told how the musical and verbal duels of her husband's sidemen overflowed into rehearsals: "Charlie Green (we called him Big Green) would be playing something wonderful and then Jimmy Harrison [the band's other star trombonist] would say, 'Huh, you think *you* done something!' and then try to cut him,"[70] provoking further banter and fueling another round in the contest.

Such wordplay was less prevalent among whites than blacks, who had grown up in a tradition that rewarded prowess in verbal games—the black community grants special recognition to the skillful talker who in the white world might be discounted as backyard lawyer, conman, or fabricator.[71] For this or other reasons, many whites could not hold their own in jive talk. They knew the right terms, but not how to use them. Registering admiration at the way his black acquaintances on Central Avenue in Los Angeles traded words, saxophonist Art Pepper wrote, "I used to stand around and marvel at the way they talked. Having really nothing to say, they were able to play those little verbal games back and forth. I envied it but was too self-conscious to do it. What I wouldn't give to just jump in and say those things. I could when I was joking to myself, raving to myself in front of the mirror at home, but when it came time to do it with people, I couldn't."[72] Pepper was reared in a repressive white family and was naturally shy; even though he knew the language he could not perform comfortably, at least among native speakers.

Yet he was right to call such banter a game, because it had all the attributes of play: its own special time, place, rules, flow, competition, chance, limitation, ecstasy, and balance of formality and spontaneity.[73] It also had play's proclivity to promote separatist and secretive social groupings. Beyond this, it sharpened wits and ears. Participants had to "get" the fast-moving messages and all their shadings quickly and send appropriate replies almost without thinking, acording to a complicated set of rules demanding, among other things, inversions of conventional proprieties. Ralph Ellison recalled standing on an Oklahoma City street corner with his "hep" young friends and responding to the music of Count Basie's band playing in a nearby dance hall:

> "Now that's the Right Reverend Jimmy Rushing preaching now, man," someone would say. And rising to the cue another would answer, "Yeah, and that's old Elder 'Hot Lips' signifying along with him; urging him on, man." And, keeping it building, "Huh, but though you can't hear him out this far, Ole Deacon Big-un (the late Walter Page) is up there patting his foot and slapping on his big belly (the bass viol) to keep those fools in line." And we might go on to name all the members of the band as though they were the Biblical four-and-twenty elders, while laughing at the impious wit of applying church titles to a form of music which all the preachers assured us was the devil's potent tool.[74]

Other games crossed conventional syntactical and morphological borderlines, twisting words into new meanings and concocting new terms. "As we played with musical notes," explained Dizzy Gillespie, "bending them into new and different meanings that constantly changed, we played with words. Say sumpn' hip Daddy-o."[75]

Jazz vocalists were especially adept at such games. Many of them could scarcely utter the banalities of popular lyrics without changing them. Assorted gestures and verbal manipulations reworked vacuous lines for new significances. By interjecting a blue note or raising an eyebrow, Fats Waller could make the sober hilarious, or the ridiculous serious. Billie Holiday breathed new life into dead stanzas with altered accents and phrasing, hornlike intonation, and omitted words. Louis Armstrong elicited double takes when he casually changed the penultimate line of "Just a Gigolo" (OK 41468) from "When the end comes I know they'll say just another gigolo" to "When the end comes I know they'll say just another jig I know."

Sometimes the alterations introduced just enough nonsense to throw the old lyrics into fresh perspective. At other times, they crossed the lines of sense altogether, as in scat singing and scat talk. The scat idiom contains all the characteristics of extreme verbal ritual: special styles and registers, fast delivery, high pitches, broken rhythms, grunts, anomalous mumbo jumbo, and prosaical repetitions.[76] We can hear a good deal of this in the *reet-a-voutee* routines of Slim Gaillard and the bop utterances of Dizzy Gillespie in songs like "Oop-Bop-Sha-Bam" and "Oop-Sho-Be-Do-Bee." And the same qualities are evident in the early singing of Louis Armstrong, most notably in "Heebie Jeebies" (OK 0300), which inaugurated the scat craze of the Twenties. After a perfectly comprehensible rendition of the first chorus, he departed from the Tin Pan Alley doggerel entirely with:

> Eef, gaff, mmff, dee-bo, dee-la-bahm,
> Rip-rip, de-do-de-da-do, do-de-da-de-da-doe,
> Ba-dode-do-do, ba-ro-be-do-be-do,
> Geef-gaf, gee-bap-be-da-de-do, d-da-do,
> Rip-dip-do-dum, so come on down, do that dance,
> They call the Heebie Jeebies dance, sweet mammo,
> Poppa's got to do the Heebie Jeebies dance.

These lines made an overwhelming impression upon his followers. "I brought the record home to play for the gang," wrote Mezz Mezzrow, "and, man, they almost fell through the ceiling. . . . [We] almost wore it out by playing it over and over until we knew the whole thing by heart. Suddenly, Tesch [clarinetist Frank Teschmacher] jumped to his feet, his sad face all lit up for once, and yelled, 'Hey, listen, you guys. I got an idea! This is something Bix should hear right away! Let's go out to Hudson Lake and give him the thrill of his life!' " Almost before these words were out, they had piled into Mezzrow's car for the fifty-mile trip. "All the way there," reported Mezzrow, "we kept chanting Louis' weird riffs, while I kept the car zigzagging like a roller-coaster to mark the explosions." Beiderbecke responded similarly, rushing off to wake up his friends so they could hear the record.[77] Before long, the lines became a form of street greeting among the initiated.

Like other such nonsense, this language transformed or contrasted with a common source and was readily decipherable to insiders. Attuned listeners responded to it as to other systems of signs and took pleasure in its defiance of the seemingly trynannical order of standard English. As one youngster told Jablow and Withers, "We like nonsense because all the squares think something has to *mean* something all the time."[78]

Aside from being an outlet for complaint, nonsensical wordplay provided kicks. Pianist Hoagy Carmichael declared that Louis Armstrong's "blubbering, cannibalistic sounds tickled me to the marrow."[79] At a college dance in the Twenties he and his friends, including Bix Beiderbecke, went into hysterics when a vocalist performed scat routines with "off color inanities in staccato [that] baffled the chaperones." After the dance the group repaired to a local hangout where, Carmichael related, Monk Moenkhaus, a dadaistically inclined would-be musician and writer, "composed one of his greatest lines for Bix, *'One by one a cow goes by.'* Bix's eyes popped, he turned his head a little to the side as he did on the bandstand when great things were coming from his horn, and murmured happily once again his entire vocabulary of praise and admiration. 'I am not a swan.' "[80] Twenty years later, singer Ella Fitzgerald reveled in the nonsense of Dizzy Gillespie, particularly the verbal games he played with his friends after hours. "It was quite an experience," she wrote, "and he used to always tell me, 'Come up and do it with the fellas'. . . . That to me was my education in learning how to really bop. We used to do 'Ooo-Bop-Sha-Bam-a-Klook-a-Mop' . . . that's one of the things I remember he used to do. And 'She-bop-da-ool-ya . . . She-bop-da-ool-ya . . . ' and that fascinated me. When I felt like I could sing like that, then I felt that I was in, in [*sic*]. And I followed him everywhere they went."[81] Such nonsense was autotelic. It existed in and of itself, following its own mysterious rules, its semantics resting entirely on process. It *did* what it meant.[82] And like other "incomprehensible" ritual language it implied a mysterious "other" reality.[83] To use it was to touch upon the sacred, to celebrate the separateness and solidarity of brotherhood, and to demonstrate qualifications for membership in the gnostic fellowship.

Humor

The comic element in jazz wordplay often enhanced its sacred nature. This may seem odd to those of us brought up in the sobrieties of the Judeo-Christian tradition, but it is no secret that humor has a refreshing, revitalizing power which can put even the most earnest, the most sacred, into balanced perspective. And as already noted, the lighthearted and sober are by no means enemies in the religious rituals of many cultures. We can see this link in the parodical sermon of the medieval Feast of Fools whose variations survive, among other places, in the writings of Bertolt Brecht and W. H. Auden, as well as in the mock sermons of jazzmen like Jimmy Harrison and Louis Armstrong that lampoon the phoniness and avarice of the hustler-preacher.[84]

Some of the greatest jazzmen have been at least part-time clowns. Before the advent of bop, the role of fool or clown went well with the image of jazzman as entertainer, an image the savvy performer exploited profitably. And despite their insistence that jazzmen were serious artists, boppers were not averse to onstage foolishness. In an earlier time, true believers took great pains not to compromise the purity of the music or gnosis. Louis Armstrong was quick to reassure friends that his notorious minstrel antics did not distract from his performances or from his devotion: "When I pick up that horn, that's all. The world's behind me, and I don't concentrate on nothing but that horn."[85] Dizzy Gillespie, also famous for his clowning, felt the same way. When told it might hurt his reputation among jazz purists, he rejoined that he was dead "*serious* as far as the music is concerned. . . . I don't put the music on. . . . There's no B.S. about the music. The music is extremely important."[86]

Gillespie and others knew full well the serious functions of humor. Among other things, it could loosen up both artist and performer. Gillespie, who consciously modeled his clowning after pianist Fats Waller's, explained that "comedy is important. As a performer, when you're trying to establish audience control, the best thing is to make them laugh if you can. That relaxes you more than anything. A laugh relaxes your muscles;

it relaxes muscles all over your body. When you get people relaxed, they're more receptive to what you're trying to get them to do. Sometimes, when you're laying on something over their heads, they'll go along with it if they're relaxed. Sometimes I get up on the bandstand and say 'I'd like to introduce the men in the band' . . . and then introduce the guys to one another. There's a reason for that. I just don't come out with it to get a laugh."[87] He used this little ritual almost nightly, but it continued to work, even among those who heard it again and again. No matter how stale, it continued to divert, cutting tension and loosening inhibition so that the magic could flow back and forth across the bandstand. Other musicians had different ice-breaking routines, but all had a similar purpose. As Charlie Parker told an admirer, "If you come on a band tense, you're going to play tense. If you come on a little bit foolish, act just a little bit foolish, and let yourself go, better ideas will come."[88]

Musicians knew that the performer who could not relax might well lose control. Reedman Don Menza, who had seen his share of performance stress, put the problem as follows: "There are a lot of pressures on an honest player . . . pressures of having to create and perform. Some musicians [like] Dizzy Gillespie can be a clown, make it look as if it's really easy and fun. However, a lot of people don't have that outlet, and when things really get bad on the stage, they don't know how to grab a handle on it, how to hold it together. Dizzy can just loosen up immediately. And then there are people that do the total opposite; there are the Charlie Minguses [who] take the bass and break it over the piano player's back, you know?"[89]

It was not enough just to start relaxed; one had to stay loose all evening. Musicians found various ways to do so, sometimes employing comic relief of the sort already mentioned. Dizzy Gillespie occasionally ended a set by telling the audience, "Now, ladies and gentlemen, I would like to turn you over. . . ." and walking off the stage without another word.[90] Other musicians indulged in what Erving Goffman calls "role distancing," like surgeons under operating-room pressures who withdraw momentarily between procedures into humor or nonsense in order to "objectify" before returning to their tense, absorbing work.[91] It was customary for jazzmen to spend their breaks loosening up in a convivial, neighborhood bar, but others sought more exotic ways to release pressure. Charlie Parker told a colleague, "If you do something out of the ordinary between sets, when you come back you will have a different thought and it will come out in your playing."[92] He tried a number of things, from sexual ploys to practical jokes and zany tricks—riding a horse into a bar, or challenging a friend to a water-drinking contest. Still others shared a form of manic humor. Pianist Art Hodes recounted going backstage during a break in a Louis Armstrong appearance with his friend Wingy Manone (a one-armed trumpeter with a reputation as a joker): "There'd be a lot of good feeling in the room. And somebody would say something funny, and that would give Louis an opening and you couldn't beat Louis at being funny—not even Wingy. And we'd laugh through the whole intermission, and then walk Louis slowly back to the stand. . . . Man, the guy could really blow then."[93]

Aside from easing the flow of magic from the jazzman's horn, his humor had a more profound role: to comment, however indirectly or unconsciously, on the nature of humanity. Insofar as he was a clown, he joined the numerous fools who peer conspicuously from our novels, poems, plays, paintings, films, and television sets—despite, or perhaps because of, the brutalities and other horrors of the twentieth century—revealing man's ludicrous contradictions, posturings, and embarrassments. In the words of Samuel H. Miller, "The clown, by his excessive exaggeration and gross simplicity, touches the hem of the metaphysical, that realm which tends to be smothered in ages proud of their pragmatic and utilitarian efficiency. He . . . like the saint, extends the dimension of consciousness beyond its normal limits. His ritual has its own sanctity."[94]

The jazzman as clown (and musician) operated at the edge of awareness and understanding in rituals full of surprise, incongruity, and catharsis, hovering ambiguously between known and unknown, sophistication and naiveté, playfulness and seriousness, the sacred and the profane. Like his musical and linguistic practices, the true believer's uses of humor implied a second or "other" reality. A Freudian would explain them as regression to a primitive or childlike mental state free from conventional responsibilities and limitations. In this interpretation, the clown, retreating to a realm of illusion, escapes from the confinements of ordinary logic and propriety into a liberating mental state, rising above frustrations and stimulating creativity and humor. Whatever the case, devout jazz followers found in the clown a liberating symbol who helped give them a seemingly universal perspective.[95]

In addition, the jazzman's humor had a social role familiar in liminal groups where the absence of ordinary rules invites common regression or transcendence. Many of his jokes made fun of nonbelievers in ways that defined and solidified the elite, but celebrated clowns like Armstrong, Gillespie, Joe Venuti, and Wingy Manone did not limit their barbs to the squares; fringe sectarians, fellow musicians, and others also felt the sting of their wit. Some insiders liked to lead naive followers by the nose with tall stories received as gospel from the lips of prophets. Nat Hentoff told of a zealous record collector trying to pick the memory of a white-haired, New Orleans musician for a definitive discography of a memorable, early recording session and getting a cock-and-bull story replete with fictitious dates and personnel, which the collector took down in detail while gratefully feeding the narrator drinks.[96] Dizzy Gillespie was a grand master of the elaborate "put on." In 1963, he arrived unannounced at San Francisco International Airport masquerading as one Prince Ibo in Nigerian robes, tarboosh on his head, and three dark-suited sidemen following at a respectful distance. To the bemusement of officials, the party swept through the lobby, parting crowds on the way to the taxi stand. Then, according to Patricia Willard, the musicians gave their white cabby

> a slip of paper bearing the name of a hotel where they held reservations, and proceeded into a violent and extended argument among themselves in pseudo-African double talk all the way there. The driver began to show signs of nervous uneasiness. At the hotel, the passengers looked uncomprehendingly when the fare was quoted. Everybody 'Ungawa'-ed. The cabby began raising his voice and pointed to the meter. The passengers got more excited and more confused. In desperation, the man held

up eight fingers and slowly counted them to indicate the dollars owed.

"Man, why didn't you say so in the first place?" Diz smiled warmly as he handed him a ten dollar denomination in United States currency and gestured that no change was necessary.[97]

The "put on" was but a variant of one of the clown's ancient tricks: to make fun of pretension and go unpunished. "In every epoch of history," wrote Freud, "those who have had something to say but could not say it without peril have eagerly assumed the fool's cap. The audience at whom their forbidden speech was aimed tolerated it more easily if they could at the same time laugh and flatter themselves with the reflection that the unwelcome words were clearly nonsensical."[98] At the same time, the joker earned the esteem of those who shared his viewpoint, recognizing him as no fool but a smart operator who got away with doing things they dared not do. The boppers knew that Gillespie was "dizzy like a fox"[99] and found him a reassuring symbol of hip superiority.

Finally, the jazzman's rituals of humor provided safety valves for aggression as well as a form of social control. The play of nicknames and various kinds of needling and josh- ing were a sort of privileged insult, useful when confined to approved rituals but divisive and destructive if permitted to get out of hand.[100] With its own logic and sanctity, this humor bound users to tacitly understood limits of ridicule which, if skillfully employed, had a devastating power to en- force conformity.

Many a deviant was brought into line after becoming the butt of a joke. A turning point in Charlie Parker's career came in 1937 when, as a teenager too big for his boots, he came to grief during a solo in a Kansas City jam session and was "gonged off" the stand by a cymbal that drummer Jo Jones scaled across the dance floor. Parker departed to the sound of humiliating guffaws, badly hurt, but resolving to return when he had learned his musical lessons.[101] A few years earlier, a cocky fifteen-year-old clarinetist, Artie Shaw, was cut down to size by persistent ridicule of older bandsmen in New Haven. "It took me quite a while to learn to keep my mouth shut and never ask questions about anything that did not directly and immediately concern me—and even at that I still kept putting my foot into it for some time." A sideman would ask the leader about a job at a marvelous place called "Webb Inn," and this would start a series of spirited discussions about the night of the booking. It was all news to Shaw, who was pointedly left out of the conversations and began to fear that he was not included. Finally, he asked, "Where *is* Webb Inn?" Whereupon, everybody else would "break into a loud chorus, 'Up the spider's ass!'" "Through all this," he related, "I began to learn a little about what was what." Equally educational, if more embarrassing, was the ridicule he faced on the bandstand, where things were taken more seriously. At one point, he began to use an improvised "lick" which quickly became the butt of merciless humor, underscoring, as he said, that "in jazz music there are certain things that are not done. . . . I managed somehow to keep from bursting into tears of rage and humiliation, and, of course, I never did play that particular phrase again. But there were a number of such lessons to learn . . . to distinguish between what is jazz and what is 'corn'. . . . The one thing I knew for sure was that so far as any of these older colleagues of mine were concerned, anger or tears would have been just about the biggest joke of all. . . . Anyway, one way or the other through all this stuff, I began to learn a little about what was what."[102]

Like Parker and many another youngster, Shaw discovered that those who stepped beyond the bounds of accepted practice invited withering ridicule which dramatized the rules and discouraged further violations.

Not that the jazzman's humor always had such a sharp edge. In friendlier circumstances, it could reinforce values and relationships more positively. Jokes about mistakes, one's own or others', prevented gaffes from being taken too seriously, providing a form of protection, and way of asking for, and giving, reassurance. And senior members used gentle humor to guide and control juniors' attitudes and behavior on and off the bandstand. Humor, then, tactfully smoothed over rough edges and molded opinion and activity along acceptable lines. Bergson called the humorist a "disguised moralist," and the jazzman was often such—defining, teaching, and enforcing the gnosis and its practices.[103]

Initiation

J. H. Kwabena Nketia points out that musical training in West Africa "is not generally organized on a formal, institutional basis, for it is believed that natural endowment and a person's ability to develop on his own are essentially what is needed. . . . The principle seems to be that of learning through social experience. Exposure to musical situations and participation are emphasized more than formal teaching."[104] While most jazzmen received at least some formal training during their careers, their initiations reflected the informality Nketia speaks of, an informality encouraging individual learning and discovery. And it is this fostering of self-discovery, of searching into the self and learning ways to express its secrets with minimal guidance, that gives jazz much of its fascination. As pianist Cecil Taylor observed, "The thing that makes jazz so interesting is that each man is his own academy."[105]

But for all their informality, the jazzman's initiation rituals were not without structure or rigor. Usually they fitted a common pattern which Mircea Eliade identifies with transitions into adulthood, secret societies, and mystical vocations—rites . of passage that often occur simultaneously and have much in common. All include the familiar three stages outlined by Arnold van Gennep: separation (from prior role and status), *limen* (literally "threshold"—Turner's concept of liminality begins here), and aggregation (reentry into the world of conventional rules and expectations). The second stage, according to Eliade, involves segregation from the opposite sex; hours of solitary meditation and study; the guidance of a master who serves variously as godfather, teacher, examiner, and accreditor; periods of trial and testing; and symbolic death and rebirth, sometimes resulting in a new name for the initiand, whose passage teaches him specialized techniques, language, and lore, and also the mystical truths of ecstasy, visions, and dreams. The initiate is above all the one who *knows.*[106]

As adolescents who sought recognition as adults, accreditation in a mystical calling, and membership in a recondite elite, apprentice jazzmen often went though all these rites of passage at the same time. Take Louis Armstrong, living on the streets of New Orleans while still in knee pants, yet not without adult models. Like most jazzmen, Armstrong had more than one master. The most influential was Joe "King" Oliver, the reigning cornetist before World War I, who called himself Armstrong's "stepfather."[107] He was also teacher, tester, and certifier. But long before Armstrong became Oliver's disciple, he had reverently followed the master around the city, carrying his treasured instrument between performances. Eventually, Oliver gave him a cornet and lessons which he mastered in long hours of solitary practice. In 1918, when Oliver left for Chicago, Armstrong had progressed to the point where the master could recommend him as his own replacement in the celebrated Kid Ory band. "There were many good, experienced trumpet players in town," Ory recalled, "but none of them had young Louis' possibilities. I went to see him and told him that if he got himself a pair of long trousers, I'd give him a job. Within two hours Louis came to my house and said, "I'm here. I'll be glad when eight o'clock comes. I'm ready to go."[108]

He thus became a member of the best band in the Crescent City, yet remained the enthusiastic naif, in his off-hours playing for small change and kicks in the freewheeling, liminal New Orleans jazz world whose informality and unexpected challenges stimulated technical and imaginative experiment. Prodded by his peers, he continued to strengthen his musical vocabulary, syntax, and emotional range, so that after leaving the Ory group he could get work on the Streckfus riverboats whose owners demanded a high level of musicianship. For many New Orleans jazzmen it was like "going to school," remembered bassist Pops Foster. "You had fourteen numbers to play in an evening and changed numbers every two weeks. The numbers were long. You'd play the whole number and maybe two or three encores and sometimes two choruses. . . .

The Streckfus people made musicians out of a whole lot of guys that way. Louis Armstrong, Johnny St. Cyr and I didn't know nothin' about readin' when we went on the boats, but we did when we came off."[109]

On these side-wheelers, which sometimes went as far upriver as Minneapolis, veteran performers such as Joe Howard and "Professor" David Jones taught Armstrong something about "legitimate" music. But eventually he concluded his apprenticeship with his real master. In 1922, Oliver called him to Chicago to join his Creole Band, then in the midst of its celebrated engagement at Lincoln Gardens on the South Side. "I lived for Papa Joe. So his calling for me was the biggest feeling I ever had musically," Armstrong wrote, indicating something of the sacredness of the master-neophyte relationship and his elation at having cleared a major hurdle in his initiation. But it was not over yet. He spent two more years under Oliver's wing, learning the ins and outs of the big time. "Sitting by him every night," wrote Armstrong, "I *had* to pick up a lot of little tactics he made."[110] By 1924 Armstrong, aware that the apprenticeship should end, went forth to assume his new role in the jazz world, his rebirth symbolized by his change of byname from "Little Louis" to "Satchmo."

Charlie Parker had a more disjointed initiation. He too was separated—at least spiritually—from his parents at an early age and became the disciple of several older men, including saxophonist Tommy Douglas, who had spent four years at the Boston Conservatory and taught Parker music theory, Buster Smith, who taught him about the alto saxophone, and Lester Young, his major inspiration. As a callow liminar in Kansas City, Parker was hired by Smith, who took a special interest in his second-alto player (Armstrong had played second-cornet to Oliver in the Creole band). Smith recalled, "He used to call me his dad, and I called him my boy. I couldn't get rid of him. He was always up under me. In my band, we'd split solos. If I took two, he'd take two; if I took three, he'd take three; and so forth. He always wanted me to take the first solo. I guess he thought he'd learn something that way. He did play like me quite a bit, I guess. But after a while, anything I could make on my horn he could make too—and make something better out of it."[111] Yet even before joining Smith's band in his mid-teens, Parker had fallen under the spell of Lester Young, the leading tenor player in Kansas City, then dominating the Count Basie band at the Reno Club. The underage Parker would sneak into the balcony of the Reno, where he supposedly followed Young's fingering silently on his own horn. Offstage the reclusive Young was little interested in divulging the tricks of the trade to unproven amateurs, but Parker managed to glean some of truths from him: to worry less about individual notes than about polish and sound, how to shape the air in the horn, what kind of mouthpiece was best, how stiff the reed should be, and how to whittle and sand it to the proper shape and thickness.[112]

With such lessons under his belt, Parker eventually felt confident enough to try his skills at some of the local cutting sessions. The results were not happy and, like other youngsters before him who failed such trials, he went back to solitary practicing, determined to remedy his shortcomings. In 1937, after being "gonged off" the stand by Jo Jones' cymbal, he told his friend Gene Ramey, "I'll fix those cats. Everybody's laughing at me now but you just wait and see."[113] To make good on this claim, he took a job in the Ozarks, using his free time to work on his technique with the help of Lester Young records played over and over. He learned Young's solos by heart, accompanying them on his own horn and studying how the master attacked notes, let them decay, ran triplets into dotted eighths, and the like. Gradually, he began to find his own voice and, when he returned to Kansas City at the end of the summer, Gene Ramey found that "the difference was unbelievable."[114] While still brash and callow, he could now hold his own musically with the best of the local men. Pianist Jay McShann recalled: "I was in a rhythm section one night when this cocky kid pushed his way on stage. He was a teenager, barely seventeen, and he looked like a high school kid. He had a tone that cut. Knew his changes. He'd get off on a line of his own, and I would think he was in trouble, but he was a cat landing on all four feet. And a lot of people couldn't understand what he was trying to do, but it made sense harmonically and it always swung."[115] Eventually, Parker got a chair in

McShann's big band, in which he began to make a national
reputation, and he later became a master in his own right,
having acquired the name of "Bird."

Jazz apprentices learned technical and ecstatic knowledge,
some it communicated directly, the rest indirectly. Dizzy Gillespie, who took his master's role seriously, liked to expound
on matters of technique and theory. Early on, he patiently
explained technical fine points to beginners in big bands—
rehearsing them in sections, indicating proper fingering, showing how to blow "pure" notes, and other tricks of the trade.
In the Forties, he ran informal master classes in New York.
Saxophonist Budd Johnson, often in attendance, recalled:

> Man, you'd go by Dizzy's apartment and sometimes he'd have
> as much as fifteen or twenty cats up there sitting around. And
> Diz would be walking around all open and talking. Tadd
> Dameron at that time was one of Dizzy's students. Tadd would
> say, "Well, Dizzy, I'm making an arrangement for so and so
> and . . . and I'm doing this." Dizzy would say, "Look, don't use
> these chords, Lemme show you what to do." And Tadd would
> get up from the piano. And Dizzy would sit at the piano and
> show him the changes. . . . Whether the guys wanna admit or
> not, he taught. He really taught. . . . He could set down the
> form and carry it to posterity. I mean, you know this is very
> important, I think, to pass on your knowledge to someone.[116]

Composer and bandleader Charles Mingus, concerned about
his works being played properly, was also an avid teacher.
Drummer Danny Richmond admitted that before joining him
he knew nothing about dynamics: "My playing was very flashy,
and I wanted to be very fast. You know, a young boy showing
off. It was only after Charles saw this that he was able to say,
'No, at this point you have to whisper, and there have to be
other points where there is planned chaos!' There were many
other lessons, of course, that I learned. Not only from the
musical standpoint but about living, and doing certain things
certain ways. And, of course, he would also make a point to
drop some of his philosophical things on me."[117]
Many technical lessons came without the benefit of a master,

but in the company of peers, in conversation, in performance, or in competition where ideas were exchanged and ears sharpened. Miles Davis told how, as novices, he and trumpeter Freddy Webster constantly challenged one another, and not just on their horns. At a club, between sets by Dizzy Gillespie, they would "stand at the bar, throw a quarter, and name the note it came down on. That shit be going down so fast, and we'd be testing ourselves." Later he said, "We really studied. If a door squeaked, we would call out the exact pitch. And every time I heard the chord of G, for instance, my fingers automatically took the position for C sharp on the horn—the flatted fifth—whether I was playing or not."[118]

Sometimes the lessons imparting the codes of wisdom and life-style were explicit. In the midst of showing young Hoagy Carmichael the secrets of the piano, Reggie Duval declared, "I want the harmony to *holler*. . . . I want it so it sounds right to *me*. And that is the way it sounds rightest." "It's wonderful," replied Carmichael. " 'Naw, but it's *right*,' " said Duval. " 'Never play anything that ain't right. You may not make any money but you'll never get hostile with yourself.' " His disciple was greatly impressed.[119]

At other times, the lessons were more implicit. After he had been with Mingus for a while, Danny Richmond was told, "You're doing well, but now suppose you had to play a composition alone. How would you play it on the drums? . . . OK, if you had a dot in the middle of your hand and you were going in a circle, it would have to expand and go round and round, and get larger and larger. And at some point it would have to stop, and then this same circle would have to come back around, around, around to the little dot in the middle of your hand. That did more for me, in a compositional sense, than anything else he's laid on me."[120]

Still other things required no explanation at all. No one had to tell an eager youngster that he must shape up, musically and otherwise, in order to survive in regimented big bands. No matter how eccentric, he soon had to learn how to read music passibly, know his parts, be prompt for rehearsals and performances, wear his uniform, get along with colleagues, stay reasonably sober, and be presentable onstage. As a youngster working in businesslike swing bands, saxophonist Illinois Jacquet quickly found that "Nobody else would be acting a fool and drinking. Everybody was so busy reading their music, some of that would rub off on you. And after a year or two of that, you would begin to act that way, live that way, play that way, and get more ambition about your music, your job. . . . See you need a lot of discipline out here too; all that is required in being a better musician."[121]

But if some things needed little explanation, others were inexplicable. No one could finally explain the charisma of the prophet, the ecstasies of the music, why certain notes sounded good together and others did not, or what it was to "swing." One had to learn such things intuitively. Sensitive youngsters had only to stay alert to discover many of the truths and rules. Pianist Billy Strayhorn related that his master Duke Ellington's "first, last and only formal instruction for me was embodied in one word: Observe."[122] By keeping his eyes and ears open the perceptive disciple discovered what inexplicably went where, and when, in music and other things. Like other liminars, the jazz initiand, freed from earlier cultural encumbrances, was particularly susceptible to indirect and buried meanings— significances at the edge of conventional articulation and comprehension.[123] In exploring these meanings, jazzmen regressed into mental states with deep-structured rules of associational logic and resorted to ritual and myth, the handmaidens of magic and the sacred.

Having left behind the protected world of his childhood, the apprentice quickly learned about the underside of life, including the uses of liquor and narcotics. Trumpeter Johnny Carisi, one of the few whites to find favor among the early boppers at Minton's, reported that he used to avoid the bar between sets until house pianist Thelonious Monk demanded, " 'What, you call yourself a jazz player'. . . . And the next thing you know he had me drinking double gins."[124] Dizzy Gillespie told of a similar experience: "When I first came to New York in 1937 I didn't drink or smoke marijuana. 'You going to be a square muthafucka!' Charlie Shavers said and turned me on to smoking pot. . . . Some of the older musicians had been smoking reefers forty to fifty years. Jazz musicians, the old ones and young ones, almost all of them I knew smoked pot."[125] In the Forties and Fifties, when indulgence in hard drugs reached its peak, there was considerable pressure to use heroin, even in established big bands, as long as it did not detract noticeably from musicianship. "When I was in Woody Herman's band," wrote reedman Jimmy Giuffre, "eight were on at one time. They thought it was hip and they were putting on the squares. It's like when you're very young and smoke cigarettes and drink coffee to be hip. Junk was a strong force around that time."[126]

For many neophytes there seemed little reason to stay straight when all the hip people were high. If Louis Armstrong declared that marijuana "makes you feel good, man. It relaxes you, makes you forget all the bad things that happen to a Negro. It makes you feel wanted, and when you're with another tea smoker it makes you feel a special kinship"[127]—what inducement was there for the anxious novice not to indulge? And if Charlie Parker could illuminate the jazz world with the help of, or despite, his habit, why couldn't his eager admirers? One night an impressionable young Hampton Hawes went up to Parker's room and witnessed one of his pre-performance routines that included eleven shots of whiskey, a handful of "bennies," and a heroin fix—while smoking marijuana. "He sweated like a horse for five minutes," Hawes reported, "got up, put on his suit and half an hour later was on the stand playing strong and beautiful." The lesson was clear. "Those of us who were affected strongest felt we'd be willing to do anything to warm ourselves by that fire, get some grease pumping through our veins. He fucked up all our minds, it was where the ultimate truth was."[128]

But once induced to explore drugs, the tyro had to learn the appropriate rituals and attitudes. Beginners often came away disappointed until taught the techniques. With marijuana the lessons were simple enough. In the Fifties one initiate told Howard S. Becker, a sociologist and musician: "I was smoking like I did an ordinary cigarette [until taken in hand by a friendly veteran]. He said, 'No, don't do it like that. . . . Suck it, you know draw in and hold it in your lungs . . . for a period of time.' I said, 'Is there any limit or time to hold it?' He said, 'No, just until you feel that you want to let it out, let it out.' So I did that three or four times."[129] Stronger drugs required more elaborate procedures, such as those singer Sheila Harris taught Art Pepper when she introduced him to heroin. Pepper related:

> She had a little glass vial filled with white powder, and she poured some out into the porcelain top of the toilet, chopped it up with a razor blade and separated it into piles, little lines. She asked me if I had a dollar bill. She told me to get the newest one I had. I had one, very clean and very stiff. I took it out of my pocket and she said, "Roll it up." I started to roll it but she said, "No, not that way." She made a tube with a small opening at the bottom and a larger opening at the top. Then she went over to the heroin and she said, "Now watch what I do and do this." She put one finger on her left nostril and she stuck the large end of the dollar bill into her right nostril. She put the tube at the beginning of one pile, made a little noise, and the pile disappeared. She said, "Now you do that." I closed my nostril. I even remember it was my left nostril. I sniffed it, and a long, thin pile of heroin disappeared. She told me to do the same with the other nostril. I did six little lines and then she said "Okay, wait a few minutes."[130]

Subsequently he learned the more direct practice of "mainlining," cooking the drug in a spoon and injecting it into the proper vein.

The user also had to learn how to perceive and appreciate the drug. Most marijuana smokers did not know they were high until at least their second indulgence. In their initial experience they might have extraordinary sensations of hunger or thirst, but they did not necessarily connect these with the chemical. "It was only after the second time I got high that I realized I was high the first time. Then I knew something different was happening," a musician told Becker. "We played the first tune for almost two hours—one tune! Imagine, man! . . . Almost two hours on one tune. And it didn't seem like anything. . . . I knew I must really be high or something if anything like that could happen. See, and then they explained to me that that's what it did to you, you had a different sense of time and everything. So I realized that that's what it was."[131] Others, too, had to be told what and how to feel. After Art Pepper first "horned" heroin, he was not sure what to make of the effect until Sheila Harris exclaimed, "Look at yourself in the mirror! Look in the mirror!" He did not want to for fear of finding the wretched figure he had become accustomed to seeing there. "But she kept saying, 'Look at yourself! Look how beautiful you are! Look at your eyes! Look at your pupils!' I looked in the mirror and I looked like an angel. I looked at my pupils and they were pinpoints; they were tiny, little dots. It was like looking into a whole universe of joy and happiness and contentment. . . . I looked at myself and said, 'I'm beautiful.' "[132]

The pharmacological effects of drug use are undeniable, but social circumstances greatly shape the user's response to it. As Becker argues, a drug can evoke a variety of feelings, so the user learns to select those that suit him and his climate of feeling, itself influenced heavily by social interaction and need.[133] Thus, the apprentice jazzman discovered the significance of drugs through ritualistic experience with fellow believers for whom the chemicals provided reinforcement of gnostic feelings and relief from stress.

Despite the communitas of the jazz novice's world his apprenticeship could be harrowing and lonesome. Much of the time he was isolated in solitary practice, learning his parts, mastering his scales, memorizing chord sequences, and strengthening his execution, tone, and ability to read. Whereas the novice in archaic societies repaired to the woods or initiation lodge to study and meditate, the jazzman went to the "woodshed." Most musicians had to put in thousands of hours there before they could be called professionals and, once they found work, might still be banished for further practice before they played acceptably. Cuba Austin, the drummer for McKinney's Cotton Pickers in the Twenties, stated that the band consisted of "a pretty scrubby bunch" of boys who "should have been in school still, and all of them were wearing knickers." Veteran John

Nesbitt rode herd on these youngsters, teaching them the rudiments of the music and acting as disciplinarian, tester, and accreditor. "When one of the gang wanted to rehearse his part," said Austin, "he would go off in the woods until he had made it. If anyone would biff a few too many, Nesbitt would send him to the woods for a private rehearsal. Sometimes more than half the band would be woodshedding."[134] Charlie Parker, as we saw, did an extended tour in the "woodshed" in the Ozarks after his humiliation at the Reno Club in 1937.

It was one thing to play among fellow neophytes, but attempts to break into the big time, to hold one's own with the established men, was another matter, particularly in agonistic cutting sessions. Even attempts to sit in informally could be traumatic, what with veterans setting up outlandish barriers or ambushes to discourage intrusions. To succeed in these ordeals the newcomer needed strong motivation, talent, and sometimes tremendous gall. Parker, again, is an obvious case in point. So is pianist Walter Bishop, Jr., who eventually made the grade in Manhattan. As he recalled: "It was around 1944. I was a young kid with more courage than knowledge. I was going all around, sitting in and jamming. I had such a strong desire to learn and become part of the scene. I suffered all sorts of indignities. I was chased off the set or somebody would call a tune I didn't know or I could be sitting up there at the piano and a horn man would call down to a friend, 'Hey, Joe, come up and play piano with us.' As if I was not sitting there at all. These things were perhaps good in a way. They made me vengeful and competitive. I would go home, lock myself in my room and practice for hours on end. If there was a certain tune that they caught me on, they would never catch me on that tune again. . . . That's the way I learned as fast as I did."[135] Artie Shaw's indignities at the hands of veterans had similar results: "It . . . gave me a strong competitive drive, a terribly urgent need to keep working at what I was doing until I simple *had* to learn something about it," he wrote. "All of my early out-group conditioning, plus this direct competition with older and more experienced men, combined to channelize all my waking (and perhaps even some sleeping) energies into an overwhelming need to prove my validity, to be accepted on the basis of my skills."[136]

Other gifted youngsters, shy and more vulnerable, did not come along as quickly. Pianist Hampton Hawes, fresh from California, where he had developed a strong, local reputation, told of being frightened away from the bandstand at Minton's: "It was like an initiation, a ceremonial rite *(chump, jump or I'll burn you up, you don't know nothin'),* calling out fast tunes in strange keys with the hip changes at tempos so fast if you didn't fly you fell. . . . For a week I had watched these cats burning each other up, ambushing outsiders, fucking up their minds so bad they would fold and split the stand after one tune. Surprised by their coldness because they were so friendly off the stand, I peeked that I wasn't ready, maybe they could get me."[137] His confidence dissolving, he departed. Like many before him, he suffered from a case of New York nerves. Coleman Hawkins, who reigned without peer as master tenor player in Manhattan for two generations and witnessed a long parade of pretenders come and go, explained, "This place makes all musicians sound kind of funny when they come around. When they first come here, I don't care what they were in their home towns, when they come here, they get cut. . . . They have to come and learn all over again, practically. Then when they come back, they are all right. Or, if they stay around they can develop to be all right."[138] Of course, not everybody returned, but Hawes did. Two years later, having sharpened his skills and shored up his courage, he came back to Minton's and triumphed. "A drummer paid me the ultimate compliment following the set," he related. " 'We been hearing about you on the coast, you a bad motherfucker.' My days of being scared were over."[139]

Hawes had passed a critical test and was now recognized in the profession and the elite. But he had failed to complete one of his initiatory transitions: he remained immature emotionally, and in his own eyes was yet to be a man—at least his own man. The pressures and anxieties of his vocation continued to overwhelm him after he became recognized, as with many other initiates who found new success. Discussing the roots of her heroin addiction, Sheila Jordan recalled her early diffidence and added, "Looking back, I also realize that I was always alone, fending for myself, doing the best I could without the family support a seventeen-year-old ordinarily gets. Smoking pot, drinking, playing it cool were my ways of hiding the pain and deprivation I wouldn't let myself realize."[140] And referring to Stan Getz's celebrated drug problem, drummer Don Lamond noted, "He was a featured tenor when he was sixteen years old: Hell, he never had a chance to grow up."[141] In familiar fashion, he had been torn prematurely from home and school to become a nomadic night-person in a mercurial profession that offered notoriety at one moment and relative obscurity or anomie the next. These circumstances were hardly conducive to maturation, and the regressive frame of mind so useful when creating led to unfortunate consequences in other areas of behavior.

All this indicates that initiation helped professional rather than personal development. "Don't forget," wrote pianist Billy Taylor in connection with the drug problem, "that the time involved in studying is huge for a musician. There must be no less than four hours of practice a day plus time for lessons, plus a couple of hours for other studies connected with music. So figure eight or ten hours of music a day, added to eating and sleeping, and there is not much time for other things that would broaden a man."[142] Many a liminal tyro was psychologically unprepared for the difficulties of the jazz life. Lacking sufficient intermediate goals and also adequate guidance and support, the player often succumbed to the immediate gratification offered by drugs, which only aggravated his problems. In her 1956 study of Harlem addicts, including musicians, psychologist Marie Nyswander found that "So great is [the drug taker's] need for immediate recognition, for *being* . . . that he does not allow himself a period of *becoming*. . . . He cannot take present deprivation in the hope of building toward security in the indefinite future but must continually bolster his self-esteem with immediate proof of present success."[143] Not all desperate young musicians succumbed to narcotics; many found other ways to cope with their stress. But Nyswander's conclusion indicates how the apprentice's initiation inhibited his emotional growth.

The need for a remedy has long been obvious, and some argue that it should come from the musician's union. Unfortunately, the American Federation of Musicians, an old-style, craft union not averse to rough tactics, has been little interested in the jazzman except to collect his dues or to retard his admittance with troublesome restrictions, including long waiting lists for membership cards and strictures against sitting in. In recent years the musicians themselves have sought to improve matters by forming their own organizations. The best known have been the short-lived Jazz Composers Guild in the Sixties, a cooperative, led by trumpeter Bill Dixon, which sought to take over key aspects of production and marketing, and the more successful AACM (Association for the Advancement of Creative Music), another avant-garde group founded in the Sixties. Guided by pianist Muhal Richard Abrams, the AACM has spawned several musical groups, including the well-known Art Ensemble of Chicago, and, aside from handling the creation and distribution of its music, has played an important role in initiating young performers, taking them off the streets and infusing them with a sense of purpose. As saxophonist Roscoe Mitchell claimed, "Until the first meeting with Richard Abrams, I was like all the rest of the 'hip' ghetto niggers; I was cool, I took dope, I smoked pot, etc. I did not *care* for the life that I had been given. In having a chance to work with the experimental band with Richard and the other musicians there I found the first something with reason/ meaning for doing. That band and the people there was the most important thing that ever happened to me." Another disciple, drummer Alvin Fiedler, said that the AACM "was like a church—it *was* my church. Music is my church and, of course, the AACM was my denomination."[144]

Among other things, Abrams organized classes, open rehearsals, and concerts in which neophytes were instructed in his special balance of individualism and cooperation. His emphasis on emotional development is evident in an AACM manifesto that read in part: "Our curriculum is so designed as to elicit maximum development of potential within the context of a training programme that exposes youngsters to constructive relationships with artistic adults. Superimposed over our training framework is our keen desire to develop within our students the ability to value *self*, the ability to value *others* and the ability to utilize the opportunities they find in society. It is felt that such values should be based on the cultural and spiritual heritage of the people involved."[145] The idea, then, was to train not just inspired professionals but also mature men who could be proud of their African tradition and their roles and relationships with their fellows, men who could handle the shocks and tribulations of their vocation. The success of AACM encouraged imitators in other parts of the country.

By the Sixties, in addition to these avant-garde efforts there was a growing number of more conservative institutions, schools and colleges devoted wholly to jazz or giving it a place of honor in their curricula in ways suggesting something like a hardening denominational dogma. In their sometimes self-conscious desire for legitimacy, these schools presented students with highly rationalized theories and techniques, emphasizing the respectable, often commercial, aspects of the music. For the most part, they underplayed its unsavory associations, ignoring some and treating others as avoidable pitfalls. "We are naturally concerned with the moral character of students as well as their ability to play," explained an administrator at one of the more successful colleges. "A guy may be a fine musician, but if he is going to get involved with a lot of off-color dealings, we don't want him."[146] Such a policy excluded some talented youngsters and increased the difficulties for matriculants with severe personal problems. It accentuated the technical rituals of initiation but unlike the program of the AACM and its imitators ignored those leading to emotional maturity. Separated from childhood circumstances and enrolled in institutions which did not act *in loco parentis*, the initiand had to learn about manhood and the deeper mysteries of the music without a traditional master and could turn only to his peers when trouble arose. In general, many traditional initiation practices had lost their currency and accredited educational institutions provided little to renew or replace them.

The rituals and related matters dealt with here relate mainly to musicians. I will show later that other followers had similar, if less demanding, practices. Yet in every case, whether at the hard core of the sect or at its fringes, rituals told the believer what to do and how to do it; they helped orient and structure activity, shape experience, and quell doubt. Selecting, limiting, and encouraging, they celebrated the separateness and solidarity of rapidly changing sects, giving them what custom gives to more static groups—a sense of uniformity and propriety that, in turn, fostered a common sensibility and a stable point of view.

Myth

Rituals are repeated practices and patterns related to the sacred; myths are stories about sacred heroes and origins, sometimes fanciful tales taken seriously by the faithful. It is not always clear to what extent jazz rituals emerge as the enactment of myth, or to what degree myth develops as the rationalization of ritual, but there is little question that psychologically and culturally the two are closely linked, mutually supplemental and reinforcing, and that they arise from similar anxieties and needs.[1]

Consider two heroes. First, King Oliver, the shaman of Lincoln Gardens and mentor of Louis Armstrong. Like the images of most other storied figures, his remains fuzzy and lends itself to different typologies. Frederic Ramsey, Jr., saw him as a noble martyr, patient and long suffering.[2] Martin Williams cast him as a culture hero, more pathetic than tragic, whose story echoes the medieval tale of success undone by capricious fate, in this case fickle public taste.[3] Whitney Balliett regarded him as nearly primordial, "mysterious, almost primeval."[4] Oliver, in fact, had all these faces and they came together in the image of him as "the King," who inherited the title from Buddy Bolden and passed it on to Louis Armstrong. In jazz royal titles are sometimes a form of wordplay, but to his ardent followers Oliver was truly sovereign and, *mutatis mutandis*, he fitted into a familiar stereotype.[5]

Like other kings, the Oliver of the mythical stories had a mysterious potency and moral force. And like other monarchs his word (in the jazz world) was law, his acts beyond judgment so long as he maintained the supernatural aura found in stories attesting to his larger-than-life abilities. He was said to have

the appetite of a giant, eating enough at one sitting to fill the
bellies of several ordinary men. According to one tale he
devoured twelve pies in succession, on a bet, to the astonish-
ment of onlookers. But his superhuman powers had mainly
to do with music. His lungs and embouchure were reputedly
so strong that he blew a cornet out of tune every four months.
And there were the inexplicable tricks he performed with
mutes, making uncannily convincing human and animal sounds.
Fellow cornetist Mutt Carey said, "Joe could make his horn
sound like a holy roller meeting."[6] Equally mysterious were
his impromptu duets, unaccountably coordinated and flawless,
with second-cornetist Louis Armstrong in the Creole Jazz Band.
But most fascinating was the magic warmth of his intense
sound, said to charm patrons out of neighboring clubs, van-
quish all comers in agonistic encounters, send dancers into
ecstasies, and enrapture the tight ring of disciples around the
bandstand.[7]

  Unhappily, the King's reign was short. By the end of the
Twenties, his style superseded by later fashions and his crown
passed to his former protégé, he began a painful decline which
ended in an unmarked grave in 1938. His anguish on the way
down and the way he bore it were well publicized in biograph-
ical narratives which emphasized the difficulties of endless
tours of one-night stands, broken-down transportation, ruined
instruments, canceled jobs, infighting among bandsmen, con-
tinual debts, brushes with the law, racial discrimination, ragged
clothes, wretched food, bedbugs, and then poor health—
frequent colds, the pyorrhea that destroyed his teeth, hyper-
tension, and, finally, heart disease. These same accounts also
stress the dignity and grace with which he confronted his fate.

  In the familiar fashion of the martyr, Oliver's suffering and
noble forbearance helped sanctify his image and his agonies
were particularly touching because dealt by bad luck. There
were stories of buses stalling on desolate roads in the middle
of winter, desperate bandsmen setting tires on fire to stay
warm, accounts of hopeless sidemen enduring all sorts of
privations until forced to leave, men like Paul Barnes, who
wrote: "I will never forget that moment when I quit the band
because things were just going too bad. King was so sad that

he had tears in his eyes. He could stand losing anyone but me. I left the band very sad and that was the last time I saw the great King who had shaken the whole United States with his jazz orchestra."[8] These stories were supplemented by Oliver's well-known letters written toward the end of his life. One reads, in part:

> Pops, breaks come to cats in this racket only once in a while and I guess I must have been asleep when mine came. I've made lots of dough in this game but I didn't know how to take care of it. I have been under the best management in the country but didn't know how to stay under it.
>
> I have helped to make some of the best names in the music game, but I am too much of a man to ask those that I have helped to help me. Some of the guys that I have helped are responsible for my downfall in a way. I am the guy who took a pop bottle and a rubber plunger and made the first mute ever used in a horn, but I didn't know how to get the patent for it and some educated cat came along and made a fortune off of my ideas. I have written a lot of numbers that someone else got the credit and the money for. I couldn't help it because I didn't know what to do.
>
> I am in terrible shape now. I am getting old and my health is failing. Doctors advised me a long time ago to give up and quit but I can't. I don't have any money and I can't do anything else, so here I am.[9]

More widely known were Oliver's letters to his sister, telling how he faced death alone and penniless in Savannah. Here is part of one:

> Dear Sister:
>
> I open the pool rooms at 9 A.M. and close at 12 midnite. If the money was only 1/4 as much as the hours I'd be all set. But at that I can thank God for what I am getting. Which I do night after night. I know you will be glad when the winter say goodbye.
>
> Now Vick before I go further with my letter I'm going to tell you something but don't be alarmed. I've got high blood pressure. Was taking treatment but had to discontinue. My blood was 85 above normal. Now my blood has started again and I am unable to take treatments because it cost $3.50 per treatment and I don't make enough money to continue my

treatments. Now it begins to work on my heart. I am weak in my limbs at times and my breath but I am not asking you for money or anything. A stitch in time save nine. Should anything happen to me will you want my body? Let me know because I won't last forever and the longer I go the worst I'll get unless I take treatments.

It's not like New York or Chicago here. You've got to go through a lot of red tape to get any kind of treatment from the city here. I may never see New York again in life. . . .

Don't think I'm afraid because I wrote what I did. I am trying to live near to the Lord than ever before. So I feel like the Good Lord will take care of me.

Good night, dear . . .[10]

For many, Louis Armstrong spoke the truth when he said of Oliver's death, "Most people said it was a heart attack. I think it was a broken heart. Couldn't go no further with grief."[11]

It goes without saying that the Oliver stories, based partly on the emotional needs of devotees, did not necessarily correspond with fact. Although generally good-natured and generous, Oliver was no saint, especially as he got older. He could be jealous, stubborn, and suspicious. Occasionally he cheated his men out of wages and otherwise treated them roughly. He was known to throw his horn at the wall in a fit of rage and to carry a pistol which he put on the table at rehearsals before asking if all were present. Yet devotees did not dwell on the hero's failings. As biographer Walter C. Allen stated, "We prefer to pass over these aspersions against an old man soured by adversity and remember the Grand King of the Lincoln Gardens and Plantation Cafe, setting Chicago back on its heels with his powerful 'trumpet of gold.' "[12] For the faithful Oliver was more than human, a noble giant who looked from his photographs with Buddhist composure, in proud command of those around him, a strong, primitive figure of stoic resolution whose head was neither turned by his early successes, nor bowed by the miseries that followed. He appeared as a demigod, possessed of mystical knowledge and of magical powers.

How do the Oliver stories gibe with general theories about myth? Carl Jung maintained that mythical tales present "psychological realities" in a "collective unconscious" reflecting "archetypes," which are inherited "primordial images" given specific content by each culture.[13] Oliver stories held a vivid reality for true believers and can be seen as variants of king and martyr archetypes, but whether or not they bespeak a collective unconscious is far from clear. Bronislaw Malinowski regarded myths as lived realities which may have fictional aspects but correspond closely to cultural experience and function as charters for existing customs and institutions.[14] Since many details in Oliver's stories mirrored those of the jazz life, they were culturally real and to some extent offered charters and sanctions for it. Thus the jazzman fallen upon troubled times might well rationalize his miseries and take courage by considering the King's sufferings. Mircea Eliade argued that myths are not so much psychological or cultural as spiritual realities, sacred accounts which depict primordial origins and heroes, provide paradigms for earthly activities, and imply an "other" or higher reality.[15] For some devotees the Oliver tales were semi-sacred with larger-than-life events and settings reflecting a higher order and offering models for worldly behavior.

If such explanations seem partial or vague it is because myths are variable and often unfathomable. Still, these hypotheses indicate how jazz tales account for and justify the music, and dramatize its mystique. But there is another side to jazz mythology that they leave out and which I want to examine now in connection with another hero, Charlie Parker.

The Parker stories present a character with many honorable faces—admirers compared him to Jupiter, Hercules, Paul Bunyan, and John Henry[16]—but he comes through most strongly as a trickster, that complicated figure who has appeared variously in stories all over the world. Part human, part animal, part supernatural, he or she may take the role of raven, mink, spider, rabbit, or bird with strange powers to perform magic feats, not necessarily with happy results. He is an ambivalent, ambiguous figure full of contradiction and irony—in one moment charming, altruistic, intelligent, and creative and in the next gross, stupid, and deceptive, a liar, thief, or seducer. He may have uncertain sexual status or outlandish appetites symbolized sometimes by outsize genitals, for instance, a snake-like penis wrapped around his neck. He may combine black and white symbolism in clever chicanery, marked by a childishness that can be his undoing. Among American blacks he has appeared, *inter alia*, as Br'er Rabbit, Tar Baby, and the spider, Aunt Nancy, characters who emerge victorious in encounters with more powerful adversaries.[17]

In the jazz world this typology is evident in tales of men like pianist Jelly Roll Morton, the notorious conman, pimp, hustler, braggart, and musical genius; or Dizzy Gillespie, the wise fool and masterful artist of the put-on who could prick the pretentious balloons of convention and escape with impunity. But the best example of the jazz trickster is Parker, appropriately known as "Bird." Parker stories, collected in Robert Reisner's *Bird: The Legend of Charlie Parker* (1962),[18] reveal an amorphous mixture of human, animal, and deific characteristics, a figure whose overweening hungers and raw aggression could negate his artistic brilliance. His myths are full of contradictions: on the one hand benevolence, sensitivity, and genius, and, on the other, gargantuan appetites, treachery, zaniness, and smashed taboos which outraged respectability but intrigued insiders.

He took special pleasure in violating conventional pollution codes. Ross Russell, who sometimes uses poetic license in his biography of Parker, *Bird Lives!* (1973), tells of a night in 1948 at the Argyle Lounge, an expensive Chicago club, when "Charlie finished a set and placed his horn on the top of the piano. Then he stepped off the bandstand, walked past the tables on the main floor, into the foyer, entered the pay telephone booth, closed the door and proceeded to urinate on the floor. The yellow stream gushed forth as from a stallion, its pool dark and foaming as it spread under the door of the telephone booth and into the foyer. He came from the booth laughing. There was no explanation or apology."[19]

On other occasions, however, his code violations were more meaningful and ironic. When a club owner in St. Louis warned the band to use the back entrance and not to fraternize with the white customers, Parker seized the first opportunity to bring the performers noisily in through the front door and at intermission led them down to sit conspicuously among the patrons. The owner was beside himself. Drummer Art Blakey recalled:

> The guy was about to wig. . . . He told someone, "You gotta get this band the hell outa here." The guys were carrying on something fierce despite the fact that gangsters were walking around with big guns on their hips. They didn't scare Bird or anyone. Tadd Dameron was drinking a glass of water. Out of one of the beautiful glasses they had to serve the customers. Bird walked over to him saying, "Did you drink out of this, Tadd?" "Tad says "Yeah." Bam! He smashes it. "It's contaminated. Did you drink out of this one?" "Yeah," Tadd says. Bam. "It's contaminated." He broke about two glasses. A guy was glaring at Bird; he just looked back cooly. "What do you want? Am I bothering you?" Bird asks him. "Are you crazy?" the guy asks. "Well, if you want to call me crazy," Bird replies. Then once again he turns to Tadd, "Did you drink out of this glass?" Bam. "It's contaminated." They put us out.[20]

Equally symbolic was his well-advertised pleasure in sleeping with white women, one of whom bore him children in a common-law marriage. By the same token, he habitually mixed huge quantities of heroin and alcohol, often without apparent effect.

But Parker's wile was not directed entirely at the square world. It also victimized admirers. His friend and business associate, Robert Reisner, was not alone in finding him impossible to deal with at times, "the most difficult person I have ever met," said Reisner. "He was suave, cunning, urbane, charming, and generally fiendish—too much. He could butter me up, lull me into position, and then bang!—a great betrayal."[21] Nor were fellow musicians safe from his treachery. Trumpeter Kenny Dorham remembered that once, when he was a member of a Parker group, "I had drawn $20 in advance, and when the time came to receive the balance, Parker claimed, 'You drew $100.' 'What!' I said in amazement. 'What proof do you have got that you didn't draw $100?' It looked like we were going to fight all night. In this instance, I circumvented a long fight against Charlie's persuasiveness and strong debating technique. I picked up a blade and I said, 'I am going to cut you with this razor blade, Bird.' He paid me begrudgingly, turning the whole thing around with the statement: 'I wanted to see where you was.' "[22]

Tales of Parker's irresponsibility were legion; he was always late, failed to show up, pawned his friends' instruments and clothes, borrowed money with no intention to repay, threatened violence or suicide to get his way. Bassist Gene Ramey related that once Parker went to the Apollo Theatre in New York to borrow a horn from Sonny Stitt, a disciple whose reverence for the master was qualified by earlier victimizations. When Stitt said no, Parker retorted:

> "You stole my horn in Detroit when you were strung out. I never said anything to you. You've got three horns on stage." Sonny said, "This is my band, and I'm featuring three horns." Bird turned and said, "You have your day; I'll have mine."
>
> But he didn't leave it at that. He went around to the back of the theatre, climbed up the fire escape in an attempt to break into Sonny's room. He was drunk and fell into the wrong dressing room, where some girl was changing clothes. She gave a yelp. I came in and so did the manager. Bird was lying on the floor. He groaned, "I think I have broken my ankle." We all became a little concerned about him, which is what he wanted so that his crime would be forgotten. When I took off his shoe to examine his foot, he winked at me—"I was doing my best to steal Sonny Stitt's horn."
>
> I helped him into the hall, and, there, the theatre manager asked him what it was all about. Charlie told him that he wanted to see him, but he never could get to him in his office. Bird's fanciful alibi did not wholly placate the man, and a few unpleasantries were exchanged, culminating in a dramatic pose of Charlie's in which he removed the fire axe from the wall and threatened to hit the guy over the head with it. I unruffled everyone and led Bird outside. I said to him, "You are acting awful mean today."[23]

No matter how outrageous or self-defeating, Parker's misadventures did not permanently damage his image. In the end, no amount of boorishness or deceit could dim his personal charisma or demystify the magic of his music, whose appeal seemed independent of his earthly behavior. Despite all his trouble with Parker, Kenny Dorham continued to speak of him as the embodiment of jazz and "a high starred person."[24] Reisner, who put up with far more of Parker's trickery, also remained in awe of the man, explaining that the faithful overlooked his sins because "he had so much soul. . . . They forgave him his trespasses when, at times, Bird felt evil, because they knew he poured so much soul into his art that it must have created an imbalance at times."[25]

Fascinated by his mysterious ambivalences, followers juxtaposed stories of his transgressions with those of his generosity, sensitivity, intelligence, or clairvoyance, thus dramatizing him as part devil and part god. Gene Ramey told how Parker, eating dinner in the kitchen of a club, showed no inclination to take the stage: "The manager came into the kitchen and told Bird he was on. Bird, his jaws champing, kept on eating. The manager waited a bit and then said, 'Please Bird finish later; the crowd is getting restless.' No response from Bird. This went on until the manager was almost in tears, imploring him to go on, and Bird turned around and said, 'Man, why don't you try one of these sandwiches? They're crazy.' " Then without any transition, Ramey added, "What amazed me about his playing was that he was one of the great creative people on that higher level of creation that has something mysterious about it. There are many who play creatively, but in their cases you can always trace where they learned and how they were formed. With Charlie Parker, it was as if he had come full-grown out of the head of Zeus. I never could figure out where what he was playing came from. Sure, there were small things you could trace back, but his main creativity was on that mysterious level, the greatest of them all."[26] Paul Radin pointed out that the reaction to the trickster in aboriginal societies "is one of laughter tempered by awe,"[27] and clearly this is true of the responses to Parker and some of the other tricksters in the jazz world.

But sometimes the awe was tinged with uneasiness, even fear. Roger D. Abrahams maintains that the trickster "is always presented as a creature with many human characteristics, but one who lacks exactly those features which would qualify him as a member of the tribe. Specifically, he often is shown to be a lawbreaker; the fact is, however, that he is too minatory, too childlike, too intense to be conscious of the law."[28] While Parker seemed conscious enough of the law, he was too childlike, irresponsible, or crazy, to honor it except when it suited him. And while his lawlessness and nonsense generally earned credit among insiders, they could also find them too strange for comfort, as when he engaged in insane shouting matches, mad water-drinking contests, bizarre sexual exploits, threats of violence, and so forth, which placed him eerily out of touch with ordinary human feelings and expectations—"out of this world" in a frightening way. Once, he disappeared from the bandstand after the first set, not to return until three in the morning when the other musicians were packing up, and, looking around bewildered, took out his horn to play exclaiming, "[L]et's get this show on the road."[29] While such behavior could sometimes be put down to drugs, too often it bordered on the demonic.

But in less troubling episodes, his transgressions delighted devotees, who found in them something their own lives lacked. Classicist Karl Kerenyi theorized that the trickster provides the audience's lives with a sense of disorder which balanced conventional demands for order, thus making "possible within the bounds of what is permitted an experience of what is not permitted."[30] The Parker myths did this in dramatic, compelling fashion, striking a sympathetic, regressive chord in those who shared in the liminality he personified. In liminality, according to Victor Turner, we see "naked, unaccommodated man, whose nonlogical character issues in various modes of behavior: destructive, creative, farcical, ironic, energetic, suffering, lecherous, submissive, defiant but always unpredictable."[31] Parker was all of these, but above all he was free, as his nickname, "Bird," suggests, a liberated and liberating symbol common to trickster stories with transcendent meanings. It is a function of myth, Turner argued, to evoke feelings of the "high and deep mysteries [of] primordial, generative powers of the cosmos [in] acts which transcend, rather than transgress, the norms of human secular society." Thus, although they may provide negative examples, trickster stories are not merely cautionary tales, but dramatizations of potency and potentiality in which "the elements of culture and society are released from their customary configurations and combined in bizarre and terrifying imagery."[32]

The Parker stories are often weird or bizarre, touching upon cosmic powers and mysteries, but they sometimes show a benevolent, quasi-deific figure who, like Oliver, taught less experienced men the expedients of the calling, overwhelmed formidable adversaries in cutting sessions, inaugurated new rituals, and redefined old ones. They show, in short, a super-human who was the embodiment of certain ideals, a psychological (Jung), cultural (Malinowski), and sacred (Eliade) presence providing sanctions and models for the jazz life. Like the Oliver tales, Parker's gained in popularity after his death. This was true with other departed jazz heroes, of course, but in Parker's case the posthumous, supernatural aura was especially strong. "Bird is not dead; he's hiding out somewhere, and he'll be back with some new shit that will scare everybody to death," declared bassist Charlie Mingus.[33] He was not alone in his belief in Parker's immortality, as numerous "Bird Lives" graffiti on urban walls testified long after his death.

Mythical stories demand extraordinary settings where heroes can perform superhuman acts comfortably and convincingly, settings which, like their inhabitants, help to explain the origins of the mysterious or sacred. Often these were cities, most obviously New Orleans, which early-jazz exponents imbued with exotic magic. In jazz mythology it was a wondrous place, a "land of dreams" where the extraordinary seemed common-place. As guitarist Danny Barker put it, "One of my greatest memories as a kid growing up in New Orleans was how a bunch of us kids, playing, would suddenly hear sounds. It was like a phenomenon, like the Aurora Borealis—maybe. The sounds of men playing would be so clear, but we wouldn't be sure where they were coming from. So we'd start trotting, start running—'It's this way!' 'It's that way!' and sometimes, after running for a while, you'd be nowhere near that music. But the music would come on you any time like that. The city was

full of the sounds of music."[34] This mysterious environment
spawned larger-than-life musicians—clarinetists with incredibly
rich tones and brass players whose pure sounds carried unbelievable distances. On still nights Buddy Bolden's horn
supposedly could be heard ten miles away. The social climate,
too, was extraordinary. Sidney Bechet remembered the New
Orleans of his childhood, "where music was as natural as the air,
the people were ready for it like the sun and the rain. . . .
The people were waiting for it, wanting it."[35] It was as if they
had been prepared for its magic by a benevolent creator.
Stories told of colorful rituals in "bucking contests" (battles
between bands), parades, funerals and carnivals, and of marvelous streets and neighborhoods, Basin Street and Storyville.
The latter, then known as "The District," has taken a familiar
place in American (not just jazz) mythology as the home of
exotic prostitutes, pimps, gamblers, as well as the "primitive"
musical geniuses who brought forth a new art form.

Stories about the origins of Kansas City jazz in the Twenties
and Thirties also focused on underworld activities, fabulous
clubs, serendipitous jam sessions, band battles, incredible feats,
and inspired musicians—all flourishing in a marvelous environment which bred "that Kansas City feeling." Pianist Mary
Lou Williams remembered how "In those years around 1930,
Kaycee was really jumping—so many great bands have sprung
up there. . . . It was a ballin' town, and it attracted musicians
from all over the South and Southwest. . . . I've known
musicians so enthused about playing that they would walk all
the way from the Kansas side to attend a jam session. Even
bass players, caught without street-car fare, would hump their
bass on their back and come running. That was how music
stood in Kansas City."[36] She found it a "heavenly city—music
everywhere in the Negro section of town, and fifty or more
cabarets rocking on Twelfth and Eighteenth Streets."[37] In such
circumstances an enigmatic Lester Young could believably
perform his extraordinary heroics and the inexplicable genius
of a young Charlie Parker could develop in ways which would
change the face of jazz.

New York also had its mythical aura. Harlem in the Twenties
was known for its fabulous clubs, ubiquitous music, all-night

jam sessions, and liminal climate. Duke Ellington remembered it as "the world's greatest atmosphere . . . like the Arabian nights."[38] Here was the fabulous Savoy Ballroom and Minton's Playhouse which, along with Monroe's Uptown House, was a nursery for early bop before the music moved downtown to Fifty-second Street. In the early Forties "the Street," as it was called, was the Mecca of jazz with its own special magic, attracting the faithful from all over the world who came to hear the giants of the day in clubs along a two-block area west of Fifth Avenue. "There was something about that street," claimed New Orleans trumpeter Louis Prima. "I can't find words for it. It always reminded me of old Bourbon Street in New Orleans. But it was not just the music. It was a feeling it gave you."[39]

In retrospect, such places were states of mind where the extraordinary happened, where the supernatural seemed natural.

Historical accounts of the heroes and origins of jazz have barely dented the credibility of jazz mythology among the faithful. However intertwined, history and myth exist in different ways, performing largely different functions and satisfying different needs. History is based upon worldly fact accessible through what passes for objective perception and comprehension. Myths, on the other hand, refer to worldly happenings but deal more with the cosmic, with appearances of the supernatural beyond the human senses and logic. Rooted in belief rather than reason, myths are told and interpreted accordingly, bending fact to faith.

Circumstances which produce myths are seldom conducive to detached observation and clear recollection. Take, for instance, the events at Minton's during its heyday as a cradle of bop. In his remarkable article, "The Golden Age, Time Past," Ralph Ellison shows how he and other habitués had trouble recalling events witnessed there. Even with his novelist's eye and ear he retained only a fuzzy recollection some fifteen years after his frequent visits. What lingered was an overall impression of the room, with its mural depicting jamming musicians seen through a smoky veil of soft, red light, and the smells of down-home food, alcohol, tobacco, sweat, and perfume, all mingling with the sounds of talk, laughter, music, and dancing to evoke a "mysterious spell" of ecstasy, communitas, and memory. For its patrons, many of them recent migrants alone and adrift in the bewildering city, Minton's provided a transcendent interval of festivity linking past and present. "In the noisy lostness of New York," writes Ellison, "they rediscovered community of the feasts evocative of the South, of good times, the best and most unselfconscious of times." Such symbolic moments were not experienced or recalled with detachment. Removed from worldly matters, the celebrants, "black and white alike, were hardly aware of where they were or what time it was; nor did they wish to be. They thought of Minton's as a sanctuary, where in an atmosphere blended of nostalgia and music-and-drink-lulled suspension of time they could retreat from the wartime tensions of the town. The meaning of time present was not their concern; thus when they try to tell it now the meaning escapes them." Ellison concludes, "That which we remember is, more often than not, that which we would have liked to have been or hoped to be. Thus our memory and identity are ever at odds; our history ever told by inattentive idealists."[40] With the passage of sanctifying time, our recollections of emotionally charged experience conform to our fondest needs.

And even when participants could recall original circumstances, details seemed unimportant. Hence the disdain of musicians for avid discographers eager to know the exact personnel and dates of past recording sessions. What counted was the music and the feelings it aroused, not details of time and place. Edward Nichols, researching his Bix Beiderbecke article for *Jazzmen* (1939), found that the witnesses "sometimes get impatient with your questions and then say, 'Listen, how do I remember where it was? Maybe it wasn't 'Dinah' and maybe it was only ten choruses, but you hadda hear that horn. If you heard the horn, that's all there is. That's Bix and you don't need any more.' "[41]

Nor were jazz writers themselves always concerned with fact. Their gnostic enthusiasm especially in the early stages of sectarian development, often led away from history and in the direction of myth. This was notably true of *Jazzmen*, edited by Frederic Ramsey, Jr., and Charles Edward Smith, which more than any other book served as the bible of the dixieland revival of the Forties. In a gospel-like chapter on King Oliver, Ramsey reworked a tale of the cornetist in ways revealing how part of the mythopoetic process worked. The original story, set in pre–World War I New Orleans and told by pianist Richard M. Jones, went as follows: "Freddy Keppard was playin' in a spot across the street and was drawin' all the crowds. I was sittin' at the piano, and Joe Oliver came over to me and commanded in a nervous, harsh voice, 'Get in B-flat.' I did, and Joe walked out on the sidewalk, lifted his horn to his lips, and blew the most beautiful stuff I have ever heard. People started pouring out of the other spots along the street to see who was blowing all that horn. Before long, our place was full and Joe came in smiling, and said, 'Now, that . . . [*sic*] won't bother me no more.' From then on, our place was full every night."[42] Ramsey found an epiphany here. Note the tone and rhetoric:

> Jones says something got into Joe one night as he sat quietly in the corner and listened to the musicians who were praising Keppard and Perez. He was infuriated by their tiresome adulation; didn't they know that Joe Oliver could play a cornet, too? So he came forth from his silence, strode to the piano, and said, "Jones, beat it out in B Flat." Jones began to beat, and Joe began to blow. The notes tore out clear as a bell, crisp and clean. He played as he never had before, filling the little dance hall with low, throbbing blues. Jones backed him with a slow, steady beat. With this rhythm behind him, Joe walked straight through the hall, out onto the sidewalk. There was no mistaking what he meant when he pointed his cornet, first towards Pete Lala's, where Keppard played, then directly across the street, to where Perez was working. A few hot blasts brought crowds out of both joints; they saw Joe Oliver on the sidewalk, playing as if he would blow down every house on the street. Soon every rathole and crib down the line was deserted by its patrons, who came running up to Joe, bewitched by his cornet. When the last joint had poured out its crew, he turned around and led the crowd into Aberdeen's, where he walked to the stand, breathless, excited, and opened his mouth wide to let out the

big, important words that were boiling in his head. But all he
could say was, "There: that'll show 'em!"

    After that night, they never called him anything but "King"
Oliver.[43]

Altering dialogue, character, event and setting, Ramsey's version employs immediate and personal language of speech to
turn the tale into a "cult story," a solemn variant of the magic-
piper narrative to be taken on faith.[44]

    When *Jazzmen* appeared in 1939, Storyville had been closed
only twenty-two years and King Oliver had lain in his grave
only one, but the book casts on both a warm, pristine light
that makes them seem extraordinarily distant. The book was
enormously influential and remains a fascinating mixture of
symbolically charged narrative and poetry befitting a sectarian
testament. It is still in print (1987), despite manifest excesses
and errors long perpetuated in writings by the faithful, writings
whose credibility among devotees has been little disturbed by
recent revisionist accounts. In the late Seventies, two versions
of Buddy Bolden's career were in print. One was Michael
Ondaatje's highly mythical narrative, *Coming Through Slaughter*
(1975), a novel elaborating on material found in *Jazzmen*.
Impressionistic and romantic, Ondaatje's book depicted Bolden
as a larger-than-life cornetist, demonic barber, gossip-sheet
editor, and notorious ladies' man who moved mysteriously
through a Crescent City dreamscape. The other book was
Donald J. Marquis' *In Search of Buddy Bolden* (1978), a sober,
thoroughly researched historical version that viewed Bolden
as a more ordinary man—a marvelous musician, handy with
the ladies but without supernatural qualities, and neither a
barber nor editor. The two versions have little in common,
aside from superficial details. The mythical and the historical,
however intertwined, exist on different planes—a point reinforced by Marquis' failure even to mention Ondaatje's book.

It is no secret that story and song are sister arts, mutually
interacting to loosen tongues and heighten effects. Understandably, there is no lack of evidence of this in the jazz world. In

1938, when folkorist Alan Lomax arranged for pianist and raconteur Jelly Roll Morton to record some of his music and reminiscences at the Library of Congress, published in 1950 as *Mr. Jelly Roll*, Morton had a highly uncharacteristic attack of nerves when he sat down at the piano and microphone. He stumbled for a moment, at a loss for words, but after playing a few bars, his imagination came alive and, according to Lomax, the narrative flowed "as if all his life he had been waiting for this moment and treasuring up the sentences—Jelly Roll began to think out loud in a biblical, slow-drag beat":

> As I can understand,
> My folks were in the city of New Orleans
> Long before the Louisiana Purchase
> And all my folks came directly from the shores of France,
> That is, across the world in the other world,
> And they landed in the New World
> Years ago. . . .

"A throbbing stream of tropic chords flowed softly behind the deep voice and the husky voice spun out a story like a song of Louisiana live-oaks on a lazy afternoon. The warm magic caught Jelly and transformed the almost icy auditorium." Out poured recollections of fabulous times and fascinating characters, many of whom live on in American folklore. Lomax listed some: "Mimi and Laura in their black shawls, Eulalie holding a John-the-Conqueror root, Mamie Desdoumes smiling a fuzzy drunken smile, King Bolden with his red undershirt showing and his stubby cornet under his elbow, Gypsy Schaeffer in her notoriety diamonds, Aaron Harris and Boar Hog in their box-back coats and Stetsons, Bad Sam and Benny Frenchy, King Porter and Scott Joplin, Stavin Chain and Clark Wade, Albert Cahill and Tony Jackson, a company of young octoroons whispering 'Look Yonder at Winding Boy' "—all of whom Morton and his piano brought to life with extraordinary vividness.[46] Morton's music and tales reaffirmed, in his mind at least, that he was an important figure, an actor in an epic which gave his personality and acts significance.

More revealing are Sidney Bechet's reminiscences in *Treat It Gentle* (1960). During his New Orleans childhood, Bechet had been filled with portentous stories of how Negroes and their music had migrated from Africa to the New World, where they found a unique voice in men like his ancestor Omar, a prophetic slave who combined mysterious musical gifts and dreams in a new song that became the basis for jazz and, like the stories which went with it, expressed the black man's fondest hopes and needs. Both music and words dealt heavily in memory and sorrow. "It's a remembering song," Bechet said of his music. "There's so much to remember. There's so much wanting, so much sorrow, and there's so much waiting for the sorrow to end."[47] Within this heritage of waiting and sorrow, jazz and its myths provided sources of identification and meaning. As Bechet said, "My story goes a long way back. It goes further back than I had anything to do with. My music is like that. . . . I got it from something inherited, just like stories my father gave down to me. And those stories are all I know about some of the things bringing me to where I am. And all my life I've been trying to explain about something . . . the part of me that was there before I was. It was there waiting to be me. It was waiting to be the music. It's that part that I've been trying to explain to myself all my life."[48] The stories, together with the music, indicated where he had come from and who he was, and implied what he should expect and do in the future. They gave life continuity and direction.

Other myths did the same for other followers. And however we understand the nature and role of these stories, their basic contribution was to give coherence and significance, not only to isolated followers in search of meaning and purpose, but to whole movements, even a whole people, fitting them into a cosmic context that explained and justified their existence and their music.

7 *Followers*

Like religious sects, jazz movements have little organization at first and only highly generalized or simplified forms later on. Still, from the beginning there were certain distinctions of status and role. So far, I have dealt mainly with the most prestigious figures—the better known musicians and their closest associates—who crucially determined the norms and pace of sect-like development. But an important part was played by some of the followers: critics, aficionados, hipsters, beats, and dancers.

Critics

According to the Weberian model, the priest emerges after the successful prophet has made his revelation and his apostles have expanded their circle into a congregation. The functions of prophet and priest overlap at times, but in general the prophet, with his extraordinary powers to evoke ecstasy, deals more directly with the beyond, whereas the priest is more the custodian of sacred beliefs and practices based on the prophet's word. As interpreter, propagandist, educator, and conservator, the priest rationalizes the message—clarifying, specifying, and systematizing. Initially, he brings together and writes down material concerning belief and rituals, reconciling inconsistencies and demystifying the unacceptable—in short, shaping a doctrine or dogma to meet the ongoing needs of the following. Later, he guards the canon against the claims of false prophets while certifying the revisions of duly recognized authorities. In doing so he cannot wander too far from the ideology, lest he be heretical, yet his interpretations cannot be too narrow for fear of losing the loyalty of the laity he serves.[1]

Weber found that when a priesthood fails to develop, or emerges in a fragmentary fashion, lay members—schismatic intellectuals and others—move in to perform priestly functions.[2] This applies in jazz sects which, lacking official priesthoods, found intellectual followers, sometimes with orthodox credentials, to define, propagate, and defend new mystiques. In a sense, jazz critics were acting priests seeking to rationalize the music and, more especially, the gnoses of successive sects, analyzing, classifying, and judging. In the early sectarian stages, they gathered, organized, and wrote down evidence of the revelations, giving them a certain logical consistency and demystifying seemingly impure myths and rituals. And, as the doctrine hardened, the critic continued to examine and interpret the canon, adjusting it to the changing needs of believers and protecting it from the claims of latter-day pretenders.

His task was not easy. On one side, he faced musicians often suspicious of his skin color, intellectualizing, and qualifications ("I don't pay no attention to these white critics about my music," said Miles Davis in 1958. "Be like somebody from Europe coming criticizing Chinese music. They don't know about that.")[3]; and on the other, listeners who could find him arbitrary and pretentious. Part of his problems stemmed from the chaos of the jazz world. In its mercurial and often frantic climate, in which styles and substyles developed with extraordinary rapidity, one following the next before the first could be fully digested by age-linked audiences seeking to break with the past, there was a premium on novelty and a careless casting aside of the old. Lacking a clear professional tradition with adequate tools, discipline, and a reassuring sense of continuity, the jazz critic was often less an interpreter, evaluator, and educator than a reporter, partisan, or publicist attempting to survive the storms of fashion.[4]

Still, from the outset, informed critics helped create and defend a growing jazz tradition. We find them writing about ragtime before World War I and again in the Twenties, when a few white listeners were beginning to regard jazz as something more than popular music. But it was not until the Thirties that actual jazz critics, virtually all white, appeared to proclaim jazz as a powerful new art. This was news even to most of its practitioners. When pianist Lil Hardin Armstrong, who played in many of her husband Louis' ground-breaking recordings in the Twenties, was asked how the band felt about these performances at the time, she recalled, "We didn't think anything about it. He just played like that and we liked it fine, but it wasn't until the white folks started to write about it later on and saying it was so artistic that we really thought about it as unusual or special."[5]

One of the first "real-jazz" critics was Charles Edward Smith who, in "Jazz: Some Little Known Aspects," an article that appeared in *Symposium* in 1930, argued authoritatively that what had passed for jazz up until then was not the real thing, and that "the men of jazz, those of the authentic minority, have remained obscure to the last."[6] He analyzed and classified the various forms of the music and showed how commercial and symphonic jazz, so popular in the Twenties, were in fact dilutions of the pure expression. Then he outlined the history of the true music, maintaining that it was art and defending it against orthodox barbs.

Later critics elaborated on these points. The best known early figure was Hugues Panassié, a Frenchman whose *Hot Jazz* (Paris, 1936; New York, 1938) went beyond Smith's brief article. "My single aim here," he wrote in his foreword, "is to give a precise idea of jazz in its definitive form, to put an end to the deplorable misunderstandings about jazz. . . . All I ask of the reader is that he free himself of all prejudices he has thus far acquired and that he pay attention to the opinions which are not so much mine as a faithful expression of the opinions of the great jazz musicians."[7] Relying particularly on the word as given by Louis Armstrong, Panassié described the nature and merits of pure jazz, cataloguing the leading tendencies, bands, performers, and recordings, and defending the music against conservative detractors. This sort of rationalization was repeated by critics in later sects. In the Forties Barry Ulanov, Leonard Feather, and others interpreted and

justified bop for a growing following, and in the Sixties Martin
Williams, Nat Hentoff, and Don Heckman, among others, did
the same for free jazz.

Needless to say, the tone and procedures of priestly writing
varied according to time and individual temperament, but
even critics given to emotional outbursts did not overlook the
importance of reasoned analysis and "objective" judgment.
Bop exponent Leonard Feather, unmatched for passionate
advocacy in the heat of intersectarian squabbles during the
Forties, complained about the irrational excesses of the early-
jazz old guard, insisting that "jazz, seen from the inside looking
out, is a matter of notes, chords and facts . . . expert analysis
in place of emotional ecstasies."[8] Other critics went into the
matter more deeply. In 1958 Martin Williams, shortly to
become co-editor (with Nat Hentoff) of the highly influential
Jazz Review, wrote an article, "Criticism: The Path of the Jazz
Critic," in *Down Beat*, maintaining that jazz criticism should not
be a journalistic sideline or form of public relations but a
special calling with its own muse and gifts "to be trained,
explored, disciplined and tested like any other talent." Williams
urged that part of the critic's initiation should include reading
master thinkers and writers from Plato and Aristotle, to T. S.
Eliot and Jung. Then he could knowledgeably apply to jazz
the questions Matthew Arnold said should be posed of literature: What is the work trying to do? How well does it do it?
How and why? Is it worth doing? And finally the critic should
compare the work to the best he knows, if such comparison is
fair and illuminating. As he analyzed a piece, he needed to
remember the fundamentally emotional appeal of the music,
though it also could be understood in a logical framework:
"Value is based in the final analysis on feeling, not reason,"
Williams argued. "But by feeling I mean a rational, conscious,
individual function. I do not mean emotion which is irrational,
impersonal, and can be irresponsible."[9] Few other jazz critics
had such a carefully elaborated philosophy or approached
their work with this Arnoldian "high seriousness." Yet Williams
was not alone in his desire to establish criticism on a formal
and methodical base and his attempts to do so indicate the
increasing sophistication of the following.

Williams' writing had mainly to do with aesthetic analysis
and evaluation but, like other critics before and after him, he
sought to define an overall jazz tradition and place it against
a broad cultural background that included other forms of
music and art, as well as social considerations. Jazz critics and
historians eagerly marked significant events and epochs and
certified heroes, lines of succession, and influence. While
sharply distinguishing between classical music and jazz, and
African and European legacies, they took pains to find universal elements in the new music, relating it to the ongoing
humanistic heritage of Western civilization. The results of all
this effort were twofold: it sharpened and hardened gnostic
doctrine which, once settled into the sectarian mind, strongly
resisted change; and it helped legitimize the music and mystique among a growing number of sympathizers and tolerant
outsiders.

The defense of the faith sometimes led to absurd excesses,
as evangelical feelings overpowered reason and judgment. In
the Forties, early-jazz critic Art Hodes assailed his bop counterparts: "And so the New Order boys go merrily on their
way, increasing the sale of the mags they write for. They're
happy—they've found a minority to pick on, just as Hitler
made use of a minority in his country. . . . They haven't wasted
their time fighting for beliefs that didn't pay off in cash. The
register rang loud and lustily for them."[10] One of his targets,
Leonard Feather, charged that the "Moldy Figs," as the boppers
called the old guard,

> are to music what Rankin and Bilbo are to politics and Pegler
> to the press. They are the extreme right-wingers of jazz, the
> voice of reaction in music. Just as the fascists tend to divide
> group against group and distinguish between Negroes, Jews,
> Italians, and "Real Americans," so do the Moldy Figs try to
> categorize New Orleans, Chicago, swing music, as "the real
> jazz." Just as the fascists have tried to foist their views on the
> public through the vermin press of *Social Justice*, *The Broom*, and
> *X-Ray*, so have the Figs yapped their heads off in The *Jazz
> Record*, *Jazz Session*, and *Record Changer*. Just as the Gerald
> L. K. Smiths regard America as a private club to which refugees
> and members of various races cannot be admitted, so does the

right-wing jazz group limit itself to a clique in which a nineteenth century birth certificate from New Orleans is almost the only admission ticket, while all young, aspiring musicians of today are barred and branded as "riff musicians" or jump and jive men.[11]

But usually the rhetoric of intersectarian disputes was more moderate. In general, avant-garde critics argued that the old music was overripe and stood in the path of the new revelation. To their eyes, the conservatives were closed-minded reactionaries vainly seeking to stem the inevitable change. For their part, the conservatives confronted upholders of the new with the sort of pollution behavior which treated the new music as an outrageous defilement of the sacred, a contagion infecting unquestionable standards, musical and otherwise.

Early-jazz critic and impresario John Hammond called bop "a collection of nauseating cliches, repeated *ad infinitum*." His colleague, George Frazier, thought bop infantile noise, "incredible stuff for a grown man to produce."[12] And in a 1945 review of the now celebrated record release pairing "Now Is the Time" and "Billie's Bounce" by Charlie Parker, a conservative voice in *Down Beat* claimed:

> These two sides are excellent examples of the other side of the Gillespie craze—the bad taste and ill-advised fanaticism of Dizzy's uninhibited style. Only Charlie Parker, who is a better musician and who deserves more credit than Dizzy for the style anyway, saves these from a bad fate. At that he's far off form— a bad reed and inexcusable fluffs do not add up to good jazz. The trumpet man, whoever the misled kid is [he was Miles Davis], plays Gillespie in the same manner as the majority of the kids who copy their idol do—with most of the faults, lack of order and meaning, the complete adherence to technical acrobatics. . . . Good, bad or indifferent, the mass of Gillespie followers will love these sides, for even bad music is great if it's Diz. This is the sort of stuff that has thrown innumerable impressionable young musicians out of stride, that has harmed many of them irreparably.[13]

The classical orthodoxy, of course, had leveled similar complaints against early jazz a generation earlier. On *Down Beat's* rating system, ranging from four (excellent) to one (bad),

Parker's record, now generally regarded as a classic, got zero.

By the Sixties things were different. Now bop was the entrenched force, and its critics led the charge against the pollutions of the "new thing" that had emerged in reaction to the settled nature of bop and complacency of its upholders. Reviewing a live performance by the John Coltrane quintet with Eric Dolphy, a *Down Beat* editor reported, "I listened to a horrifying demonstration of what appears to be a growing 'anti-jazz' trend exemplified by these foremost exponents of what is termed avant-garde music. I heard a good rhythm section . . . go to waste behind the nihilistic exercises of the two horns. . . . Coltrane and Dolphy seemed intent on deliberately destroying 'swing'. . . . They seemed bent on pursuing an anarchistic course in their music that can be but termed anti-jazz."[14] The term "anti-jazz" stuck. Conservative critics used it increasingly to underscore the evils of the "new thing," particularly its disregard for the harmonic sequences which seemed indispensible to true jazz. "Subservience to harmony is the only way jazz can exist," asserted English critic Benny Green, who went on to say, "The harmonic license of free jazz must be restrained, just as the Criminal Code has deprived the citizen of the freedom of knocking down some old man, emptying gas meters and walking down the street with no clothes on."[15] And writing in *Down Beat*, Clive Loveless, calling "new thingers" "fashion cultists," declared that Eric Dolphy, for all of his sincerity, played "dull, repetitious music full of shrieking dissonance . . . empty and devoid of the ideals of the jazz spirit." Leonard Feather agreed that good intentions were not enough for creative artists. "After all," he concluded, "Hitler was sincere."[16]

While such opinions could be tenaciously held for years, they were not unalterable. Some early-jazz spokesmen, initially appalled by bop, came to tolerate and even appreciate it; and certain bop hard-liners, including high priest Leonard Feather, learned to open up their minds, if not their hearts, to free jazz. Time, exposure, and economic exigency tended to melt opposition—at least if the critic sought to remain active beyond his early years. Unlike an ordained priest, he had little in the way of institutional support or security, and usually worked on a part-time or free-lance basis. In an artistic environment in which styles thrived for a generation or less, he could ill afford to limit his interest to only one, no matter how passionate his commitment. He had to stay current or end up with a shrinking audience in a backwater far from the rapidly shifting mainstream.

This is not to suggest that there was little good writing about jazz. Nat Hentoff, Martin Williams, Marshall Stearns, and Gunther Schuller, to name a few, have made lasting contributions to the understanding and growth of the music. The point is that they did so under trying circumstances, which makes their achievements all the more remarkable.

Aficionados

Complementing the critics in their rationalizations were other cognoscenti, among the most devoted of them "serious" record collectors. While all followers bought recordings within their budgets, some acquired large collections of early disks, which they carefully catalogued and maintained. These aficionados, who flourished up to the Fifties, supported newsletters and magazines, such as *The Record Changer* and *Jazz Information*, that served as clearinghouses for disks and data and defined what belonged and what did not by reviewing performances and setting a dollar value on records according to content, rarity, and condition. For the most part, collectors were white middle-class males who kept one foot in the majority culture. This, however, did not inhibit their enthusiasm—sometimes fanaticism—for jazz. They insisted on the "purity" of the "real thing," the unadulterated sounds of the Chicago, or, more rigorously, the original New Orleans tradition. Francis Newton observed that for such purists "a Calvinistic spirit" and abhorrence of heretics counted heavily; undiluted jazz was like "the ideal blood of an aristocratic family in constant danger of pollution from the floods around it. 'What is jazz?' is the single question which crops up most frequently in the discussions of the aficionados."[17] Newton spoke from an English viewpoint, but his observation applied to both sides of the Atlantic.

The fascination of jazz sometimes bespoke latter-day primitivism in rebellion against a stifling establishment. To find excitement and meaning unavailable in mainstream life, twentieth-century primitivists turned to pre-industrial peoples whose timeless rituals and myths remained spontaneous and free. These included contemporary noble savages and other earthy heroes in various out-of-the-way places, from the villages of Spain, to the deserts of Arabia, the tropics of Tahiti, or the Afro-American demimonde, where life and art seemed naturally in tune with the rhythms of nature. In Harlem and other black neighborhoods, well-to-do white Americans found an exotic alternative to conventional diversions or the attritions of nine-to-five jobs. They went uptown for entertainment and art that expressed seemingly primordial passions and appetites, and sought fleshly delights. It hardly mattered that this energetic slumming yielded few glimpses of the realities of black life.[18]

A good example of the primitivist attraction to jazz appeared in the writings of Carl van Vechten, classical-music critic turned novelist and leading white spokesman for the Harlem Renaissance of the Twenties. Greatly taken with all black art, Van Vechten was especially intrigued by Bessie Smith and faithfully collected all her recordings, which he insisted on playing for visitors at his Manhattan apartment. In 1925 he shepherded friends to the Orpheum Theatre in Newark, where Bessie proved to be the embodiment of his primitivist ideal:

> She was at this time . . . very large, and she wore a crimson satin robe, sweeping up from her trim ankles, and embroidered in multicolored sequins in designs. Her face was beautiful with the ripe beauty of southern darkness, a deep bronze, matching the bronze of her bare arms. Walking slowly to the footlights, to the accompaniment of the wailing, muted brasses, the monotonous African pounding of the drum, the dromedary glide of the pianist's fingers over the responsive keys, she began her strange rhythmic rites in a voice full of shouting and moaning and praying and suffering, a wild, rough, Ethiopian voice, harsh and volcanic, but seductive and sensuous too, released between

rouged lips and the whitest of teeth, the singer swaying slightly
to the beat, as is the Negro custom:

"Yo' brag to woman I was yo' fool, so den I got dose sobbin'
hahted blues." Celebrating her unfortunate love adventures,
the Blues are the Negro's prayer to a cruel Cupid.

Now, inspired partly by the powerfully magnetic personality
of this elemental conjure woman with her plangent African
voice, quivering with passion and pain, sounding as if it had
been developed at the sources of the Nile, the black and blue-
black crowd, notable for the absence of mulattoes, burst into
hysterical, semi-religious shrieks of sorrow and lamentation.
Amens rent the air.

Afterward, the ecstatic van Vechten went backstage to pay
homage to the "Empress of the Blues," who received him "with
just the right amount of deference," he said, adding, "I believe
I kissed her hand. I hope I did."[19] Subsequently, he invited
her to one of his pointedly biracial soirees where, after a
performance by Margarita d'Alvarez of the Metropolitan Opera, Bessie entranced the company with the blues. Van Vechten's worship grew, and he eventually donated his valuable
collection of her records (original 78's) to the James Weldon
Johnson Collection at Yale, his alma mater, carefully stipulating
that these *sacra* by played only once a year.

Van Vechten's concern with black art ranged well beyond
jazz, but other devotees limited themselves to the music, even
to one performer whom they talked about incessantly. As head
of the Hot Record Exchange, a gathering place for the faithful
in Manhattan, Stephen Smith heard a lot of such talk. He told
of one true believer who habitually interrupted discussions
with the determined announcement: " 'I am a Joe Venuti
collector. What have you got by him?' Just to keep him quiet,
we played him a record which had several fine choruses by
others than Joe, but of course he was completely bored until
Venuti took his little break in the middle of the record. Then
he went wild. *He was sent.* It is not safe to get into a conversation
with this violent type because to him everything evolves around
his pet." Such fanaticism was especially common among recent
converts, whom Smith termed "the deadliest of the lot." "There
is a peculiar fascination in the collecting of hot which causes

the beginner to become violently excited about the whole thing," he wrote. "I have never met a beginner who was not going out immediately to educate the public to the benefits of a music which he himself knew nothing about, and to warn it against the greatly overrated musicians who were 'too commercial.' "[20] Still, for all their blind evangelism, such enthusiasts played an important role. Along with more moderate devotees, they spread the word of the "real thing," its categories, definitions, and related values in simple, forceful terms easy to understand—if not always to embrace.

At the other extreme were knowledgeable collectors with a sober, methodical interest in the music and its by-products. Though moved by jazz's aesthetic appeal, their fascination was with details of recordings: sites, personnel, dates, catalogue numbers of masters, original issues, reissues, and other minutiae, a fascination that largely bewildered musicians. Trumpeter Max Kaminsky, working at Nick's in Greenwich Village at the onset of the Dixieland Revival recalled, "We were suddenly besieged with a strange new breed of fan—the record collector. Pale, intense, studious-looking young men buttonholed us when we headed for Julius's, the saloon up the street where we relaxed between sets, and plied us with questions about who played what instrument in some pickup band recorded some twenty years earlier."[21]

With antiquarian fastidiousness, collectors sifted through piles of old records in dusty basements, attics, and Salvation Army bins as if in search of splinters of the True Cross. In "Jazz Cult: I. Intimate Memoirs of an Acolyte" (1947), Ernest Borneman, an anthropologist and jazz devotee, told how as an English university student he was initiated into collecting by an old hand. During visits to the local flea market the veteran acted with the utmost seriousness, scrutinizing every disk with patient care and checking it against a large data bank in his notebook and memory. When Borneman presented him with two questionable finds, he sensed his mentor's "mental machine clicking into action:

> "Cushion Foot Stomp". . . . That's Parlorphone R3383 . . .
> that's an Oken original . . . that's not Armstrong at all . . . guess

it must be Clarence Williams' Washboard Band . . . wrong label
. . . will be a collectors' item soon . . . keep it. Now "Black and
Tan Fantasy" . . . that's Parlorphone R3492 . . . master number
81778C . . . that's Okeh 40955 in the original . . . an Ellington
tune . . . Ellington and Bubber Miley . . . that's not Miley on
trumpet though . . . Miley was sick the day they recorded . . .
probably Jabbo Smith . . . good man too . . . wrong label again
. . . keep that too.[22]

Borneman's teacher religiously read everything he could find
about his avocational passion and kept up a busy correspondence with like-minded devotees—not only in the United States
but in distant corners of the earth—who, according to Borneman, typically answered letters as follows:

Dear Norm:
   Will trade Louis' Gennett 5627 "Of All the Wrongs" with
Red Onion Jazz Babes in excellent condition (slight chip
one side not touching first groove) for mint copy Clarence
Williams' Blue 5 "Texas Moaner Blues." Also have Sippie
Wallace vocal "A Jealous Woman Like Me" with Armstrong
cornet in fair condition. What offer? Will take any Bessie
Smith with James P. Johnson on piano in good or excellent
condition.
                                        Yrs. Dr. L. Y. Yen
                              University of Canton, China[23]

Collectors behaved pretty much the same all over. They
preferred the original issue of records to later pressings in
which the true sounds of the master disk might be diluted by
dubbing or editing. A few extremists never put their precious
acquisitions on a turntable, packing them in cotton for safety
and taking them out only for inspection. Others bought old
78's mainly for commercial reasons, trading them among
themselves in frequent mail auctions.

The cognoscenti eagerly systematized and preserved knowledge of their treasures, and to this purpose kept carefully
compiled notebooks cataloguing relevant facts and eventually
pooling their information in discographies. At first these
catalogues were far from accurate or complete, but persistent,
devoted labors gradually produced reliable references. The
most famous early work was by Charles Delaunay, whose

efforts culminated in his *New Hot Discography* in 1948.[24] The son of modernist painters Charles and Sonia Delaunay and a friend of Panassié, Delaunay was converted to the music in the Twenties, when he was a fifteen-year-old schoolboy in Paris. ("Being a jazz lover in Paris in the early twenties was like being an early Christian in Rome," he later said.[25]) Troubled by the lack of information about his cherished disks, he assiduously sought out visiting American musicians, sometimes taking the records up to their hotel rooms where they helped him identify soloists, locations, and dates. In 1936, he published his first discography and after the war wrote to record companies in the United States, where later visits turned up considerable data on old union sheets. His 1948 discography, along with Orrin Blackstone's *Index to Jazz* (1945–48), were the basic guides for collectors until superseded by Jorgen Grunnert Jepson's *Jazz Records: A Discography* (1963) and then Brian Rust's more exhaustive *Jazz Records, 1907–1942* (1970; 4th Ed., two volumes, 1978).[26] In 1977 Delaunay and over twenty assistants were at work on a discography extending from 1942 onward, which he estimated would run to about 20,000 pages.[27]

Whereas the critic dealt primarily with the aesthetic and spiritual matters, the discographer, arriving later on the scene, dealt more with physical objects and had a more historical role in the rationalization process. As curator and researcher he authenticated artifacts, and fixed dates, places, and personnel in ways that lent order and legitimacy to the developing jazz tradition.

In 1943 true believer Milton Gabler published an early version of Delaunay's *Hot Discography* in New York.[28] Seven years earlier he had opened the Commodore Record Shop on West Forty-second Street, which joined the Hot Record Exchange as a headquarters for the faithful. Gabler's store was small and shabby, its entrance all but lost in the neon signs of its neighbors, but for many devotees it had a special significance. "It's a shrine," declared guitarist Eddie Condon, "the crummiest shrine in the world."[29] Gabler seemed to have a magic touch, struggling financially but keeping a large number of

records in stock and procuring rare sides on request from out
of the blue.

His reach extended to other sectarian enterprises. In 1935
he inaugurated the United Hot Clubs of America (UHCA)
with two Yale alumni, Marshall W. Stearns and John Hammond, and two years later arranged with some of the big
record companies to lease masters from their vaults for new
pressings on the UHCA label. Within five years he had reissued
fifty-seven "jazz classics," resurrecting and creating reputations
by listing names of all the performers on the labels, something
not done before on jazz records. At the same time, he began
to issue original sides on his own Commodore label, ignoring
prevailing Jim Crow customs in the recording business by
bringing together the best available black and white artists. He
seemed to cast a spell over the studio. "There's a ray that
comes out of him. You can't help doing what he wants," stated
one musician. "Here is a guy who can't read a note and he
practically tells you what register you're going to play in just
by the position of your head." Gabler admitted, "Maybe I'm
Svengali. Maybe they're more relaxed and they'll do things for
me that might give me a kick where they wouldn't for anyone
else. . . . I can never tell when I'm going to be lifted right out
of my seat."[30] He eventually produced over a hundred original
records, stimulating the emergence of other small jazz labels.

The most important was Blue Note, started in 1939 by Alfred
Lion, a German businessman who fled the Nazis and settled
in New York to be near the music he loved. With the help of
boyhood friend Francis Wolff, he introduced quality recording
to jazz. Concerned to get the real thing, "not its sensational
and commercial adornments," he unprecedentedly paid performers for rehearsals, often two or three, before everyone
was satisfied that a good session would result. At rehearsals
and recording dates he provided food and drink and urged
musicians to bring along their own material and friends who
might be added to the personnel. With the advent of long-
playing records, he urged players to take longer solos than
planned if the spirit moved them.[31] He treated his musicians
with the respect and deference customarily accorded their
classical counterparts and was rewarded with extraordinary

results up through the Sixties, strongly influencing the course of jazz and preserving the work of important figures little recognized in their day.

The growth of independents led the big companies to recall their leased masters from Gabler (who went to work for Decca) and come out with their own reissued jazz classics, starting with sides by Louis Armstrong, Bessie Smith, Jelly Roll Morton, and Bix Beiderbecke. At the same time, they took further—if still tentative—steps toward recording live jazz. All this activity met with limited commercial success but did much to spread the prophecy to the expanding following. On the other hand, the reissues cut into the value of the "collectors' items," although a core of early 78-fanciers remained, insisting on the reliquarian merits of the original issues and the purity of their sounds.

Spurred by these developments, interest in early jazz reached reached its peak in the Forties, fueling the fundamentalist Dixieland Revival spearheaded by purist critics and collectors in reaction to the commercial heresies of smooth, big band swing and, more importantly, the increasing incursions of outrageous bop. In addition to burgeoning numbers of records, publications, and organizations devoted to the old-time music, a few nightclubs started to feature it, attracting not just intellectuals and critics but listeners from many walks of life. All of a sudden, out-of-work jazzmen found themselves in the spotlight. Delighted to be working regularly again (for a modest sixty dollars a week at Nick's, the revivalist outpost in Greenwich Village), Max Kaminsky recalled, "With the sudden craze for hot jazz records we found ourselves celebrities in the highly concentrated, intense world of jazz. I didn't know what to make of it all. Here these people were beginning to write about us and talk about our records and look up to us as heroes; compliments and plaudits were showered upon us from all sides. . . . People all over the world were beginning to collect our records and idolize us as the stalwart, pure-hearted artists fighting against the commercial music world. All we were concerned about was making our band sound good."[32] Whatever the psychological distance between hero and worshipers— a distance enhancing the performer's charisma—the veteran was delighted to find his services in demand once again and to have the music treated with reverence, however extravagant it sometimes became.

In the best circumstances, revival performance-climates alternated between rapt silence and explosive enthusiasm. Such conditions prevailed at the famous Sunday afternoon jam sessions Milt Gabler began in 1939 at Jimmy Ryan's on West Fifty-second Street, where the usual nightclub atmosphere was suspended. There was a minimum of tinkling glass, talk, and ringing of the cash register while the rituals were in progress, and the nondrinking faithful paid a dollar to sit in rows in front of the band. But, wherever they sat, patrons gave their undivided attention to the music. "The audience listened hard. The feeling was that musicians and fans alike lived just for Sundays," recalled Kaminsky. "The Ryan's regulars were the most sincere and discriminating group of fans I ever played for. At Ryan's the music was the thing and when a soloist was building a solo, you never heard a sound from the audience. You could *feel* them listening."[33] From time to time, however, their restraint disappeared as the musicians broke loose in a rousing, up-tempo standard. As Kaminsky recounted, "The fans, who included specimens of all varieties—the earnest jazz purist; the jivey hep cat; the intense intellectual; extroverts from the advertising world; Broadway types; sentimental drunks; dedicated drinkers; plain people; and plain characters—were all members of the same fraternity."[34] The Sunday afternoon devotions at Ryan's continued into the Forties and spawned imitators in other large cities with similarly avid followers.

At first the musicians at such sessions were whites of the Chicago school playing their own, streamlined versions of the old New Orleans jazz. But sticklers for purity were happier with white imitators of the original Crescent City sounds, and were particularly delighted by black survivors whom they had helped rescue from obscurity, including Sidney Bechet, Jelly Roll Morton, and Bunk Johnson, whom they zealously canonized. Johnson, reputed to have played with Buddy Bolden and to have been Louis Armstrong's real mentor (false impressions which Johnson encouraged), was found through a blind letter *Jazzmen* co-editor Frederic Ramsey, Jr., sent to him in care of the postmaster in a small town outside of New Orleans. Johnson's well-publicized reply had the ring of biblical truth, in the words of Ernest Borneman, "the dignity of an Old Testament lament."[35]

> Dear Friend, your letter was received and was more than glad. . . . Now a picture of mine is what you want and that is something I haven't got. . . . I am here only making out now. For we have work only when Rice Harvest is in, and that over, things goes Real ded until Cane Harvest. I drive a truck and trailer and that only pays me $1.75 a day and that do just not last Very Long. So you all know for sure that just about how mutch money that I makes now. I made up my mind to work Hard until I die as I have no one to tell my troubles to and my children they can not help me out in this case. I have been Real Down for about Five years. My teeth went bad in 1934 so that was my finish playing music. I am just about to give it up. Now I haven't got no other way to go, but put my Sholder to the wheel and my nose to the grinding Stone and put my music down.[36]

After further correspondence—and help from *Jazz Information* editor Gene Williams, San Francisco architect Rudi Blesh, later the author of a fundamentalist account of the music, *Shining Trumpets* (1946), and New Orleans jazz historian William Russell—Ramsey got Johnson a new set of teeth and a secondhand trumpet. In 1942 he made a series of recordings and the following year was brought North for personal appearances. Acute ears found much lacking in his performances, but purists made him an overnight prophet, one of the original saints returned in the flesh, and took everything he said and played as gospel. Unhappily, he could not handle his newfound acclaim. More and more he believed his own press notices and became an overbearing alcoholic. After causing all sorts of trouble, including hard feelings among fellow musicians, he retired in 1948 and died a year later. Like some other rehabilitated veterans, he let his imagination outrun his memory, claiming, among other things, to have been the co-inventor of jazz with Buddy Bolden, a widely credited assertion made in a letter to Frederic Ramsey printed as the epigraph to *Jazzmen*.

The Dixieland Revival, like many other fundamentalist

restorations, was more notable for intensity than longevity. But by the end of the Forties, when most of its fire had died out, it had contributed heavily to the acceptance of early jazz, bringing large numbers of listeners around to the view that America developed a "unique art form." Increasingly, people found it, or its dilutions, attractive, and its superficial, upbeat dixieland version became the good-time music of middle-class America. This revival has been the most dramatic so far, but there have been others, major and minor, centering on "boogie-woogie" in the late Thirties, ragtime in the Fifties and again the Seventies, and "regressive" hard bop in the Fifties, to name the most important—all marked by evangelical zeal, demands for purity, critical touting, record reissues, the return of old heroes, and a host of youngsters imitating them.

Such renewals also fostered a growing number of concerts in halls hitherto sacred to classical music. There had been commercial- and symphonic-jazz concerts in Aeolian Hall in New York to much fanfare in the Twenties (one by Paul Whiteman in 1924 featured George Gershwin introducing his *Rhapsody in Blue*), and by the Thirties the time was ripe for real jazz in symphonic auditoriums. The most celebrated early events were produced by the indefatigable John Hammond, critic, record producer, and midwife to the careers of important early musicians and bands. He organized two Benny Goodman concerts in 1937–38 and the two more memorable "Spirituals to Swing" programs in 1938–39, bringing together stars of the Goodman and Count Basie Bands with other notable musicians. The first well-known series of concerts began in 1942 when Ernest Anderson, an advertising man and jazz devotee, helped guitarist Eddie Condon present Dixieland music in Manhattan's Town Hall. Initially, only a few diehards attended, but seven months later the concerts were regularly sold out and at one point mounted policemen had to be called in to maintain order among those turned away. In the mid-Forties, Leonard Feather brought bop concerts to Town Hall and then Carnegie Hall, demonstrating that even "far out" jazz could now get a "serious" hearing.

More significant were the promotions of Norman Granz and George Wein, both of whom had attended the Ryan's Sunday jam sessions. In 1944, Granz, an amateur musician and film editor, tried a variant of the Ryan's formula in concerts at the Los Angeles Philharmonic Auditorium. Their success led to extended foreign and domestic tours of his "Jazz at the Philharmonic" troupes. His tastes ran toward the contemporary and he knew how to put together programs which excited large, if only superficially appreciative, crowds. The same was true of Wein, a pianist also dedicated to the spread of jazz, though not always in its purest manifestations. After running clubs in Boston that held sessions like Ryan's, he started the annual Newport Jazz Festival in 1954, with the backing of local socialite Elaine Lorillard. It featured jazz and some popular music (eventually including rock) stars in crowded programs. As the audience grew in successive years (from 13,000 patrons in 1954 to 60,000 in 1959), it became increasingly difficult to control. In 1960, there was a riot when 12,000 rock fans, refused admittance to overflowing Freebody Park, over-whelmed the police with flying beer cans—many full—and went in anyway.[37] After another riot ten years later, the Festival moved to New York, where it focused more on legitimate jazz and became more decorous. In 1981, it presented some fifty concerts, as well as workshops and seminars, in different parts of Manhattan and outlying areas as far away as Saratoga, catering to the faithful from all parts of the denomination. In the meantime, Wein had started festivals in other cities and had imitators at home and abroad.

While large jazz festivals usually had a wide denominational appeal, some smaller ones had narrower interests. The Tenth Annual Bix Beiderbecke Memorial Festival took place in Beiderbecke's hometown, Davenport, Iowa, in 1981, fifty years after his death. The performers were generally amateurs playing dixieland music, including the Chicago Jazz Band, mostly University of Michigan professors, and the Natural Gas Band from San Francisco, composed of two dentists, two lawyers, and an engineer. The four-day event attracted many middle-aged, middle-class devotees, the "white pants and poly-ester crowd," as one musician called them, who talked about retirement and bowling when not attending to the music. There were also youngsters in jeans, sometimes with frisbees, who spontaneously broke into Charleston or Lindy steps, as their grandparents once might have done. The Bix Beiderbecke Memorial Society ran the Festival in ways stressing purity and discouraging excessive frivolity. Above all, they wanted to avoid a commercial, circus atmosphere and thus limited their concession booths to appropriate food, drink, and decorous posters, bumper stickers, and T-shirts proclaiming "Bix Lives." But they were not the only purists on hand. One musician complained that listeners "are always telling me that so-and-so played it better in the Thirties." Yet lighthearted or serious, they were caught up in the festivity and lifted out of their daily routines and feelings. As the clarinetist in the Chicago Jazz Band explained, "[T]his is happy music. No matter what's going on in my life it makes me feel better. The underlying rhythm is always forward and up."[38]

In 1931, when Beiderbecke died at twenty-eight of alcoholism in a seedy hotel room in New York, he was a musicians' musician, virtually unknown to the public. But fifty years later, thanks to the ongoing efforts of a growing group of aficionados, he had a firm place in the pantheon of many respectable Americans who would largely have disapproved of him during his lifetime. From the first, early-jazz cognoscenti worked to elevate and spread his image, fostering rituals and myths that gradually brought pilgrims to his grave, reissues of his recordings, a definitive biography—*Bix: Man and Legend* (1974) by Richard M. Sudhalter and Philip R. Evans—and the Memorial Society which, in addition to mounting the Annual Festival, sought to build a museum as an appropriate shrine to the cornetist.

Hipsters

The hipsters, who manned strategic street corners in urban neighborhoods in the Forties and early Fifties, were enthusiastic jazz followers but commonly got their primary kicks from drugs. Their interests intersected rather than coincided with those of true believers. Still, the area of intersection was relatively large. In "Cats, Kicks, and Color," a study of fifty black hipsters in a Chicago neighborhood during the Fifties, Harold Finestone found his subjects to be sensitive, "home-grown ghetto intellectuals" who saw little meaning or prospect in the world of convention and therefore chose to live by their wits in the fluctuating uncertainties of street life. They were artful hustlers often operating beyond the law in search of kicks.[39] In "The White Negro: Superficial Reflections on the Hipster," Norman Mailer spoke of intelligent refugees from a dying general culture devastated by twentieth-century horrors and now teetering precariously between democracy and a totalitarianism that had erased all but the most courageous moral individualism. Mailer's white hipsters were part-time psychopaths (not psychotics) who surrendered to childlike impulses for instant gratification. Like Finestone's subjects, however, they did not surrender unconditionally to the plea-sure principle, but maintained a certain detachment, a cool aloofness which lent a sense of objectivity to their stance. In Mailer's words, which smack of updated primitivism, the hipster was "a sophisticated and wise primitive in a giant jungle," not entirely without self-restraint yet seeking moments of incandescent ecstasy.[40]

This last assertion, whatever the validity of Mailer's overall argument, fits hipsters who arrived at similar liminal positions from different ethnic contexts. Black or white, they were suspended between responsibilities of childhood and adult-hood and lived for momentary ecstasies providing not only fleeting kicks but integrative and therapeutic feelings. "Jazz music gives form to my mind, forms in sound, and I feel it's better than any psychoanalysis, because art is a healer . . . it organizes my universe for me," testified one hipster.[41]

Hipster groups, like those of their jazz counterparts, were minimally structured, egalitarian bodies wherein esteem came with awareness. To be hip was to be "in the *know*," keenly sensitive to, but not overly demonstrative about, the raptures shared only by insiders. This bred a cool evangelism that hipsters found at the heart of bop. Finestone noted, "The cat's attitude toward music has a sacred, almost mystical quality.

Jazz opens doors to highly valued experience which for him can be found in no other way. It is more important than eating to him and second only to the "kick" [heroin]. He may give up his hope of dressing according to his standards but he never gives up music."[42] His idols were Charlie Parker and Dexter Gordon, the personifications of hipness, and as Finestone found, "Almost every cat is a frustrated musician who hopes some day to get his 'horn' out of pawn, take lessons, and earn fame and fortune."[43]

Mailer argued that his white hipster found in jazz the same things the Negro had found years before, things that "gave voice to the character and quality of his existence, to his rage and the infinite variations of joy, lust, languor, growl, cramp, pinch, scream, and despair of his orgasm. For jazz is orgasm, it is the music of the orgasm, good orgasm and bad, and so it spoke across the nation, it had the communication of art even where it was watered, perverted, corrupted, and almost killed; it spoke in no matter what laundered, popular way of instantaneous existential states to which some whites could respond . . . it said, 'I feel this, and now you do too.' "[44] In Mailer's interpretation, the hipster armed with the Negro's viewpoint heard in jazz not just an aesthetic message but a holy rallying cry intensifying shared feelings and confirming the validity of his outlook. Nat Hentoff has correctly pointed out that Mailer's definition is too limited, that while jazz can be intensely orgasmic, but is many other things too, depending on the performer's and listener's background, personality, and circumstances.[45] But if Mailer was unaware of the breadth of the music, so were many hipsters drawn to jazz mainly for its intensity, not necessarily orgastic, yet nonetheless powerfully ecstatic.

Hipsters thought of themselves as "somewhere," withdrawn from the "nowhere" square world, and as might be expected their withdrawal rituals resembled jazzmen's in dress and other things. In New York during the Forties, hipster fashion called for a long frock coat with "drape shape," padded shoulders, and rolled collar, also a snap-brim hat, pegged pants, tinted glasses, and sometimes a white streak of powder in the hair.[46] In Chicago the style was different. Finestone's subjects wore

conservative suits, colorful sport shirts, a tie clip—but no tie—
and expensive wide-brimmed Stetsons. They took great pains
to keep their outfits spotless, and the more affluent ostenta-
tiously changed their entire getup two or three times a day.[47]
As with many other liminars, highly distinctive dress provided
insignia of togetherness apart, symbols of conviction and
fellowship in circumstances removed from ordinary society.

Along with distinctive modes of dress went other identifying
mannerisms. Anatole Broyard wrote that the East Coast hipster
affected a look almost devoid of feeling: "His face . . . was
frozen in the 'physiognomy of astuteness.' Eyes shrewdly
narrowed, mouth slackened in the extremity of perspicuous
sentience, he kept tabs, like a suspicious proprietor, on his
environment. He always stood a little apart from the group.
His feet solidly planted, his shoulders drawn up, his elbows
in, hands pressed to sides, he was a pylon around whose
implacability the world obsequiously careened." Everything in
his pose contrived to present what Broyard called a "discrete
entity—separate, critical and defining"—illumined by an eso-
teric awareness and underscored by metonymous gestures,
brushing palms instead of handshaking, or raising an index
finger without lifting the arm, gestures which implied a prior
understanding and said "There is no need to explain, man, I
dig you."[48]

In speech as well as kinesis, performance was crucial. How
you said something was as important as what you said. Bor-
rowing heavily from the language of the jazz world, hipster
argot evolved rapidly in wordplay that only insiders could
follow, and street corner discussions or confrontations inspired
gifted improvisation, particularly among blacks—verbal bra-
vura implementing kicks and "hustles." The hippest cat talked
the best game, and his vocabulary, like the jazzman's, was
limited, abstract, and ambiguous, but remarkably flexible and
expressive. It was adaptable to many situations and meanings
where the received idiom failed to communicate, especially
meanings at the edges of ordinary understanding, between
reason and emotion or sense and nonsense. Some of this talk
was calculated gibberish, but for the most part it used familiar
words stripped of ordinary denotation. "Pecks" meant food,

"bread" money, and "flicks" movies. Many terms referred to energy or movement: "gone," "put down," "dig," and "flip"; or to existential status, "somewhere," "with it," and "out of this world." While hip usages varied according to time and place, they were essential to the hipster's role and identity. Without his jargon he was "nowhere."[49]

Beats

The beats, too, varied from place to place and turned to jazz as part of their revolt against the general culture. But they were further removed from the jazz life than the hipsters and were sometimes considered square by its elite. A cultic group with numerous transient members, the beats were, in effect, a second wave of Lost Generation bohemians, updated from the Coolidge era to the Eisenhower. Like the first wave, they were mostly young whites interested mainly in literature, but their variant of the aesthetic morality had generous helpings of Zen Bhuddism and Walt Whitman–like transcendentalism. While no strangers to alcohol, the favorite drug of their predecessors, they favored marijuana and stronger, hallucinogenic and ad-dictive substances. And instead of taking long sojourns in Europe, they generally confined their restless wanderings to this side of the Atlantic.[50]

Liminally suspended from convention, they were coolly disengaged, particularly from the drudgeries and responsibil-ities of nine-to-five jobs. But unlike the hipsters, who worked their hustles more or less furtively, the beats delighted in calling attention to their behavior, thumbing their noses at rectitude and authority in ways that made news. Jack Kerouac, Allen Ginsberg, Gregory Corso, and other spokesmen were great onstage performers, gifted in the nonsense and mockery that attracted media coverage. Their vocabulary included many boppers' words, although their borrowings did not always ring true. They also had a distinctive form of dress, resembling, as

Thomas Parkinson said, "Christ as beatnik with sandals and beard."[51]

"We're in the vanguard of a new religion,"[52] proclaimed Jack Kerouac, and in familiar fashion this faith revolved around a mystique of ecstatic moments, some triggered by jazz. "Beat means beatitude, not beat up," he explained. "You *feel* this. You feel it in a beat, in jazz—real cool jazz or a good gutty rock number."[53] While the beats' raptures over music were often intense, their tastes seemed indiscriminate to jazz aficionados, who were troubled by any linking of jazz to its commercial relatives. In Kerouac's testamentary novel, *On the Road* (1957), Dean Moriarity—the protagonist modeled on beat idol Neal Cassidy—responds to a performance by George Shearing, a cool pianist whom the author unhiply viewed as Charlie Parker's peer:

> Shearing began to rock; a smile broke over his ecstatic face; he began to rock in the piano seat, back and forth, slowly at first, then the beat went up, and he began rocking fast . . . he brought his face down to the keys, he pushed his hair back, his combed hair dissolved, he began to sweat . . . folks yelled for him to "Go!" Dean was sweating; sweat poured down his collar. "There he is! That's him! Old God Shearing! Yes! Yes! Yes!" And Shearing was conscious of the madman behind him, he could hear every one of Dean's gasps and imprecations. . . . "That's right!" Dean said. "Yes!" Shearing smiled and rocked. Shearing rose from the piano, dripping with sweat. . . . When he was gone, Dean pointed to the empty piano seat. "God's empty chair," he said.[54]

No matter how undiscriminating his taste, the beat's fascination with jazz was unswerving and raised hopes for a fusion of it and poetry. At one point Kerouac was booked into the hip Manhattan club, the Village Vanguard, an idea thought up by television personality Steve Allen, who accompanied Kerouac on the piano in regular sets with saxophonists Zoot Sims and Al Cohn. Kerouac started the evenings with stumbling, almost inaudible readings that turned into alcoholic declamations as the night wore on. Sometimes, he set his poetry aside and sang versions of jazz solos originated by Miles Davis and others.[55]

More common was the beats' use of jazz as background at
poetry readings which, with or without the music, could
resemble jam sessions. Allen Ginsberg, who presided over
some of the most memorable of these occasions was, in Bruce
Cook's words, "a sort of self-appointed shaman—intense, vol-
uble, irascible, and obviously convinced of the holiness of his
mission as a poet."[56] He was not alone in this role. At one
notable session there were five soloists, aside from Ginsberg,
whose rendition of *Howl* was the evening's climax. Jack Kerouac
described it in *Dharma Drums* (1958): "Everyone was there. It
was a mad night. And I was the one who got things jumping
by going around with . . . three huge gallon jugs of California
Burgundy and getting them all piffed so that by eleven o'clock
when Alvah Goldbrook was reading his poem 'Wail' drunk
with arms outspread everybody was yelling 'Go! Go! Go' (like
a jam session) and old Rheinhold Cacoethes, the father of the
Frisco poetry scene, was wiping his tears in gladness. . . .
Meanwhile scores of people stood around in the darkened
gallery straining to hear every word of the amazing poetry
reading as I wandered from group to group . . . giving out
little wows and yesses of approval. . . . It was a great night."[57]
Alvah Goldbrook was the code name for Ginsberg; Rheinhold
Cacoethes was Kenneth Rexroth; and "Wail" was "Howl,"
which Ginsberg had written two weeks earlier under the
influence of peyote and various amphetamines. When he read
it that night, he was, according to Kerouac, in constant movement to the rhythms of the chanted lines.

On such occasions what was said sometimes mattered less
than the way it was said. Ginsberg, Lawrence Ferlinghetti, and
other beat evangelicals had not only powerful ecstatic messages,
but also dramatic presences and deliveries. One after another
they mounted the stage, like successive jazz soloists, declaiming
their work before rapt audiences whose antiphonal responses
heightened the magic of the moment.

Dancers

Conservative churches have long found little place for dancing. Elsewhere, however, religion and the dance have had close ties. Dancing was a prominent activity in the Dionysian cults of antiquity and in the early worship of Jews and Christians. But as Christian and Jewish orthodoxies hardened, authorities frowned upon enthusiastic eurhythmics as the entering wedge of paganism—especially after the hysterias of Tarantism in the fourteenth century, interpreted by the Church as the work of the Devil. Nevertheless, dancing did not die out entirely in the rituals of Christianity and in our own time remains in the practices of Greek Orthodoxy, some Latin American Catholics, and certain evangelical groups in the United States.[58]

In archaic cultures dancing has had still closer connections with religion, and nowhere perhaps more than in West Africa, which provided the balletic traditions of American slaves. These traditions flourished freely in Catholic colonies and survived in Protestant ones, despite restrictions designed to curtail or eradicate them. The survivals tended to be interchangeable between sacred and secular circumstances. For instance, the "Eagle Rock," performed by blacks to early-jazz accompaniment, came from the Eagle Rock Baptist Church in Kansas City. Many European contributions to jazz dances also had religions origins. The "Fox Trot" evolved from an old quadrille used in totemic fertility rituals. Similarly, the "Turkey Trot" and "Grizzly Bear" hark back to emblematic practices.[59]

Curt Sachs has shown that all dances, mimetic or abstract, generate ecstasy or intimations of the sacred. In mimetic steps the performer identifies—or did originally—with the totemic figures he or she imitates. In more abstract dances he loses himself in the rhythm separating him from ordinary sensory activity,[60] for instance, in the ring shouts, derived from African circle dances, performers sang and shouted rhythmically in gathering rapture as they shuffled counterclockwise around symbolic, supernaturally charged objects in the center. In both mimetic and abstract steps the dancer ideally escapes the temporal and spatial limitations of mortality in becoming possessed by magic forces. As Sachs puts it:

Repressed powers are loosed and seek free expression; an innate sense of rhythm orders them into lively harmony. Harmony deadens and dissipates the will, the dancer gives himself over to the supreme delight of play prescribed by custom, gives himself over to the exhilaration, which carries him away from the monotony of everyday life, from palpable reality, from the sober facts of his experience—thither where imagination, fancy and vision waken and become creative.

In the ecstasy of the dance man bridges the chasm between this and the other world, to the realm of demons, spirits and God. Captivated and entranced he bursts his earthly chains and trembling feels himself in tune with all the world. . . . Every dance gives ecstasy. The adult who puts his arm around his companion in the ballroom, and the child in the roadway, skipping in a round dance—they forget themselves, they dissolve the weight of earthly contact and the rigidity of daily existence.[61]

Dancing proper was not the only source of such feelings. They emerged in other circumstances as well, in the rhythmic responses at jazz concerts and to the marching of a New Orleans funeral. William J. Shaefer calls the New Orleans street parade "a vigorous exercise in eurhythmics . . . there are no passive spectators at a New Orleans parade. Even at its most somber—in the melancholy dirges—the music stirs. Ghosts of waltzes and schottisches and quadrilles, of nineteenth-century triple-meter dances, haunt slow passages in dirges like 'Garlands of Flowers' or 'West Lawn Dirge.' The lyricism of these funeral chants is not only vocal, but in the best French manner, balletic too."[62] These processions, so memorable in the minds of early jazzmen, continue in New Orleans and still feature strutting, uniformed musicians led by a flamboyant Grand Marshal in colorful getup, his outsized sash flying wildly as he executes his high-stepping acrobatics. Sidney Bechet recalled the Grand Marshall as "a man who could prance when he walked, a man that could really fool and surprise you. He'd keep time to the music, but all along he'd keep a strutting and moving so you'd never know what he was going to do next. Naturally, the music, it makes you strut, but it's in *him* too, the way he's strutting, it gets to you."[63] Equally demonstrative were youngsters and others in the ragged "second line" who danced alongside the band in frenzied versions of the "Shudders," "Suzy Q," or "Shimmy," clapping and chanting or playing battered or homemade instruments.

The more ordinary dances done to jazz were similarly vigorous and elaborate. The "Lindy Hop," or "Jitterbug," which swept the country in the Thirties and provided the basis for the "Mambo" and "Funky Chicken" of later years, consisted of a box step, with stress on the off beat, followed by a "breakaway" in which dancers flung their partners outward in improvised "air" and "floor" steps before returning to the box configuration. The breakaway might be explosively acrobatic, but the overall effect was smooth, a horizontal flow appropriate to streamlined swing music.[64] But however slick, the "Lindy" could be as rapturous as the more frenzied, bouncy steps of the Twenties. Malcolm X attested to this in his *Autobiography*. As a teenager in Boston, appropriately dressed in a zoot suit on which he had just made the down payment, he went to the local Roseland Ballroom, and after a trip to the men's room to fortify himself with a stiff drink of whiskey (so that "everything felt right"), he descended to the dance floor where Lionel Hampton's

> band was working, and that big waxed floor was packed with people lindy-hopping like crazy. I grabbed some girl I'd never seen, and the next thing I knew we were out there lindying away and grinning at each other. It couldn't have been finer.
>
> I'd been lindying previously only in cramped little apartment living rooms, and now I had room to maneuver. Once I really got myself warmed and loosened up, I was snatching partners from a mob the hundreds of unattached, freelancing girls along the sidelines—almost every one of whom could really dance— and I just about went wild! Hamp's band wailing, I was whirling girls so fast their skirts were snapping. Black girls, brownskins, high yellows, even a couple of white girls there. Boosting them over my hips, shoulders, into the air. Though I wasn't quite sixteen then, I was tall and rawboned and looked like twenty-one; I was also pretty strong for my age. Circling, tap-dancing, I was underneath them when they landed—doing the "flapping eagle," the "kangaroo," and the "split."
>
> After that, I never missed a Roseland lindy-hop as long as I stayed in Boston.[65]

Millions of Americans experienced something of this ecstatic play, which Huizinga called the most unalloyed form of ludic expression: "Whether we think of sacred or magical dances of savages, or the Greek ritual dances, or the dancing of King David before the ark of the Covenant, or of dance simply as part of a festival, it is always and with all peoples pure play, the purest form of play that exists." The "play mood," he concluded, is one of "rapture and enthusiasm, and sacred and festive in accordance with the occasion," a mood in which "a feeling of expectation and tension accompanies the action, mirth and relaxation follow."[66]

Obviously, not all jazz dancing shows these elements to the full, but most of them are in the "Lindy" and many other steps: voluntary participation, stoppage of workaday activity; unique often inviolate, rules governing more or less orderly rituals in a special time and place; and the total absorption with attendent flow-feeling.

Here too are some of Caillois' play attributes. While jazz dances often elicited the soul of cooperative bliss, at times they were highly agonistic, whether among partners setting out playful challenges for one another, or more formal, organized dance contests which generated fierce rivalries. Moreover, they left much to chance: the choice of partners on a given night, and the chemistry between them; the nature of the music and dance floor; the proximity of other dancers who could either inhibit or exhilarate; and the mood of the evening. Then, too, jazz dancing with its dizzying, rhythmic movements also offered a good illustration of *ilynx*, a concept which, I think, can be extended beyond vertigo to describe other kinds of sense deprivation, including ecstasy. And the new steps, at least when done well, stuck a balance between the Cailloisian *paidia*, with its spontaneity and intuition, and *ludens*, stressing practiced skills and orderly procedure, so important in ritualistic, balletic formulas.

Finally, jazz dances were full of the simulation or mimicry Caillois noted in play. Many had animal names such as the "Bunny Hug" or "Lame Duck." Others purportedly imitated diabolical figures—was not jazz, after all, "the devil's music"? Then, too, one partner was usually by definition a follower, copying or complimenting the other. On a broader scale, styles were set by the leading dancers of the day, like the celebrated Vernon and Irene Castle, emulated and lionized not only for their dancing, but for their manners and appearance during the ragtime "dance craze." Thousands (including many of New York's exclusive "400") did slavish, if awkward, imitations of their "Castle Walk," and young women bravely dispensed with corsets, shortened their dresses, and bobbed their hair, the better to manage the athletic steps and demonstrate a new freedom. "Don't fasten your blouse down too tightly," Irene Castle counseled in *Modern Dancing*, the popular book she wrote with Vernon in 1914, "and be sure, in selecting one of the transparent, filmy little affairs now so much in vogue for dancing, that you can stretch your arms right above your head without difficulty. . . . The new styles of stockings, with elastic tops that hold them up snugly with the aid of only a round garter, are much better to dance in than the looser hose that require garters suspended from the corset." While this advice provoked scandal in some quarters, the Castles put some conservative minds at ease with their clean appearance, genteel demeanor, and avowed preference for restrained, elegant fox trots over what they called "ugly, ungraceful and out of fashion" steps like the "Turkey Trot" and "Grizzly Bear," so barbarous in the eyes of the older generation. Far from indecent and degenerate, the approved steps were touted as healthy and uplifting. "We are, while we dance, warring not only against unnatural lines of figures and gowns, but we are warring against fat, against sickness, and against nervous troubles," wrote Irene. "For we are exercising. We are making ourselves lithe and slim and healthy, and these are things that all the reformers in the world could not do for us." Furthermore, dancing provided an antidote to the evils of liquor: "Men and women who used to loiter in cafes, drinking and chatting, during afternoons are now dancing and drinking only a cup of tea. Young men are dancing instead of loafing in clubs and drinking, and the girls are learning the wisdom about the deadly cocktail, so that every dip and walk and glide and lock-step is really a soldier in the great army of health and beauty."[67] Along with the Castles' celebrity went a strong charisma breeding a sense of authority that helped to break down conventional barriers and to legitimize novelty. Caught up in the Castles' aura even the timidest soul felt secure following the latest fad.

Following Huizinga, the theologians Harvey Cox and Hugo Rahner speak of the sacredness of play, referring not simply to its inviolate rules but also to its uplifting, transcendent quality. In *Man at Play*, Rahner wrote:

> In the last analysis there is a secret, a mystery, at the heart of every form of play . . . a sacral secret. . . . To play is to yield oneself to a kind of manic, to enact to oneself the absolutely other, to preempt the future, to give lie to the inconvenient world of fact. In play earthly realities become, all of a sudden, things of the transient moment, presently left behind, then disposed of and buried in the past; the mind is prepared to accept the unimagined and incredible, to enter a world where different laws apply, to be relieved of all the weights that bear it down, to be kingly, unfettered and divine. Man at play is reaching out . . . for that superlative ease, in which even the body, freed from its earthly burden, moves to the effortless measures of heavenly dance.[68]

Whatever the final truth of these assertions, it is not difficult to see in them Malcolm X's Lindy ecstasies at the Roseland.

The Lindy Hop reached its height of sophistication at the Savoy Ballroom in Harlem, the "Home of Happy Feet," which hired the best bands in the country and became something of a shrine. It was cavernous, a block-long structure with a half-lit, cathedral interior and two altar-like bandstands. Patrons coming in off the street for the first time discovered a sumptuous wonderland with its thick carpets, uniformed attendants, broad expanses of mirrored walls reflecting a large cut-glass chandelier, and an ornate, marble staircase leading to the crowded dance floor. Leon James, whose Savoy experiences led to a professional dancing career, recalled his awe upon first climbing these stairs: "My first impression was that I had stepped into a different world."[69] A different world, with its own time, space, and rules, and also its own elite made up of the best dancers among the devoted habitués. In many ways this inner circle was analogous to the musicians' hard core. It emerged cult-like in 1928 around Shorty Snowden, who developed a version of the Lindy at a Manhattan dance marathon that lasted eighteen days. Movietone News recorded Snowden's winning routine, which found an ardent following after being shown in theaters across the country.

Among the elite, recognition depended on merit measured by peers in agonistic performance rituals, the most notable of which took place in the northeastern end of the Savoy. Called the "Cats' Corner," it was mentally roped off by insiders as sacred to their activities, and ritual proclaimed that it be kept empty until the "King" (the first to hold the title was Snowden) arrived. Trespassers were discouraged by various means, including painful kicks to the shins as they danced by. Once proceedings began, the least skilled dancers performed first, gradually giving way to their betters, until the King himself took command shortly before intermissions. Although these exhibitions encouraged individuality and improvisation, there were certain inviolate rules. Erstwhile King Leon James recalled, "Nobody copied anybody else or did somebody else's speciality, because he'd get whipped up, tromped in the middle of the crowd by all the others. I never could do steps like the other guys anyway. I'd just wiggle my legs and it came out different—Clock Clock they called it or sometimes legomania—so they accepted me in Cats' Corner."[70]

The rituals produced formidable contests demanding great skills and preparation. "You had to be able to dance to very fast tempos," said Leon James. "The bands seemed to swing faster every night, and all of the best dancers could follow them in new and different ways,"[71] which meant working up new steps to keep pace with the latest musical developments. Not above challenge, the King seldom rested easily on his throne. In 1937 a young pretender, Albert Mimms, temporarily interrupted his reign after a courtier divulged the secrets of the latest routines to a woman in exchange for her favors. Mimms managed to charm the secrets out of her and adapt them to his own acrobatic style. One night, just after King Leon James had performed, Mimms grabbed a partner and, defying protocol, burst into Cats' Corner with a breathtaking dance that astonished insiders immediately recognized as substantially their own. James tolerated this *lèse-majesté*, holding back lieutenants who wanted to bring it to an abrupt stop, but afterward he was frosty when Mimms came over to pay obeisance. The chill prevailed for a year, but then, unable to deny Mimms' talents, the King granted him recognition and eventually friendship. Challenges to the throne usually came from insiders, or at least local figures like Mimms, but sometimes unknowns appeared to throw down the gauntlet. Once, someone called "Little Shirley" came over from New Jersey and took the title home with him, obliging King Shorty Snowden to go to Newark the following week and bring it back to the Savoy, where it remained. Meanwhile, other Savoyards made successful forays into outside neighborhoods with similar success, proving to one and all that they were the greatest.

The unity and identity of the elite was reinforced by other practices, including withdrawal rituals, which again resembled those of the jazz hard-core, and also distinguishing habits of speech, dress, and comportment. Insiders used most of the jazz jargon and emphasized "correct" pronunciation. (The square gave himself away immediately by saying "Sa'voy" instead of "Savoy'.") It was also important to look right, particularly on Sunday night, called "Celebrity Night," when the house was reserved for the hippest dancers. Shorty Snowden explained:

> We started getting ready for Sunday on Saturday. The deal was to get our one sharp suit to the tailor to be pressed Saturday afternoon. Then we'd meet at the poolroom and brag about what we were going to do on the dance floor the next night. . . . On Saturday night we'd get dressed up and walk over to the front of the Savoy and stand on the sidewalk and wisecrack and watch the squares trip over each other trying to get in where they wouldn't see any real dancing or hear any good music either, because the bands played their best for us. Then sometimes Mister Charles Buchanan [the manager] would come running down, three stairs at a time, yelling, "Why don't you boys come on up and do a dance for the crowd?" When

he finally offered to pay us, we went up and had a ball. All we wanted to do was dance anyway.[72]

They only got pocket money for such exhibitions, but it did not matter. For those truly caught up by the ecstasy, material rewards were secondary.

By the time the Lindy had reached its stylish zenith at the Savoy, the jitterbug craze was spreading across the country, nourishing numerous big bands and exposing many youngsters to the jazz world. The most avid followers fit a familiar liminal pattern. Among them were middle-class, white teenagers dissatisfied with the world of their parents and searching for excitement. In *Jazz Dance* (1979), Jean and Marshall Stearns provide a good case in point in their friend, Ernest Smith, who ended up as an advertising man in New York, but as a fifteen-year-old in 1939 felt something missing from his comfortable suburban life in Pittsburgh. Restless and bored by the usual social outlets and entertainments, including high school dances with their cut-and-dried waltzes and fox trots, Ernest became interested in big bands, which led him to dance halls in black neighborhoods where the Lindy was done. Before long, he was trying his hand at the fascinating dance and after a little practice felt confident enough to jitterbug before his classmates, who were unimpressed, even shocked by the new steps, making it difficult for him to find partners to help polish his form. "The hardest thing to learn," he recalled, "is the pelvic motion. I suppose I always felt that these motions are obscene. You have to sway, forwards and backwards, with a controlled hip movement, while your shoulders stay level and your feet glide along the floor. Your right hand is held low on the girl's back, and your left hand down at your side enclosing her hand. At this time, the girl's at high school wouldn't or couldn't dance that way."[73] So he started running with a group of toughs who danced with working-class girls in nearby mill towns. Most of his new male friends were dropouts who let their hair grow, wore zoot suits with rolled lapels, pegged pants, and other "hep" attire, and walked in a kind of dance, sauntering cat-like, heads bobbing, shoulders hunched, and arms held close to the body with fingers snapping rhythmically. As for his newfound dance partners, they jitter-bugged uninhibitedly close to the authentic Negro style. "They were poorer and less educated than my high school friends," said Smith, "but they could really dance. In fact, at that time it seemed that the lower class a girl was, the better dancer she was. I never brought any of them home."[74]

In the next few years jitterbugging spread to respectable ballrooms across the nation, allowing the fringe of the early-jazz sect to make deep inroads into the general culture at the same time that bop, which turned jazz into a listener's music, was being born.

The loosening tie between the music and dancing, ushered in by bop, troubled many early jazzmen, and even some of the leading boppers, who felt at home playing with dancers in front of them. Many an oldtimer had eurhythmics in his blood, having started out as a general entertainer—a dancer or singer as well as an instrumentalist. Some, like pianist Sammy Price and bluesman T-bone Walker, began as dancers, and many other jazzmen, particularly drummers, naturally gestured and swayed in time to the beat. Dizzy Gillespie and Thelonious Monk relieved performance pressures with special dances in front of the band. Still others drew crucial inspiration from dancers. A performance by Carmen Amaya altered the career of pianist Cecil Taylor. "It was as though everything stopped," he told Nat Hentoff. "I mean everything *stopped*. That, to me, is the highest kind of compliment that can be paid to another artist—to make somebody else lose all sense of time, all sense of his own existence." Hentoff believes that this is what Taylor himself does in his extended, typhoon-like solos, rhythmically bouncing and thrashing on the stool while hammering per-cussively on the keyboard, pedals, and floor.[75] Like many great performers, he must be seen live, not just heard on recordings, to be fully appreciated.

And many jazzmen, even those who hardly moved when they played, liked to have dancers in front of them sharing or contributing to the ecstasy. Bix Beiderbecke remained relatively immobile when playing but enjoyed the response of enthu-siastic dancers; and Lester Young, who claimed he liked "to see a person stand flat-footed and play the instrument," declared toward the end of the swing era, "I wish jazz were played more for dancing. I have a lot of fun playing for dances because I like to dance too. The rhythms of the dancers come back to you when you're playing."[76] Great jazzmen and great dancers inspired each other.[77] Referring to the Savoy in 1937, Shorty Snowden recalled: "Dizzy Gillespie was featured in the brass section of Teddy Hill's swinging band. A lot of people had pegged him as a clown, but we [The Cats] loved him. Every time he played a crazy lick, we'd cut a crazy step to go with it. And he dug us and blew even crazier stuff to see if we could dance to it, a kind of game, with the music and dancers challenging each other."[78]

Lester Young was not the only jazzman who missed the contributions of dancers to post-Thirties music. Dizzy Gillespie shared his sense of loss and attempted to do something about it with demonstrations of bop steps. But in the end he had to admit failure. "I used to dance all the time in front of the band," he wrote in 1979. "But it was pretty difficult, really, without that strong one-two, one-two beat. They're getting back to a more definite beat because we've figured out that our music was primarily for dancing. Jazz was invented for people to dance to, and we can't get away from that. My music calls for listening, but it'll make you shake your head and pat your feet. If I don't see anybody doing that in the audience, we ain't getting to them."[79] This applied to the most avid believer, who found rapturous reaffirmations in the sounds, and to the fringe devotee momentarily caught up in a hint of the ecstasy. Either way, motor response indicated that the prophecy was getting through, the gnosis being shared.

Having originated in the underside of American life, jazz has now gained favor in the most prestigious quarters. We find it flourishing not only in major universities and conservatories, but in schools entirely devoted to it, in leading research and curatorial institutions, like the Smithsonian, and archives entirely given over to it, such as the Institute of Jazz Studies at Rutgers University, Newark—all founded or staffed by true believers. Its rapid (as such things go) acceptance attests not just to the magic of the music but to the strength of the gnosis and its sect-like following. Whether as critics, chroniclers, collectors, discographers, evangelical entrepreneurs or impresarios, cool hipsters, zealous beats, or simply anonymous dancers, club patrons, or casual record buyers—the laymen who paid the lion's share of the bills—followers have contributed interest and support, essential to the growth and acceptance of jazz as a vital artistic and social force.

Conclusion

In the last part of the nineteenth century, a white, Protestant consensus dominated the moral and spiritual life of the United States, influencing virtually every aspect of the nation's political, economic, intellectual, and social experience. It was a remarkably stable and unified consensus, with only marginal dissent and increasingly interchangeable denominations. Unchallenged as yet by growing American Catholicism and Judaism, it constituted a massive, monolithic defense of the status quo. But this dominance was steadily eroded by the drastic upheavals of the twentieth century.

Although the consensus had shown signs of strain before World War I, gaping cracks did not appear until the Twenties, when the Protestant zealotry that led to American involvement in the war and to Prohibition gave way to doubt and hedonism, undermining old taboos, especially concerning art and sex. Other erosions were implicit in conservative fears and defensiveness—in the revived evolution debate (notably in the celebrated Scopes Trial), racism (spread by the reinvigorated Ku Klux Klan, active for the first time in the North as well as in the South), and xenophobic political repression (the Red Scare and the Sacco-Vanzetti case). The Wall Street "crash" and the Depression further tested consensual values with intense economic hardships, internal migrations, and political extremism, both on the right and the left, demonstrating that American resources for fanaticism and bigotry were far from exhausted.

Although World War II again brought the nation and its churches together in a single-minded purpose, the Holocaust, atom bomb, and other horrors cast shadows on Christian notions of mortal virtue and, more significantly, of God's benevolence. On the surface the consensus seemed to solidify again in the complacent Eisenhower years, with its energy in business-oriented civil religion of 100% Americanism and the easy optimism of "positive thinking," but both of these only superficially addressed the sobering implications of McCarthyism, the Korean "police action," and the realities of the Cold War hovering darkly over the national consciousness.

In 1960 the election of John F. Kennedy, the first non-Protestant president, symbolized how far the growing pluralism had cut into the old hegemony. American society now seemed less a melting pot than a salad bowl in which different ethnic and religious groups maintained identity while striving for equality. Among these groups were newly awakened blacks, organized under their own Protestant leadership into the civil rights movement. But the hopes and expectations of the early Sixties were only partly achieved after a series of brutal assassinations (one telecast "live" before a large national audience) and yet another war (whose horrors appeared nightly in the nation's living rooms) brought the country to a boiling point which spilled over into the peace movement, Women's Liberation, and the "sexual revolution"—all challenges to the traditional Protestant ethic, as well as to conservative Catholic and Jewish tenets.

By the Seventies the old-time religion, although still influential and strident, had been shunted into subcultural status and moderate Christianity and Judaism, which had sought to keep abreast of changing times, also fell into difficulties, including losses in membership (in proportion to population growth) and declining numbers of clergymen. Despite assertions of the "Moral Majority" and like-minded groups in the Reagan years, the nation seemed to place less and less credence in religious salvation. In 1957, when a Gallup Poll asked a cross section of Americans, "Do you believe that religion can answer all or most of today's problems?," 81 percent answered yes. In 1962, 62 percent said yes, and in 1984 only 54 percent.[1] However fitfully and indirectly, we were moving ever further from our religious heritages.

This "secularization" had several causes. One was the growth of science, not only as it influenced theology through Darwin,

Freud, Einstein, and others, but in technological applications, up through the automations of the "post-industrial" computer age, which drastically changed rhythms, customs, and living standards. Another was the heavy tide of immigration—fourteen million newcomers came to our shores between 1900 and 1920. Few of them spoke English, fewer still were Protestants, and for the most part they settled into unassimilated ghettos. Another cause, closely tied to the first two, was the growth of American cities, whose atmospheres challenged many of the old religious verities. Protestantism was strongest in the nuclear families of the farms and small towns where most Americans lived in the nineteenth century. By the early 1900's, however, the balance was shifting, and the census of 1920 reported for the first time that the majority lived in cities. Long before this numerical shift, however, the city had beckoned persuasively to the young, the ambitious, and the restless. Later, urbanism infiltrated the countryside and distant towns, in suburbs, subdivisions, and shopping centers made attractive by the mass media and accessible by the automobile.

Urbanization threatened traditional habits of living. The city was bewilderingly complex, with multilayered political, economic, and social institutions; mechanized jobs with unaccustomed roles for women and children as well as for men; large blocks of leisure time and a wide range of recreational facilities; intensified pace, rhythms, and noise—all of which elbowed aside rural customs and sensibilities geared to a simpler, more intimate world. In the city man-made works crowded out the works of God and nature, as inherited notions of the supernatural, along with the moral and social order they supported, lost their grip. Increasingly, traditional churches, once sources of inspiration, guidance, and solace, seemed obstructions to pleasure, progress, and truth.

But if the decline of the old consensus liberated people from archaic beliefs and restraints, it also created a disturbing vacuum. New religious explanations and moral guidelines did not readily spring up to fill the gap, the replacements being too often arbitrary or ephemeral, without convincing authority or justification. Hence, many Americans were at loose ends, without clear social or philosophical direction or purpose, without sanctuary in times of stress. The metropolis was a collection of strangers, transients in flux, and the individual, alone or in concert, could do little to change the massive social and political machinery. Understandably, many felt alienated and alone.

Feelings of anomie were particularly strong among blacks, for whom the pain of racism was exacerbated by the speed and breadth of their urban migration. In 1890, 77 percent of American Negroes lived on Southern farms; by 1965 three-fourths of them resided in the city, half of them in the North.[2] Thus, within a single human lifetime the majority of Afro-Americans had been uprooted, most of them crowded into ghettos in worse circumstances than their white counterparts. They suffered mightily—their pay was lower, their living conditions more squalid, rents higher, families more riven, hopes more frustrated, and lives more violent. Isolated and alienated, many sought relief along marginal or deviant paths.

Negroes were not the only victims. Despair surfaced in different ways and to varying degrees throughout the urban environment, from black ghettoes to prosperous white suburbs. It was especially evident in restless adolescents who revolted against the status quo and its hypocritical upholders.

Religion offered no remedy for this malaise and even seemed irrelevant to twentieth-century life. Some people believed that God was dead or indifferent to worldly affairs. Others declared that intelligent men had long ago traded faith for reason, that lingering supernaturalism was but vestigial superstition lurking in the historical background or on the dim edges of human consciousness, that the modern world was, in effect, "desacralized." Yet such assertions are hard to credit. The older faiths may well be declining, perhaps terminally, but religion, defined broadly, is still very much with us in one form or another. We encounter it daily, if not in traditional forms, then in ways ranging from resurgent Pentecostalism, eschatological cults, and faith healing to the ancient, transcendent appeal of the arts and to ongoing loyalties to the Freudian faith, millenial Marxism, evangelical capitalism, the religion of science, and chauvinistic civil religion—all religious in so far as they hold some things sacred and uphold them with rituals and myths.

No man or society exists long without some form of religion to help them come to terms with the disturbing and inexplicable. Without beliefs and practices to deal with mystery and misfortune, the cosmos seems chaotic, filled with existential isolation and anxiety. Crises and uncertainty recur or find replacements, and require new faiths to cope with them. Thus, God may die, but religion does not; we forever seek ways to reinforce or replace old beliefs. Sociologist Robert Nisbet, remarking the persistence of the sacred in human consciousness, writes, "Note the ease with which those who abandon traditionally sacred norms or beliefs convert other norms— political, economic, scientific—from merely empirical or utilitarian significance not the less sacred because no deities or supernatural spirits are involved. . . . The appeal of religion would not appear to have greatly lessened in twentieth century industrial societies."[3] And its appeal is particularly strong among the spiritually dispossessed in metropolitan wastelands, including those who find affirmations in jazz.

Of course, not all jazz followers had been suffocating in spiritual vacuums before they heard the music. Some, especially those on the sectarian fringes, continued to find meaning in the old creeds, as, for that matter, did many jazzmen, particularly as they aged. But for all true believers jazz answered needs that traditional faiths did not address. While the music had different meanings for different followers—black or white, male or female, young or old, rich or poor, in various psychological states and social situations—for all devotees it provided some form of ecstasy or catharsis transcending the limitations, dreariness, and desperation of ordinary existence. Despite the horrors and emptiness of the wasteland, jazz not only survived but flourished, even prevailed, bringing intimations of beauty even to the least sensitive listeners, including hard-bitten criminals. As two killers explained to ragtime pianist Jimmy Durante after nearly implicating him in a murder, "Jimmy, you're the only real beauty we got in our lives. The swell tunes an' everything."[4] And on a higher level, it stimulated feelings of exultation and affirmation. Free-jazz saxophonist Archie Shepp declared, "Jazz is a symbol of the triumph of the human spirit, not its degradation. It is the lily in spite of the swamp."[5]

Yet it was more than just a passive bloom of spirituality emerging from a desolate landscape. It was also an active agent, a powerful force whose ecstasies, whether subtly insinuated or supplied in lightning illuminations, altered personality and society. As earthy blues, exalted anthem, or something in between, jazz could energize the most jaded will. In the words of one listener, speaking in 1917, "It has the power and penetration to inject life into a mummy."[6] Through cajolery, charm, warmth, surprise, shock, or outrage it could brush aside the most entrenched tradition, the most oppressive custom, and inspire subversive social behavior. Consider how jazzy music of the Twenties went hand in hand with the upheavals in manners and morals of that time, how bop was the cry of streetwise young rebels in the Forties, and how the "new thing" of the Sixties was closely allied to the "Black Power" impulses of that day. But as its styles matured jazz could have a more conservative role. In the Eisenhower era, jazz of the Twenties—or rather what was left of it—became the comfortable, "good time music" of the business community. Bop has been played in the music programs of the White House—the Reagan White House at that. And the "new thing," now old, is well on its way to being recognized by the establishment.

Clearly, then, jazz is more than a passive flower, a glorious cultural ornament affirming humanity, it is also a powerful social force which has cut broadly and deeply, its prophets, rituals, and myths touching not only individual souls but large groups, bringing intimations of magic and the sacred to an era whose enormous changes have depleted conventional faiths.

Notes

Epigraph

Marshall Stearns, *The Story of Jazz* (New York: Oxford Univ. Press, 1956), p. xi.

Preface

1. Published by Univ. of Chicago Press.

2. Most of the existing books on jazz say something about its ties with religion. The standard histories of the music—including Marshall Stearns, *The Story of Jazz* (New York: Oxford Univ. Press, 1956); Frank Tirro, *Jazz* (New York: Norton, 1977); and James Lincoln Collier, *The Making of Jazz* (Boston: Houghton Mifflin, 1978)—consider the religious origins of the music both in Africa and the New World. Sometimes the linkage is taken further. In *The Heart of Jazz* (New York: New York Univ. Press, 1956), William L. Grossman and Jack W. Farrell argue unpersuasively that Christianity lies at the base of "pure"—but only "pure"—New Orleans jazz. And in *Soul Music: Black and White* (Minneapolis: Augsburg, 1975), Johannes Riedel discusses jazz and other kinds of black music as forms of religious expression.

But few works treat the religious response to jazz. Of those that do, however briefly or implicitly, three stand out: Charles Keil's *Urban Blues* (Chicago: Univ. of Chicago Press, 1966); Ralph Ellison's *Shadow and Act* (New York: Random House, 1964); and Albert Murray's *Stomping the Blues* (New York: McGraw-Hill, 1976). All three discuss jazz or black music's connection with ethnic religion and have helped me examine its implications for a religion of art.

Still other studies investigate the jazz community from a more secular angle, but with important religious ramifications. Some writers have viewed it within a Marxist framework, notably Francis Newton (Eric Hobsbawm) in *The Jazz Scene* (London: McGibbon and Kee, 1959). Some have regarded it in terms of occupational ideology, e.g., Allen Merriam and Raymond Mack, in "The Jazz Community," *Social Forces*, XXXVIII (1960): 211–22, or within a context of deviance, for instance, Howard S. Becker in *Outsiders* (Glencoe, Ill.: Free Press, 1963). And some have pointed to its more ordinary middle-class implications. The most extensive work here is Charles Nanry, "The Occupational Subculture of the Jazz Musician: Myth and Reality," unpublished PhD diss., Rutgers Univ., 1970, and with Edward Berger, *The Jazz Text* (New York: Van Nostrand, 1979), pp. 243–55. See also Edward Harvey's "Social Change and the Jazz Musician," *Social Forces*, XLVI (Sept. 1967): 34–42; Philip S. Hughes, "Jazz Appreciation and the Sociology of Jazz," *Journal of Jazz Studies*, I (1974): 79–96; and Robert Stebbins, "The Jazz Community: The Sociology of a Musical Subculture," unpublished PhD diss., Univ. of Minnesota, 1964 (two parts appeared in *Sociological Quarterly*: "Class, Status, and Power Among Jazz and Commercial Musicians," VII (1966) and "A Theory of the Jazz Community," IX (1968). The earliest such study is Carlo Lastrucci's "The Professional Dance Musician," *Journal of American Musicology*, III (1941): 168–72. Others have looked at the jazz community anthropologically, with reference to black culture, notably Ortiz Walton in *Music: Black White and Blue* (New York: Morrow, 1972). Finally, some have illuminated it with a mixture of sociological, psychological, and humanistic insights, most importantly Nat Hentoff in *The Jazz Life* (New York: Dial, 1961) and other books.

1   *Church*

1. Trans. Paul Shores (New York: Putnam, 1930), pp. 333–34.

2. Frank Patterson, " 'Jazz'—The National Anthem(?)," *Musical Courier*, LXXXIV (May 1922): 6.

3. Ernst Troeltsch, *The Social Teachings of the Christian Churches*, trans. Olive Wyon (New York: Macmillan, 1931), Vol. I, pp. 19–21, 331–38. See also H. Richard Niebuhr, *The Social Sources of Denominationalism* (New York: Holt, 1929); and Kenneth O'Dea, "Sects and Cults," *International Encyclopedia of the Social Sciences*, David Sills, ed. (New York: Macmillan, 1968), vol. XIV, pp. 130–35.

4. Gilbert Chase, *America's Music* (New York: McGraw-Hill, 1956), p. 365.

5. Walter Damrosch, *My Musical Life* (New York: Scribners, 1923), p. 334.

6. *Ibid.*, pp. 223–24.

7. *Fourteenth Annual Census* (Washington, D.C., 1920), vol. IV, p. 42.

8. For a good discussion of this see John H. Mueller, *The American Symphony Orchestra* (Bloomington: Indiana Univ. Press, 1951), esp. pp. 380ff.

9. Theodore Thomas, *A Musical Autobiography*, ed. George Upton (Chicago: A. C. McClurg, 1905), vol. I, frontispiece, p. 251.

10. Henry T. Finck, "Music and Morals," in *Chopin and Other Essays* (New York: Scribners, 1910), 143–82.

11. David Ewen, *Music Comes to America* (New York: Allen, Towne and Hearth, 1942), pp. 96–97.

12. Deems Taylor, "Music," in Harold Stearns, ed., *Civilization in the United States* (New York: Harcourt, 1922), pp. 204–5; also D. G. Mason, *The Dilemma of American Music and Other Essays* (New York: Macmillan, 1928), p. 91.

13. Thomas, I, epigraph.

14. Here and elsewhere in this chapter I have relied heavily on Edward A. Berlin, *Ragtime: A Musical and Cultural History* (Berkeley: Univ. of California Press, 1980), esp. chap. 3.

15. Mary Douglas, *Purity and Danger* (London: Routledge, 1960) and "Pollution," *International Encyclopedia of the Social Sciences*, vol. XII, pp. 336–42.

16. Emile Durkheim, *The Elementary Forms of the Religious Life*, trans. Joseph Ward Swain (New York: The Free Press, 1965), pp. 455–56.

17. John T. Howard, *Our American Music* (New York: Crowell, 1931), p. 185.

18. "Musical Impurity," *Etude*, XVII (Jan. 1900): 16.

19. Leo Oehmler, "Ragtime: A Pernicious Evil and Enemy of True Art," *Musical Observer*, XI (Sept. 1914): 15.

20. "Enjoin 'Jazz' Palace to Protect New-Born; Salvation Army Fears Effect on Babies," *The New York Times*, Feb. 4, 1926, p. 4; see also Karl Muck, "The Music of Democracy," *Craftsman*, Dec. 1915: 227.

21. Philip Gordon, "Ragtime, Folksong and the Music Teacher," *Musical Observer*, VI (1912): 724–5.

22. "Damrosch Assils Jazz," *The New York Times*, Apr. 17, 1928, p. 26.

23. "Where Is Jazz Leading America?" (first installment), *Etude*, XLII (Aug., 1924): 518.

24. Statement by George Cobb in 1919, reprinted in *Ragtimer*, Nov.–Dec. 1968: 5.

25. Oehmler, p. 15.

26. Paul Whiteman and Mary Margaret McBride, *Jazz* (New York: J. H. Sears, 1926), pp. 137–38; see also "Wants Legislature to Stop Jazz as an Intoxicant," *The New York Times*, Feb. 12, 1922, p. 1.

27. "Music in America," *The New York Times*, Oct. 9, 1921, p. 10.

28. Francis Toye, "Ragtime: The New Tarantism," *English Review*, XIII (1913): 654.

29. Walter Winston Kenilworth, "Demoralizing Ragtime Music," *Musical Courier*, XLVI (May 21, 1913): 22–23.

30. Whiteman and McBride, pp. 139–40.

31. See Richard Christie and Peggy A. Cook, "A Guide to Published Literature Relating to the Authoritarian Personality Through 1956," *Journal of Psychology*, VL (1958): 171–99; T. W. Adorno *et al.*, *The Authoritarian Personality* (New York: Harpers, 1950); Otto Klineberg, "Prejudice: The Concept," *International Encyclopedia of the Social Sciences*, vol. XII, pp. 439–47; and George E. Simpson and J. Milton Yinger, *Racial and Cultural Minorities: An Analysis of Prejudice and Discrimination* (New York: Harper and Row, 1972), pp. 526–27.

32. Roger Bastide, "Color, Race, and Christianity," in John Stone, ed., *Race, Ethnicity and Social Change* (North Sicuate, Mass.: Duxbury Press, 1977), pp. 286–97.

33. For a summary of these attitudes see Oscar Handlin, *Race and Nationality in American Life* (New York: Doubleday/Anchor, 1957), pp. 119–22, 125–28.

34.   Ronald L. Morris, *Wait Until Dark* (Bowling Green, Oh.: Popular Press, 1980), p. 76.

35.   Nat Shapiro and Nat Hentoff, eds., *Hear Me Talkin' to Ya* (New York: Dover, 1966), p. 332.

36.   John R. McMahon, "Our Jazz-Spotted Middle-West," *Ladies' Home Journal*, XXXIX (Feb. 1927): 38.

37.   H. O. Brunn, *The Original Dixieland Band* (Baton Rouge: Louisiana State Univ. Press., 1960), p. 173.

38.   Morris, 77.

39.   "Canon Assails Our New Dances," *The New York Times*, Aug. 25, 1913, p. 3; "Canon Newboldt's Warning," *The New York Times*, Aug. 26, 1913, p. 8.

40.   "Judge Rails at Jazz and Dance Madness," *The New York Times*, Apr. 14, 1926, p. 15.

41.   Hiram Moderwell, "Ragtime," *New Republic*, IV (1915): 285.

42.   "The Musical Possibilities of Ragtime," *Metronome*, XIX (Mar. 1930): 11.

43.   "Jazz and Its Victims," *The New York Times*, Oct. 7, 1928, Sect. V, p. 19.

44.   Chris Goddard, *Jazz Away from Home* (New York: Paddington, 1979), p. 261.

45.   William L. Grossman and Jack R. Farrell, *The Heart of Jazz* (New York: New York Univ. Press, 1956), p. 62; see also Albert Murray, *Stomping the Blues* (New York: McGraw-Hill, 1976), pp. 23–42.

46.   Ralph Ellison, *Shadow and Act* (New York: Random House, 1964), p. 238.

47.   Nat Hentoff, "Garvin Bushell and New York in the Thirties," *Jazz Review*, II (Jan. 1959): 11–12.

48.   Shapiro and Hentoff, p. 198.

49.   "Our Musical Condition," *Negro Musical Journal*, I (1903): 137–38.

50.   Leroi Jones, *Black Music* (New York: Morrow, 1968), p. 11.

51. Billy Taylor, "Negroes Don't Know Anything About Jazz," in Don Cerulli *et al.*, eds., *The Jazz Word* (New York: Ballantine, 1960), p. 40.

52. Ellison, p. 239.

2 *Sect*

1. Dizzy Gillespie with Al Fraser, *To Be, Or Not . . . to Bop* (New York: Doubleday, 1979), p. 141.

2. Ernst Troeltsch, *The Social Teachings of the Christian Churches*, trans. Olive Wyon (New York: Macmillan, 1931) I, pp.19–21, 331–38; for a summary of scholarship on sects see Kenneth O'Dea, "Sects and Cults," *International Encyclopedia of the Social Sciences*, David L. Sills, ed. (New York: Macmillan, 1968), vol. XIV, pp. 130–35.

3. "Bop Will Kill Business, Unless It Kills Itself First," *Down Beat*, Apr. 7, 1948, p. 42.

4. Max Kaminsky and V. E. Hughes, *Jazz Band: My Life in Jazz* (New York: Da Capo, 1981), p. 193.

5. Both quotations appear in Arnold Shaw, *52nd Street* (New York: Da Capo, 1977), p. 268.

6. Nat Hentoff, *The Jazz Life* (New York: Dial, 1961), p. 228.

7. Bryan Wilson, *Religious Sects* (New York: McGraw-Hill, 1970), pp. 26–28, 36–167.

8. Linda Dahl, *Stormy Weather* (New York: Pantheon, 1984), pp. ix–x, 3.

9. See Curt Sachs, *The History of Musical Instruments* (New York: Norton, 1940), *passim*; Sally Placksin, *American Women in Jazz* (New York: Wideview, 1982); and Dahl, pp. 25–44, for documentation of sexual differentiation.

10. Max Weber, *The Sociology of Religion*, trans. Ephraim Fischoff (Boston: Beacon, 1963), pp. 104–5, 239; see also Ortiz Walton, *Music: Black, White, and Blue* (New York: Morrow, 1972), p. 35; and Leroi Jones, *Blues People* (New York: Morrow, 1963), pp. 91–92.

11. Valerie Wilmer, *As Serious As Your Life* (Westport, Conn.: Lawrence Hill, 1980), p. 206.

12.   See Charles Nanry and Edward Berger, *The Jazz Text* (New York: Van Nostrand, 1979), p. 247.

13.   Turner's ideas on liminality are developed in *The Forest of Symbols* (Ithaca, N.Y.: Cornell Univ. Press, 1967); "Myths and Symbols," *International Encyclopedia of the Social Sciences*, X, pp. 576–81; *The Ritual Process* (Chicago: Aldine, 1969); and *Dramas, Fields, and Metaphors* (Ithaca, N.Y.: Cornell Univ. Press, 1974). His concept of the "liminoid," dealing with practices of play in post-industrial societies, can be found in "Frame, Flow, and Reflection: Ritual Drama as Public Liminality," in Michael Benamou and Charles Camarello, eds., *Performance in Postmodern Culture* (Madison, Wis.: Coda, 1977), pp. 33–55, and *From Ritual to Theatre* (New York: Performing Arts Journal Publishers, 1982), pp. 52–54. In all of this he started from Arnold van Gennep, *The Rights of Passage*, trans. Monika Vizedom and Gabriella Chaffee (Chicago: Univ. of Chicago Press, 1960).

14.   *Louis Armstrong—A Self-Portrait and Interview*, interview by Richard Meryman (New York: Eakins, 1970), pp. 23–24.

15.   Nat Shapiro and Nat Hentoff, *Hear Me Talkin' to Ya* (New York: Dover, 1966), p. 119.

16.   *Ibid.*, pp. 317–18.

17.   Turner, *Ritual Process*, pp. 128–29; *From Ritual to Theatre*, pp. 47–52. In the latter Turner distinguishes three kinds of communitas: spontaneous, ideological, and normative. The first and third seem especially applicable here.

18.   Artie Shaw, *The Trouble with Cinderella* (New York: Da Capo, 1979), pp. 148–49.

19.   Kitty Grime, *Jazz Voices* (London: Quarter, 1983), p. 93.

20.   Weber, *Sociology of Religion, passim*; also Weber, *The Theory of Social and Economic Organization*, trans. A. M. Henderson and Talcott Parsons (New York: Free Press, 1964), esp. "The Routinization of Charisma," pp. 358–72; for application to music see Weber, *The Rational and Social Foundations of Music*, trans. and ed. Don Martindale, Johannes Riedel, and Gertrude Neuwirth (Carbondale, Ill.: Southern Ill. Univ. Press, 1958); see also Walton, esp. pp. 14–17.

Anthony F. C. Wallace in his well-known article, "Revitalization Movements," *American Anthropologist*, LVIII (Apr. 1956), 264–81, describes movements, religious and otherwise, which are "deliberate, organized, conscious," efforts at renewal. His model works well with groups that develop consciously and purposefully, but jazz sects are usually minimally organized, highly spontaneous, and relatively un-self-conscious bodies which evolve with great rapidity and therefore do not fit comfortably into Wallace's pattern of "processual structure." This has five stages: 1. Steady State; 2. Period of Individual Stress; 3. Period of Cultural Distortion; 4. Period of Revitalization (in which occur the functions of mazeway reformulation, communication organization, adaption, cultural transformation, and routinization); and 5. "New Steady State." I discuss the notion of "mazeway" in Chapter Four, but in general, Wallace's processional stages, though present in the swift growth of jazz sects, blur indistinguishably. Individual stress, cultural distortion, and mazeway reformulation seem to go on simultaneously or to recur amid ongoing creative challenges in fluctuating circumstances and styles.

For a review of material on Wallace's paradigm see Weston LeBarre, "Crisis Cults," *Current Anthropology*, XXI (Feb. 1971), 3–44. Also of interest in connection with sectarian development is Mary Douglas and Aaron Wildavsky, *Risk and Culture* (Berkeley: Univ. of California Press, 1982), a look at cultic behavior among environmentalists.

21.   This definition comes from Leopold von Wiese and Howard Becker, *Systematic Sociology* (New York: Wiley, 1932), *passim;* see also Milton Yinger, *Religion, Society and the Individual* (New York: Macmillan, 1957), p. 154; and Yinger, *Religion in the Struggle for Power* (Durham, N.C.: Duke Univ. Press, 1946), p. 22.

22.   Liston Pope, *Millhands and Preachers* (New Haven: Yale Univ. Press, 1942), pp. 117–40.

23.   John Pareles, "Jazz Swings Back to Tradition," *The New York Times Magazine*, VI (June 17, 1984), 23, 54, 61; also Pareles, "Pop Life: Jazz Service Group Formed," *The New York Times*, May 1, 1985, C 25.

24.   John Rockwell, *All American Music* (New York: Knopf, 1983), p. 190.

25.   Pareles, "Jazz Swings Back to Tradition," C 23, 54, 61.

3   *Prophets*

1.   Mircea Eliade, *Shamanism: Archaic Techniques of Ecstasy*, trans. Willard Trask (Princeton: Princeton Univ. Press, 1964), pp. 446–47, and

passim; Eliade, *The Myth of Eternal Return*, trans. Willard Trask (New York: Pantheon, 1954), pp. 92–94; Eliade, *Rites and Symbols of Initiation*, trans. Willard Trask (New York: Harper and Row, 1958), pp. 85–87; see also Willard Z. Park, *Shamanism in Western North America* (New York: Cooper Square, 1975).

2. See Waldemar Bogoras, "Shamanistic Performance in the Inner Room," in William A. Lessa and Evon Z. Vogt, eds., *Reader in Comparative Religion: An Anthropological Approach*, 3rd ed. (New York: Harper and Row, 1972), pp. 283–87; Andrew Neher, "A Physiological Study of Universal Behavior in Ceremonies Involving Drums, *Human Biology*, XXXIV (1962), 151–60; Rodney Needham, "Percussion and Transition," in Lessa and Vogt, 391–97.

3. Nat Hentoff and Nat Shapiro, eds., *Hear Me Talkin' to Ya* (New York: Dover, 1966), p. 100.

4. Eliade, *Shamanism*, p. 180.

5. Max Weber, *The Theory of Social and Economic Organization*, ed. and trans. Talcott Parsons (New York: Free Press, 1957), esp. 358–63, 368–92; and Edward Shils, "Charisma," in *International Encyclopedia of the Social Sciences*, David L. Sills, ed. (New York: Macmillan, 1968), vol. II, pp. 386–90.

6. Shapiro and Hentoff, p. 176.

7. Eddie Condon and Thomas Sugrue, *We Called It Music* (New York: Holt, 1947), p. 107.

8. Jack Chambers, *Milestones, I* (Toronto: Univ. of Toronto Press, 1983), pp. 79–80.

9. Shapiro and Hentoff, p. 255.

10. Derek Jewell, *A Portrait of Duke Ellington* (New York: Norton, 1971), p. 31.

11. Robert Reisner, *Bird: The Legend of Charlie Parker* (New York: Citadel, 1962), pp. 144–45.

12. Ira Gitler, *Jazz Masters of the Forties* (New York: Macmillan, 1974), p. 151.

13. Shapiro and Hentoff, pp. 341–42.

14. *Ibid.*, pp. 151–52.

15. Reisner, p. 56.

16.   Shapiro and Hentoff, p. 39.

17.   John Hammond, "Lester Young," *Jazz*, III (1959): 181–83.

18.   Shapiro and Hentoff, p. 164.

19.   Erving Goffman, *The Presentation of Self in Everyday Life* (New York: Doubleday/Anchor, 1959), pp. 67–70.

20.   Charles Cooley, *Human Nature and the Social Order* (New York: Scribners, 1922), p. 351.

21.   Ross Russell, *Bird Lives* (New York: Charterhouse, 1973), p. 324.

22.   Nat Hentoff, *Jazz Is* (New York: Random House, 1976), p. 24.

23.   Arnold Shaw, *52nd Street* (New York: Da Capo, 1977), p. 63; Rex Stewart, *Jazz Masters of the Thirties* (New York: Macmillan, 1974), p. 183.

24.   Reisner, pp. 121, 13.

25.   Anthony F. C. Wallace, "Revitalization Movements," *American Anthropologist*, LVIII (Apr. 1956): 272.

26.   Len Lyons, *The Great Pianists* (New York: Quill, 1983), p. 127.

27.   Kitty Grime, *Jazz Voices* (London: Quartet, 1983), p. 76.

28.   John Litweiler, *The Freedom Principle* (New York: Morrow, 1984), pp. 167–68.

29.   James L. Collier, *The Making of Jazz* (Boston: Houghton Mifflin, 1978), p. 488.

30.   Dizzy Gillespie with Al Fraser, *To Be, Or Not . . . to Bop* (New York: Doubleday, 1979), p. 474.

31.   Valerie Wilmer, *As Serious As Your Life* (Westport, Conn.: Lawrence Hill, 1980), p. 44.

32.   Ralph Ellison, *Shadow and Act* (New York: Random House, 1964), p. 236.

33.   Shapiro and Hentoff, p. 206.

34.   J. C. Thomas, *Chasin' the Trane* (New York: Da Capo, 1976), p. 127.

35.   Mezz Mezzrow and Bernard Wolfe, *Really the Blues* (New York: Random House, 1946), p. 83.

36. Condon and Sugrue, p. 102.

37. Shapiro and Hentoff, p. 161.

38. Reisner, p. 80.

39. Alan Lomax, *Mr. Jelly Roll* (New York: Grove, 1950), p. 36.

40. Shapiro and Hentoff, p. 206.

41. *Ibid.*, p. 39.

42. *Ibid.*, p. 153.

43. Gitler, *Jazz Masters*, p. 26.

44. Nat Hentoff, *The Jazz Life* (New York: Dial, 1961), pp. 144–45.

45. Emile Durkheim, *The Elementary Forms of the Religious Life,* trans. Joseph Ward Swain (New York: Free Press, 1965), pp. 351–55.

46. Reisner, pp. 32–33.

47. Bill Cole, *John Coltrane* (New York: Schirmer, 1976), p. 5.

4   *Gnosis*

1. Ross Russell, *Bird Lives* (New York: Charterhouse, 1973), p. 270; and Linda Dahl, *Stormy Weather* (New York: Pantheon, 1984), p. 234.

2. R. Murray Schafer, *The Tuning of the World* (New York: Knopf, 1977), *passim.*

3. Nat Shapiro and Nat Hentoff, *Hear Me Talkin' to Ya* (New York: Dover, 1966), p. 37.

4. *Ibid.*, p. 410.

5. Dizzy Gillespie with Al Fraser, *To Be, Or Not . . . to Bop* (New York: Doubleday, 1979), pp. 30–31.

6. Nat Hentoff, *The Jazz Life* (New York: Dial, 1961), p. 161.

7. See Charles Keil, *Urban Blues* (Chicago: Univ. of Chicago Press, 1966), p. 164; and Albert Murray, *Stomping the Blues* (New York: McGraw-Hill, 1976), pp. 9–42. Each indicates how the preacher deals in trance and the bluesman in dance. In fact both do both, and so does the jazzman.

8. Shapiro and Hentoff, p. 243.

9.   Nat Hentoff, *Jazz Is* (New York: Random House, 1976), p. 164.

10.   *Ibid.*, p. 206.

11.   Phyl Garland, "Requiem for 'Trane," *Ebony*, XXIII (Nov. 1967): 72.

12.   Willie "The Lion" Smith with George Hoefer, *Music on My Mind* (New York: Doubleday, 1964), p. 129.

13.   Shapiro and Hentoff, pp. 246–47; see also Lawrence W. Levine, *Black Culture and Black Consciousness* (New York: Oxford Univ. Press, 1977), pp. 212–13.

14.   Eddie Condon and Thomas Sugrue, *We Called It Music* (New York: Holt, 1947), p. 107.

15.   Hentoff, *Jazz Life*, p. 246. Beyond this, much of Murray's *Stomping the Blues* involves jazz as affirmation.

16.   Brian Priestly, *Mingus* (London: Quartet, 1982), pp. 114, 192.

17.   Art Hodes and Chadwick Hansen, eds., *Selections from the Gutter* (Berkeley: Univ. of California Press, 1977), p. 18.

18.   Robert Reisner, *Bird: The Legend of Charlie Parker* (New York: Citadel, 1962), p. 233.

19.   Shapiro and Hentoff, p. 406.

20.   Sidney Bechet, *Treat It Gentle* (New York: Hill and Wang, 1960), p. 124.

21.   Benny Goodman and Irving Kolodin, *The Kingdom of Swing* (New York: Stackpole, 1939), p. 101.

22.   Arnold Shaw, *52nd Street* (New York: Da Capo, 1977), p. 283.

23.   Ira Gitler, *Swing to Bop* (New York: Oxford Univ. Press, 1985), p. 84.

24.   J. B. Figi, "Cecil Taylor: African Code, Black Methodology," *Down Beat*, April 10, 1979, p. 12.

25.   Reisner, p. 71.

26.   Emile Durkheim, *The Elementary Forms of the Religious Life*, trans. Joseph Ward Swain (New York: Free Press, 1965), p. 380; see also Mircea Eliade, *The Sacred and Profane*, trans. Willard Trask (Harcourt, Brace, and World, 1959), pp. 9–19.

27.   Howard S. Becker, *Outsiders: Studies in the Sociology of Deviancy* (New York: Free Press, 1963), pp. 95–100.

28.   Becker, pp. 96–97.

29.   Hentoff, *Jazz Life*, p. 25.

30.   Victor W. Turner, "Religious Specialists: I, Anthropological Study," *International Encyclopedia of the Social Sciences*, David Sills, ed. (New York: Macmillan, 1968), vol. XIII, p. 438. For other treatments of this much discussed subject see, *inter alia*, Durkheim, pp. 339ff; James Frazer, *The Golden Bough* (New York: Macmillan, abridged ed., 1955); Bronislaw Malinowski, *Magic, Science and Religion, and Other Essays* (Glencoe, Ill.: Free Press, 1948), pp. 1–71; Claude Lévi-Strauss, *The Savage Mind* (Chicago: Univ. of Chicago Press, 1966).

31.   Hentoff, *Jazz Is*, p. 225; Robert Palmer, "Cecil Taylor Group at New Village Club," *The New York Times*, Jan. 8, 1982, C 24; Len Lyons, *The Greatest Pianists* (New York: Quill, 1983), p. 306.

32.   Lyons, p. 261.

33.   Priestly, *Mingus*, p. 137.

34.   James Lincoln Collier, *Louis Armstrong* (New York: Oxford Univ. Press, 1983), p. 197.

35.   Sally Placksin, *American Women in Jazz* (New York: Wideview, 1982), p. 68.

36.   Hentoff, *Jazz Is*, p. 11.

37.   Bill Cole, *John Coltrane* (New York: Schirmer, 1976), pp. 32, 60.

38.   Gunther Schuller, *Early Jazz* (New York: Oxford Univ. Press, 1968), p. 55.

39.   This summary draws on Marghanita Laski, *Ecstasy* (London: Cressett, 1961); Abraham Maslow, *Religious Values and Peak Experiences* (Columbus, Oh.: Ohio State Univ. Press, 1964); I. M. Lewis, *Ecstatic Religion* (Harmondsworth, Eng.: Penguin, 1971); and Robert Jay Lifton, "A Kind of Everyday Ecstasy," *The New York Times Book Review*, Aug. 19, 1979, p. 9. The concept of "otherness" comes from Rudolf Otto, *The Idea of the Holy*, trans. John W. Harvey (New York: Oxford Univ. Press, 1958).

40.   Laski, *passim*.

41.   Hentoff, *Jazz Life*, p. 88.

42. Max Kaminsky and V. E. Hughes, *Jazz Band: My Life in Jazz* (New York: Da Capo, 1981), p. 40.

43. Hentoff, *Jazz Is*, p. 164.

44. Laski, pp. 370–71.

45. Russell, p. 127.

46. Evelyn Underhill, *Mysticism* (London: Methuen, 1911), p. 77.

47. Laski, pp. 66–70; Lewis, pp. 119ff, 189.

48. Shapiro and Hentoff, p. 245.

49. *Ibid.*, p. 247.

50. I have taken this quotation and some of the ideas in this paragraph from Johannes Riedel, *Soul Music: Black and White* (Minneapolis: Augsburg, 1975), pp. 64–65, 78–79.

51. Quoted by Nat Hentoff in Notes for "Into the Hot," Gil Evans Orchestra, Impulse: A 9.

52. Frederic Ramsey, Jr., and Charles Edward Smith, eds., *Jazzmen* (New York: Harcourt Brace, 1939), p. 118.

53. Whitney Balliett, "Hodes Blues," *New Yorker*, LVII (Mar. 30, 1981): 104.

54. Placksin, p. 294.

55. Hentoff, *Jazz Is*, p. 26.

56. Valerie Wilmer, *As Serious As Your Life* (Westport, Conn.: Lawrence Hill, 1980), p. 198.

57. Wilmer, pp. 201–2.

58. *Ibid.*, p. 199.

59. A. B. Spellman, *Black Music: Four Lives* (New York: Schocken, 1970), p. 139.

60. Wilmer, pp. 206–7.

61. John Chilton, *Billie's Blues* (New York: Stein and Day, 1975), p. 45.

62. Hentoff, *Jazz Is*, p. 71.

63. Wilmer, p. 194.

64.   Kitty Grime, *Jazz Voices* (London: Quartet, 1983), pp. 143–44.

65.   Wilmer, p. 193.

66.   Carol Easton, *Straight Ahead: The Story of Stan Kenton* (New York: Da Capo, 1981), p. 21.

67.   Anthony F. C. Wallace, "Revitalization Movements," *American Anthropologist*, LVIII (1958): 266; Wallace, "Mazeway Resynthesis: A Biocultural Theory of Religious Inspiration," *Transactions of the N.Y. Academy of Sciences*, Series 2, XVIII (1956): 602–38.

68.   See Joel Allison, "Adaptive Regression and Intense Religious Experience," *Journal of Mental Disease*, CVL (1968): 452–63; C. W. Christiansen, "Religious Conversion," *Archives of General Psychiatry* (Chicago), IX (1963): 207–16; H. Fingerette, "The Ego and Mystic Selfishness," *Psychoanalytic Review*, XLV (1958): 5–40; Abraham H. Maslow, "Cognition of Being in a Peak," *Journal of Genetic Psychology*, XLIV (1959): 43–67; also in this connection Wallace, "Mazeway Resynthesis," 636–37; and William James, *The Varieties of Religious Experience* (New York: Modern Library, 1929), p. 86.

69.   Hentoff, *Jazz Life*, pp. 15–16.

70.   Priestly, pp. 47–48.

71.   Hoagy Carmichael, *The Stardust Road* (New York: Rinehart, 1946), pp. 6–7.

72.   Barry Ulanov, *History of Jazz in America* (New York: Viking, 1952), pp. 130–31.

73.   Russell, p. 324.

74.   Bechet, p. 201.

75.   Milton Mezzrow and Bernard Wolfe, *Really the Blues* (New York: Rinehart, 1946), p. 182.

76.   Valerie Wilmer, *The Face of Black Music* (New York: Da Capo, 1976).

77.   Ian Carr, *Miles Davis* (New York: Morrow, 1982), p. 179.

78.   Shapiro and Hentoff, p. 159.

79.   Shaw, *52nd Street*, p. 234.

80.   Ira Gitler, *Jazz Masters of the Forties* (New York: Macmillan, 1974), p. 152.

81. Gillespie and Fraser, p. 142.

82. Hentoff, *Jazz Life*, p. 74.

83. Bechet, pp. 176–77.

84. Kaminsky and Hughes, p. 113.

85. Hentoff, *Jazz Is*, pp. 27–8, 33.

86. Rex Stewart, *Jazz Masters of the Thirties* (New York: Macmillan: 1972), p. 196.

87. Ralph Ellison, *Shadow and Act* (New York: Random House, 1964), p. 344.

88. Reisner, p. 85.

89. Stewart, p. 147.

90. Gitler, *Swing to Bop*, pp. 307–8.

91. Alan Lomax, *Mr. Jelly Roll* (New York: Grove, 1950), pp. 93–94.

92. Gitler, *Swing to Bop*, p. 169.

93. Frank Kofsky, *Black Nationalism and the Revolution in Music* (New York: Pathfinder, 1970), p. 226.

5 *Rituals*

1. This is adapted from William A. Lessa and Evon Z. Vogt's definition in their *Reader in Comparative Religion: An Anthropological Approach*, 3rd ed. (New York: Harper and Row, 1972), p. 134. I discuss it further in connection with myth in Chapter 6.

2. Dell Hymes, "The Breakthrough into Performance," in Dan Ben-Amos and Kenneth Goldstein, eds., *Folklore: Performance and Communication* (The Hague: Mouton, 1975), pp. 18–20; see also Richard Bauman, *Verbal Art as Performance* (Rowley, Mass.: Newbury, 1977); Erving Goffman, *Presentation of Self in Everyday Life* (New York: Doubleday/Anchor, 1959); and Goffman, *Interaction Ritual* (New York: Doubleday/Anchor, 1967).

MUSICAL PERFORMANCE

3.   Art and Laurie Pepper, *Straight Life* (New York: Schirmer, 1979), caption to plate opposite, p. 279.

4.   Nat Hentoff, *Jazz Is* (New York: Random House, 1976), pp. 25–26.

5.   Mezz Mezzrow and Bernard Wolfe, *Really the Blues* (New York: Random House, 1946), pp. 72–73.

6.   Quoted in Nat Hentoff, *The Jazz Life* (New York: Dial, 1961), p. 92.

7.   Hampton Hawes, *Raise Up off Me* (New York: Coward-McCann and Geoghegan, 1974), p. 20.

8.   Kitty Grime, *Jazz Voices* (London: Quartet, 1983), pp. 147, 180.

9.   Hentoff, *Jazz Life*, pp. 88–89.

10.   Whitney Balliett, "Jazz: Little Jazz," *New Yorker*, LVI (Dec. 16, 1985): 155.

11.   Ira Gitler, *From Swing to Bop* (New York: Oxford Univ. Press, 1985), p. 33.

12.   *Ibid.*, p. 171.

13.   Brian Priestly, *Mingus* (London: Quartet, 1982), p. 144.

14.   Valerie Wilmer, *Jazz People*, (Indianapolis: Bobbs-Merrill, 1970), p. 123.

15.   Whitney Balliett, *Improvising* (New York: Oxford Univ. Press, 1977), p. 112.

16.   Whitney Balliett, "Profiles: Easier Than Working (Dick Wellstood)," *New Yorker*, LVI (Mar. 3, 1980): 48.

17.   Mihaly Csikszentmihalyi, *Beyond Boredom and Anxiety* (San Francisco: Jossey-Bass, 1975), *passim.*

18.   Victor W. Turner, "Frame, Flow, and Reflection: Ritual and Drama as Public Liminality," in Michel Benamou and Charles Camarello, eds., *Performance in Post Modern Culture* (Madison, Wis.: Coda, 1977), p. 33; and more recently Richard Schechner, *Between Theater and Anthropology*, (Philadelphia: Univ. of Pennsylvania Press, 1985), *passim.*

19.   Grime, pp. 120–21.

20. Harvey Cox, *The Feast of Fools*, (Cambridge, Mass.: Harvard Univ. Press, 1969), pp. 70–5; see also Victor Turner, ed., *Celebration: Studies in Festivity and Ritual* (Washington D.C., 1982), esp. pp. 201–19.

21. Alan Lomax, *Mr. Jelly Roll* (New York: Grove, 1950), pp. 14–15; see also Marshall Stearns, *The Story of Jazz* (New York: Oxford Univ. Press, 1956), p. 62; Melville Herskovits, *Dahomey* (New York: Augustine, 1938), pp. 385, 387, 402.

22. Stearns, pp. 57–63, 311–12 (quotation on p. 61); see also Lyle Saxon, Edward Dreyer, and Robert Tallant, eds., *Gumbo Ya-Ya* (Boston: Houghton Mifflin, 1945), p. 61.

23. Al Rose, *Eubie Blake* (New York: Schirmer, 1979), p. 12.

24. Emile Durkheim, *The Elementary Forms of the Religious Life*, Joseph Ward Swain, trans. (New York: Free Press, 1965), pp. 383, 470.

25. Cox, p. 18; see also Joseph Pieper, *In Time with the World: A Theory of Festivity*, Richard and Clara Wilson, trans. (New York: Harcourt Brace, 1965), *passim*.

26. Ralph Ellison, *Shadow and Act* (New York: Random House, 1964), p. 244.

27. *Ibid.*, p. 243.

28. Nat Shapiro and Nat Hentoff, eds., *Hear Me Talkin' to Ya* (New York: Dover, 1966), p. 338.

29. Johan Huizinga, *Homo Ludens: A Study of the Play Element in Culture* (Boston: Beacon, 1955), pp. 13, 132; for a useful review of early scholarship on play see David L. Miller, *Gods and Games* (Cleveland: World, 1969).

30. Roger Callois, *Man, Play, and Games*, Meyer Barash, trans. (Glencoe, Ill.: Free Press, 1961), pp. 4–5, 11–36; see also in these connections Owen Aldis, *Play Fighting* (New York: Academic Press, 1975); M. J. Ellis, *Why People Play* (Englewood Cliffs, N.J.: Prentice-Hall, 1973); and Jerome S. Bruner, Alison Jolly, and Kathy Silva, eds., *Play—Its Role in Development and Evolution* (New York: Basic Books, 1976).

31. Art and Laurie Pepper, *Straight Life* (New York: Schirmer, 1979), pp. 475–76.

32. Huizinga, pp. 9, 34.

33. Hugo Rahner, *Man at Play* (New York: Herder and Herder, 1967), p. 21.

34. Shapiro and Hentoff, pp. 286.

35. *Ibid.*, p. 292.

36. *Ibid.*, p. 284.

37. See Lawrence W. Levine, *Black Culture and Black Consciousness* (New York: Oxford Univ. Press, 1977), pp. 233–4; also Sidney Bechet, *Treat It Gentle* (New York: Hill and Wang, 1960), pp. 61–64.

38. Shapiro and Hentoff, pp. 292–93.

39. Rex Stewart, *Jazz Masters of the Thirties* (New York: Macmillan, 1972), pp. 149–50.

40. *Ibid.*, pp. 141–5, quotation p. 144.

41. Ira Gitler, *Swing to Bop*, p. 82.

42. Ross Russell, *Bird Lives* (New York: Charterhouse, 1973), p. 139.

43. Robert Reisner, *Bird: The Legend of Charlie Parker* (New York: Citadel, 1962), p. 136.

44. Gitler, *Jazz Masters of the Forties* (New York: Macmillan, 1966), p. 178.

45. William Bruce Cameron, "Sociological Notes on the Jam Session," *Social Forces*, XXXIII (1954): 177–78.

46. Shapiro and Hentoff, p. 195.

47. Huizinga, pp. 50, 63–73.

48. Russell, p. 139.

49. Samuel Charters and Leonard Kunstadt, *Jazz: A History of the New York Scene* (New York: Da Capo, 1981), p. 189.

50. *Ibid.*, pp. 291, 197.

APPEARANCE

51. For a discussion of the jazzman's dress and general image see Albert Murray, *Stomping the Blues* (New York: McGraw-Hill, 1976), pp. 227–54.

52. For a discussion of these see Herbert G. Blumer, "Fashion," in *International Encyclopedia of the Social Sciences*, David L. Sills, ed. (New

York: Macmillan, 1968), vol. V, pp. 541–45; also René Koenig, *The Restless Image*, F. Bradley, trans. (London: Allen and Unwin, 1973); and T. C. Fliegel, *The Psychology of Clothes* (London: Hogarth, 1950).

53.   Reisner, p. 124.

54.   Blumer, pp. 542–43; Georg Simmel, "Fashion," *American Journal of Sociology*, LXII (1957); 541–58.

55.   Jack Chambers, *Milestones, I* (Toronto: Univ. of Toronto Press, 1983), p. 17.

56.   Pepper and Pepper, p. 44.

LANGUAGE

57.   See Robert S. Gold, *Jazz Talk* (Indianapolis: Bobbs Merrill, 1975), p. ix.

58.   Louis Armstrong, *Swing That Music* (New York: Longmans Green, 1936), p. 78.

59.   Mezzrow and Wolfe, p. 142.

60.   Robert Reisner, *The Jazz Titans* (New York: Doubleday, 1960), p. 147.

61.   Paul Van Buren, *The Edges of Language: An Essay in the Logic of Religion* (New York: Macmillan, 1977), pp. 4–5, 98.

62.   Gold, p. ix; Shapiro and Hentoff, p. 232.

63.   Reisner, *Jazz Titans*, p. 179.

64.   See I. A. Richards, *The Philosophy of Rhetoric* (New York: Oxford Univ. Press, 1936), p. 13; and Kenneth Burke, *Language As Symbolic Action* (Berkeley: Univ. of California Press, 1968), pp. 44–62, 391.

65.   Shapiro and Hentoff, p. 236.

66.   For a review of the scholarship on nicknames see Barbara Kirshenblatt-Gimblett, *Speech-Play* (Philadelphia: Univ. of Pennsylvania Press, 1976), pp. 198–201; see also Alan P. Merriam and Raymond W. Mack, "The Jazz Community," *Social Forces*, XXXVIII (1960): 218.

67.   See Charles Keil, "Emotion and Feeling through Music," in Thomas Kochman, ed., *Rappin' and Stylin' Out* (Urbana, Ill.: Univ. of Illinois Press, 1972), pp. 83–100; see also Richard Bauman, *Verbal Art as Performance* (Rowley, Mass.: Newbury, 1977), pp. 10–11; and Ray

L. Birdwhistell, *Introduction to Kinesics* (Louisville: Univ. of Louisville Press, 1952), *passim*.

68. In connection with linguistic performance see, among other things (in addition to Bauman above), Dell Hymes, "The Breakthrough into Performance," in Dan Ben-Amos and Kenneth Goldstein, eds., *Folklore: Performance and Communication*, (The Hague: Mouton, 1975), pp. 18–20; and Erving Goffman, *Forms of Talk* (Philadelphia: Univ. of Pennsylvania Press, 1981).

69. Roger D. Abrahams, *Deep Down in the Jungle* (Chicago: Aldine, 1970), *passim*; see Kirshenblatt-Gimblett, pp. 5–7, 184–87, for an excellent survey of the writing on agonistic wordplay.

70. Shapiro and Hentoff, p. 219.

71. Abrahams, pp. 39–60, see also his "Pattern of Performance in the West Indies," in Norman E. Whitten, Jr., and John F. Szwed, eds., *Afro-American Anthropology* (New York: Macmillan, 1970), pp. 164–65.

72. Art and Laurie Pepper, *Straight Life* (New York: Schirmer, 1979), p. 44.

73. See Huizinga, esp. pp. 9, 13, 34, 50, 63–73; Caillois pp. 4–5, 11–36; and Csikszentmihalyi, *passim*.

74. Ralph Ellison, *Shadow and Act* (New York: Random House, 1964), p. 243.

75. Gillespie and Fraser, p. 281.

76. See William J. Samarin, "The Language of Religion" in Samarin, ed., *Language in Religious Practice* (Rowley, Mass.: Newbury, 1976), pp. 8–9.

77. Mezzrow and Wolfe, p. 120.

78. Alta Jablow and Carl Withers, "Social Sense and Verbal Nonsense in Urban Children's Folklore," *New York Folklore Quarterly*, XXI (1965): 255; see also Kirshenblatt-Gimblett, pp. 10–11; Michael Holquist, "What Is a Boojum? Nonsense and Modernism" in Peter Brooks, ed., *The Child's Part* (Boston: Beacon, 1972), pp. 145–64; and Elizabeth Sewell, *The Field of Nonsense* (London: Folcroft, 1970).

79. Hoagy Carmichael, *The Stardust Road* (New York: Rinehart, 1946), p. 140.

80.   Carmichael, pp. 116–17.

81.   Gillespie and Fraser, p. 272.

82.   Here I paraphrase Holquist, pp. 159, 161.

83.   See Kirshenblatt-Gimblett, p. 11; also William J. Samarin, *Tongues of Men and Angels* (New York: Macmillan, 1970).

HUMOR

84.   See M. Carroll Hyers, ed., *Holy Laughter* (New York: Seabury, 1969); also Sander Gilman, *The Parodic Sermon* (Wiesbaden: Franz Steiner, 1974), pp. 11ff, 130ff; for a limited view of humor in jazz see Leonard Feather and Jack Tracy, *Laughter from the Hip* (New York: Horizon, 1963); see Murray, pp. 181–200, for an incisive discussion of this subject.

85.   Hentoff, *Jazz Is*, p. 71.

86.   Gitler, p. 81.

87.   Gillespie and Fraser, pp. 303–4.

88.   Hentoff, *Jazz Is*, p. 179.

89.   Pepper and Pepper, p. 472.

90.   J. C. Thomas, *Chasin' the Trane* (New York: Da Capo, 1975), p. 46.

91.   Erving Goffman, *Encounters* (Indianapolis: Bobbs Merrill, 1961), pp. 85–152, and esp. pp. 115–32.

92.   Reisner, *Bird*, p. 125.

93.   Art Hodes and Chadwick Hansen, eds., *Selections from the Gutter* (Berkeley: Univ. of California Press, 1977), p. 18.

94.   Samuel H. Miller, "The Clown in Contemporary Art," in Hyers, pp. 90, 100–101.

95.   Sigmund Freud, "Jokes and Their Relation to the Unconscious," in *The Standard Edition of the Complete Psychological Works of Sigmund Freud* (New York: Macmillan, 1960), vol. VIII; see also Jacob Levine, *Motivation in Humor* (New York: Atheneum, 1969); and J. H. Goldstein and P. E. McGhee, eds., *The Psychology of Humor* (New York: Academic Press, 1972), which presents an annotated bibliography of the subject.

96.   Hentoff, *Jazz Life*, pp. 18–20.

97. Gitler, p. 107.

98. Quoted in Jacob Levine, "Humor," *International Encyclopedia of the Social Sciences*, vol. VII, p. 7.

99. Shapiro and Hentoff, p. 346; also William P. Gottlieb, *the Golden Age of Jazz*, (New York: Simon and Schuster, 1979), p. 21.

100. See Kirshenblatt-Gimblett, pp. 202–5.

101. Reisner, *Bird*, pp. 185–86.

102. Artie Shaw, *The Trouble with Cinderella* (New York: Da Capo, 1979), pp. 180–81.

103. Rose L. Coser, "Laughter Among Colleagues," *Psychiatry*, XXIII (1960): 81–89; also Coser, "Some Social Functions of Laughter," *Human Relations*, XII (1959): 171–82.

INITIATION

104. James Lincoln Collier, *The Making of Jazz* (Boston: Houghton-Mifflin, 1978), p. 45.

105. Wilmer, *Jazz People*, p. 21.

106. Mircea Eliade, *The Quest* (Chicago: Univ. of Chicago Press, 1969), esp. pp. 112–26.

107. *Louis Armstrong—A Self-Portrait*, interviewed by Richard Meryman (New York: Eakins, 1970), pp. 13, 17; see also Armstrong, *Satchmo* (New York: Prentice-Hall, 1954), pp. 17, 27.

108. James Lincoln Collier, *Louis Armstrong* (New York: Oxford Univ. Press, 1983), p. 71.

109. *Ibid.*, p. 79.

110. Meryman, p. 29.

111. Reisner, *Bird*, p. 214.

112. Russell, p. 68ff.

113. Reisner, *Bird*, p. 186.

114. *Ibid.*, p. 186.

115. Russell, p. 93.

116. Gillespie and Fraser, pp. 217–18.

117. Priestly, pp. 75–76.

118. Chambers, p. 33.

119. Carmichael, p. 17.

120. Priestly, pp. 85–86.

121. Gillespie and Fraser, p. 145.

122. Shapiro and Hentoff, p. 237.

123. Victor Turner, *Drama, Fields, and Metaphors* (Ithaca, N.Y.: Cornell Univ. Press, 1974), pp. 238–40.

124. Gillespie and Fraser, p. 144.

125. *Ibid.*, p. 283.

126. Hentoff, *Jazz Life*, p. 88.

127. Collier, *Armstrong*, p. 221.

128. Chambers, p. 17.

129. Howard Becker, *Outsiders: Studies in the Sociology of Deviance* (New York: Free Press, 1963), p. 47.

130. Pepper and Pepper, pp. 83–4.

131. Becker, p. 51.

132. Pepper and Pepper, pp. 84–85.

133. Becker, p. 42. His argument follows George Herbert Meade's hypothesis that the meaning of an object depends mainly on social relationships and the uses to which it can be put. See Meade's *Mind, Self, and Society* (Chicago: Univ. of Chicago Press, 1934), pp. 277–80; also Peter L. Berger and Thomas Luckmann, *The Social Reconstruction of Reality* (New York: Doubleday Anchor, 1967). For a basic definition of deviance see Edwin M. Lemert, *Social Pathology* (New York: McGraw-Hill, 1951) and also Lemert, *Human Deviance, Social Problems, and Social Control* (Englewood Cliffs, N.J.: Prentice-Hall, 1967).

134. Shapiro and Hentoff, p. 190.

135. Reisner, *Bird*, p. 45.

136. Shaw, *The Trouble with Cinderella*, p. 83.

137. Hawes, pp. 20–21.

138.   Hentoff, *Jazz Life*, p. 21.

139.   Hawes, p. 22.

140.   Grime, p. 147.

141.   Shapiro and Hentoff, p. 372.

142.   *Ibid.*, pp. 377–8.

143.   Hentoff, *Jazz Life*, p. 85.

144.   Wilmer, p. 116–17.

145.   *Ibid.*, pp. 118–19.

146.   Edward Harvey, "Social Changes and the Jazz Musician," *Social Forces*, VIL (1967): 40.

6   *Myth*

1.   See William A. Lessa and Evon Z. Vogt, eds., *Reader in Comparative Religion: An Anthropological Approach*, 3rd. ed. (New York: Harper and Row, 1972), p. 134ff. This volume contains Clyde Kluckhohn's essential essay, "Myth and Ritual: A General Theory," which originally appeared in *Harvard Theological Review*, XXXV (Jan. 1942): 45–79. For distinctions between myth and legend see William Bascom, "The Form of Folklore: Prose Narratives," *Journal of American Folklore* LXXVIII (1965): 3–20.

2.   Frederic Ramsey, Jr., and Charles Edward Smith, eds., *Jazzmen* (New York: Harcourt Brace, 1939), pp. 59–91.

3.   Martin Williams, *King Oliver* (New York: A. S. Barnes, 1960), pp. 2, 34.

4.   Whitney, Balliett, *Improvising* (New York: Oxford Univ. Press, 1977), p. 23.

5.   See S. H. Hooke, ed., *Myth, Ritual, and Kingship* (New York: Oxford Univ. Press, 1958).

6.   Nat Shapiro and Nat Hentoff, *Hear Me Talkin' to Ya* (New York: Dover, 1966), p. 42.

7.   See, for example, *ibid.*, pp. 45–46, 98–100.

8. Walter C. Allen and Brian Rust, *King Joe Oliver* (London: Sidgwick and Jackson, 1958), p. 40.

9. Shapiro and Hentoff, p. 184–5.

10. *Ibid.*, pp. 186–7.

11. *Louis Armstrong—A Self-Portrait*, interviewed by Richard Meryman (New York: Eakins, 1970), pp. 49–50.

12. Allen and Rust, p. 46; see also *Pops Foster, Autobiography*, as told to Tom Stoddard (Berkeley: Univ. of California Press, 1971), pp. 180–81; also Martin Williams, *Jazz Masters of New Orleans* (New York: Macmillan, 1967), p. 80.

13. Jung's notions of myth can be found in *Psychological Reflections: An Anthology of His Writings*, Jolande Jacobi, ed. (New York: Harpers, 1953).

14. For Malinowski's theories about myth see *Magic, Science and Religion, and Other Essays* (Glencoe, Ill.: Free Press, 1948), pp. 1–71.

15. See Eliade, *Myth and Reality*, trans. Willard R. Trask (New York: Harpers, 1963).

16. See, for instance, Ross Russell, *Bird Lives* (New York: Charterhouse, 1973), pp. 34, 323; and Robert Reisner, *Bird: The Legend of Charlie Parker* (New York: Citadel, 1962), p. 228.

17. See Victor W. Turner, "Myths and Symbols," *International Encyclopedia of the Social Sciences*, David L. Sills, ed. (New York: Macmillan, 1968), vol. X, pp. 580–81; Paul Radin, *The Trickster* (Westport, Conn.: Greenwood, 1969); Roger D. Abrahams, "The Outrageous Hero," in Tristram P. Coffin, ed., *Our Living Tradition* (New York: Basic Books, 1968), pp. 173ff; and Lawrence W. Levine, *Black Culture and Black Consciousness* (New York: Oxford Univ. Press, 1977), pp. 121–32, 370–85.

18. A remarkable collection of sometimes contradictory accounts, full of mythopoetic implications.

19. Russell, p. 257.

20. Reisner, p. 51.

21. *Ibid.*, p. 12.

22. *Ibid.*, p. 80.

23. *Ibid.*, p. 189.

24. *Ibid.*, p. 80.

25. *Ibid.*, p. 15.

26. *Ibid.*, p. 191.

27. Radin, p. 185.

28. Abrahams, p. 173.

29. Reisner, p. 14.

30. Radin, p. 185.

31. Turner, p. 580.

32. *Ibid.*, pp. 577, 580–81.

33. Reisner, p. 152.

34. Shapiro and Hentoff, p. 3.

35. Sidney Bechet, *Treat It Gentle* (New York: Hill and Wang, 1960), p. 215.

36. Shapiro and Hentoff, pp. 284–85.

37. *Ibid.*, p. 287.

38. Willie "The Lion" Smith, *Music on My Mind* (New York: Da Capo, 1978), p. 131.

39. Arnold Shaw, *52nd Street* (New York: Da Capo, 1977), p. 126.

40. Ralph Ellison, *Shadow and Act* (New York: Random House, 1964), pp. 199–201, 206.

41. Ramsey and Smith, p. 143.

42. Shapiro and Hentoff, pp. 45–46.

43. Ramsey and Smith, pp. 62–63.

44. Amos Wilder, *The Language of the Gospel* (New York: Harper and Row, 1964), pp. 38–39, 51.

45. Ondaatje's novel was published in New York by Norton; Marquis' study, in Baton Rouge by Louisiana State Univ. Press.

46. Alan Lomax, *Mr. Jelly Roll* (New York: Grove 1950), pp. 226–27.

47. Bechet, pp. 202–3.

48. *Ibid.*, p. 4.

7 *Followers*

CRITICS

1. Max Weber, *The Sociology of Religion*, trans. Ephraim Fischoff (Boston: Beacon, 1963), pp. 67–68; Victor Turner, "Religious Specialists: Anthropological Study," in *International Encyclopedia of the Social Sciences*, David L. Sills, ed. (New York: Macmillan, 1964), vol. XIII, pp. 130–35.

2. Weber, pp. 125–26.

3. Amiri Baraka, "Miles Davis," *The New York Times Magazine*, June 16, 1985, Sect. VI, p. 50.

4. See Ortiz Walton, *Music: Black, White, and Blue* (New York: Morrow, 1972), pp. 118–20; and Nat Hentoff, "Jazz and the Intellectuals: Somebody Goofed," *Chicago Review*, III (1955): 110–21.

5. Max Kaminsky and V. E. Hughes, *Jazz Band: My Life in Jazz* (New York: Harper and Row, 1963), p. 39.

6. Charles Edward Smith, "Jazz: Some Little Known Aspects," *Symposium*, I (1930): 502; for 1920s background see Roger Pryor Dodge, "Consider the Critics" in Frederic Ramsey, Jr., and Charles Edward Smith, eds., *Jazzmen* (New York: Harcourt Brace, 1939), pp. 301–27.

7. Hugues Panassié, *Hot Jazz*, trans. Lyle and Eleanor Dowling (New York: Doubleday, 1936), p. xvi.

8. Ernest Borneman, "The Jazz Cult," in Eddie Condon and Richard Gehman, eds., *Eddie Condon's Treasury of Jazz* (New York: Da Capo, 1977), pp. 49–50. This material first appeared in *Harpers*, CXCIV (Feb. 1947): 141–47; and (March 1947): 261–73.

9. Martin T. Williams, "Criticism: The Path of the Jazz Critic," *Down Beat*, XXV (Aug. 21, 1958): 11.

10. Borneman, p. 64.

11. *Ibid.*, p. 65.

12. Both quotations appear in Leonard Feather, *Inside Jazz* (New York: Da Capo, 1977)—originally *Inside Be-Bop* (New York: J. J. Robbins, 1949), epigraph; see also John Hammond with Irving Townsend, *On Record* (New York: Ridge, 1977).

13. Ross Russell, *Bird Lives* (New York: Charterhouse, 1973), p. 197.

14. For this quotation and responses see Don De Michael, "John Coltrane and Dolphy Answer the Jazz Critics," *Down Beat*, XXIX (Apr. 12, 1962): 20–22.

15. Benny Green, "A Matter of Form," *Jazz Journal* XV (June 1962): 11.

16. Clive Loveless, "Outward Bound with Eric Dolphy," *Down Beat*, XXX (July 1963): 1, 17.

AFICIONADOS

17. Francis Newton, *The Jazz Scene* (London: MacGibbon and Kee, 1959), p. 232.

18. Neil Leonard, *Jazz and the White Americans* (Chicago: Univ. of Chicago Press, 1962), pp. 70–71; Newton, pp. 264–65.

19. Chris Albertson, *Bessie* (New York: Stein and Day, 1972), pp. 106–7.

20. Stephen W. Smith, "Hot Collecting," *Jazzmen*, pp. 290–91; see also Charles Edward Smith, "Collecting Hot," *Esquire*, I (Feb. 1934): 79ff.

21. Kaminsky and Hughes, p. 115.

22. Borneman, p. 38.

23. *Ibid.*, p. 38.

24. There were earlier editions published in Paris in 1936, 1938, 1943, and in New York in 1943.

25. This quotation and relevant material appeared in Whitney Balliett, "Profiles: Panassié, Delaunay et Cie," *New Yorker*, LII (Feb. 14, 1977): 45–52.

26. The Jepson was published by Knudsen in Holte, Denmark; the Rust, by Arlington House, New Rochelle, N.Y.

27. Balliett, p. 52.

28. New York: Commodore Record Co.

29. Gilbert Millstein, "The Commodore Record Shop and Milt Gabler," in *Condon and Gabler*, p. 96.

30. *Ibid.*, pp. 98–99.

31. Robert Palmer, "Jazz's Bluenote Label Comes Back to Life," *The New York Times*, Feb. 10, 1985, H 23–24.

32. Kaminsky and Hughes, p. 117.

33. *Ibid.*, pp. 122–23.

34. *Ibid.*, p. 122.

35. Borneman,pp. 52–57.

36. For this letter and related material see Tom Bethell, *George Lewis: A New Orleans Jazzman* (Berkeley: Univ. of California Press, 1977), pp. 122–40.

37. See John S. Wilson, "Good-by Newport Blues," *The New York Times*, July 10, 1960, Sect. II, p. 9; Whitney Balliett, "Musical Events," *New Yorker*, CCCLXVIII (July 16, 1960): 84ff; Gene Lees, "Newport, The Trouble," *Down Beat*, XXVII (July 18, 1960): 20–23.

38. This account of the Beiderbecke Festival is from Meg Cox, "Bix Beiderbecke: Sweet Sounds of Jazz Revisited," *The Wall Street Journal*, Aug. 7, 1981, p. 19.

HIPSTERS

39. Harold Finestone, "Cats, Kicks, and Color," *Social Problems*, V (Summer 1957): 356–57; see also Newton, pp. 220–21; Mezz Mezzrow and Bernard Wolfe, *Really the Blues* (New York: Random House, 1946), chap. 3; Orrin E. Klepp, *Heroes, Villains, and Fools* (Englewood Cliffs, N. J.: Prentice-Hall, 1962), pp. 125–41.

40. Norman Mailer, "The White Negro: Superficial Reflections on the Hipster," *Dissent*, V (1957): 269, 280–81.

41. Lawrence Lipton, *The Holy Barbarians* (New York: Messner, 1959; New English Library ed., 1962), p. 19.

42. Finestone, p. 361.

43. *Ibid.*, p. 361.

44. Mailer, p. 279.

45. Nat Hentoff, *The Jazz Life* (New York: Dial, 1961), p. 142.

46. Anatole Broyard, "A Portrait of the Hipster," *Partisan Review*, XV (1948): 722–23.

47. Finestone, p. 357.

48. Broyard, p. 722.

49. *Ibid.*, p. 723.

BEATS

50. See Bruce Cook, *The Beat Generation* (New York: Scribners, 1971); Thomas Parkinson, ed., *A Casebook on the Beats* (New York: Crowell, 1961); Francis J. Rigney and L. Douglas Smith, *The Real Bohemia* (New York: Basic Books, 1961); and John Tytell, *Naked Angels* (New York: McGraw-Hill, 1976).

51. Parkinson, "Phenomenon or Generation," in Parkinson, p. 278.

52. Herbert Gold, "The Beat Mystique," in Parkinson, p. 248.

53. Jack Chambers, *Milestones, I* (Toronto: Univ. of Toronto Press, 1983), p. 247.

54. Jack Kerouac, *On the Road* (New York: Viking, 1958), p. 106.

55. Chambers, p. 248.

56. Cook, p. 7.

57. *Ibid.*, pp. 63–64.

DANCERS

58. See E. Louis Backman, *Religious Dances in the Christian Church and in Popular Medicine*, trans. E. Claussen (London: Allen and Unwin, 1952), pp. 1ff, 154ff, 190–257, 328, 334.

59. Marshall and Jean Stearns, *Jazz Dance* (New York: Schirmer, 1979), pp. 26–27; also see William O. E. Oesterly, *The Sacred Dance* (Cambridge, Mass.: Cambridge Univ. Press, 1923), pp. 22ff and *passim*; and Gerardus van der Leeuw, *Religion in Essence and Manifestation*, (Gloucester, Mass.: Peter Smith, 1967).

60. Curt Sachs, *World History of the Dance* (New York: Norton, 1963), pp. 9–16, 49–138.

61. Sachs, pp. 4, 49.

62. William J. Schaefer, *Brass Bands and New Orleans Jazz* (Baton Rouge: Louisiana State Univ. Press, 1977), p. 94.

63. Sidney Bechet, *Treat It Gentle* (New York: Hill and Wang, 1960), pp. 67–68.

64. Stearns and Stearns, p. 325.

65. *Autobiography of Malcolm X* (New York: Grove, 1966), pp. 58–59.

66. Johan Huizinga, *Homo Ludens* (Boston: Beacon, 1955), p. 132, 164.

67. Vernon and Irene Castle, *Modern Dancing* (New York: Harpers, 1914), p. 141, 143, 145–46, 154.

68. Hugo Rahner, *Man at Play*, trans. B. Battershaw and E. Quinn (New York: Herder and Herder, 1969), p. 85; for Cox's notion of the sacredness of play see *Feast of Fools* (Cambridge, Mass.: Harvard Univ. Press, 1969), pp. 2ff and *passim*.

69. Stearns and Stearns, p. 321.

70. *Ibid.*, p. 323.

71. *Ibid.*, p. 323.

72. *Ibid.*, p. 323.

73. *Ibid.*, p. 330.

74. *Ibid.*, p. 330.

75. Nat Hentoff, *Jazz Is* (New York: Random House, 1976), p. 225.

76. Nat Shapiro and Nat Hentoff, eds., *The Jazz Makers* (New York: Rinehart, 1957), pp. 264, 267.

77. Stearns and Stearns, p. 325.

78. *Ibid.*, p. 325.

79. Dizzy Gillespie with Al Fraser, *To Be, Or Not . . . to Bop* (New York: Doubleday, 1979), p. 304.

Conclusion

1. "Of God, Man, Politics, and the First Amendment," *The New York Times*, Mar. 11, 1984, E22.

2.   For these figures and related material, I have relied on Sidney Ahlstrom, *A Religious History of the American People* (New Haven: Yale Univ. Press, 1972), pp. 1055–56 and *passim*. Further figures on the migration and economic and social conditions among blacks appear in Giles Oakley, *The Devil's Music* (New York: Harcourt Brace & Jovanovich, 1978), pp. 63–64, 161–62, 166–68.

3.   Robert Nisbet, *The Social Bond* (New York: Knopf, 1970), pp. 239–40; for a general discussion of this subject see Andrew M. Greeley, *Unsecular Man* (New York: Schocken, 1972).

4.   Gene Fowler, *Schnozzola, The Story of Jimmy Durante* (London: Hammond, 1952), p. 32.

5.   Valerie Wilmer, *The Face of Black Music* (New York: Da Capo, 1976).

6.   Chris Goddard, *Jazz Away from Home*, (New York: Paddington, 1979), p. 30.

Index